T0299551

MOTHERLAND

LUKE PEPERA is a writer, broadcaster, historian and anthropologist dedicated to sharing his passion for African history and cultures. He was born in Ghana and has a degree from St Peter's College, Oxford, where he read Archaeology and Anthropology and studied ancient and medieval African history. He has worked at the Pitt Rivers Museum, *The Times* and *Tatler*, and has written and presented *Africa: Written Out of History*, a documentary for History Hit.

MOTHERLAND

**A Journey through 500,000
Years of African Culture and Identity**

W&N
WEIDENFELD & NICOLSON

First published in Great Britain in 2025 by Weidenfeld & Nicolson,
an imprint of The Orion Publishing Group Ltd
Carmelite House, 50 Victoria Embankment
London EC4Y 0DZ

An Hachette UK Company

The authorised representative in the EEA is Hachette Ireland,
8 Castlecourt Centre, Castleknock Road, Castleknock, Dublin 15, D15 XTP3,
Republic of Ireland (email: info@hbgi.ie)

1 3 5 7 9 10 8 6 4 2

Copyright © Luke Pepera 2025

The moral right of Luke Pepera to be identified as
the author of this work has been asserted in accordance
with the Copyright, Designs and Patents Act of 1988.

All rights reserved. No part of this publication may be
reproduced, stored in a retrieval system, or transmitted
in any form or by any means, electronic, mechanical,
photocopying, recording, or otherwise, without the
prior permission of both the copyright owner and the
above publisher of this book.

A CIP catalogue record for this book is
available from the British Library.

ISBN (Hardback) 978 1 3987 0736 8
ISBN (Export Trade Paperback) 978 1 3987 0737 5
ISBN (Ebook) 978 1 3987 0739 9
ISBN (Audio) 978 1 3987 0740 5

Typeset by Input Data Services Ltd, Bridgwater, Somerset

Printed in Great Britain by Clays Ltd, Elcograf, S.p.A.

MIX
Paper | Supporting
responsible forestry
FSC
www.fsc.org   FSC® C104740

www.weidenfeldandnicolson.co.uk
www.orionbooks.co.uk

To my father, for his unyielding
love and support.

CONTENTS

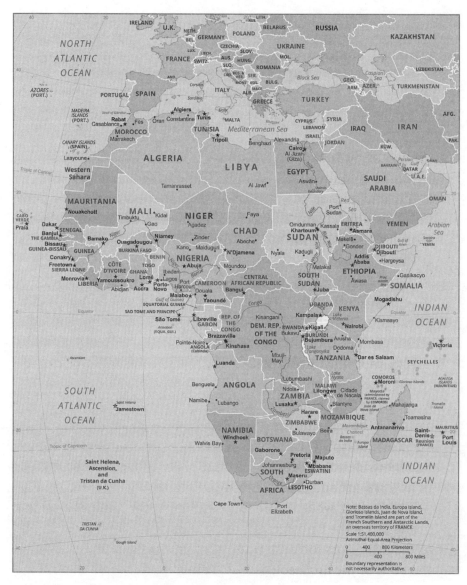

A map of contemporary Africa.

INTRODUCTION

In the summer of 2012, I visited the National Museum of Ghana. I was at home in Ghana for the school holiday, catching up with family and friends. Since I was in my second-last year of school, I had to complete my Extended Project – an independent school project that counts towards your final grades. The subject can be anything you want.

Being interested in history, Africa and storytelling, I decided to write a short history of the Kwahu – one of the ethnic groups I belong to, which is also a subgroup of the better-known Akan ethnic group. I thought I might begin my research at the museum.

However, when I got there, I was a little disappointed.

Just like in my history lessons at school, the documentaries I watched and the books I read, there wasn't much on African – let alone Ghanaian – history, except for the Transatlantic Slave Trade and colonialism. (Thankfully, today, the museum's collection is much broader, featuring, for instance, chiefs' regalia and indigenous tools, art and crafts, including instruments and textiles.)

Not finding what I needed at the museum, I contacted some professors at the University of Ghana. There I had better luck. One of the professors took me round a small museum tucked away at the back of the archaeology department and showed me, among other things, iron artefacts dating to around 500 AD that were made and found in Ghana. Another invited me to her lecture on the history of Akan chieftaincies.

This, plus some articles they recommended to me, gave me all I needed to complete my project. But having been exposed to just a little of the deeper African past and shown that there was still so much to discover and learn about it, I became keenly interested in doing so.

I applied to study archaeology and anthropology at university. In my third year, I took a module on the formation of African states. I was exposed even more to the richness of Africa's past. I learnt about ancient East African trade and architecture, medieval West African empires and Central African kingdoms' crafts and religions, to name a few. I also became compelled to pass on this knowledge, which is so little known and appreciated.

That's where this book comes in.

It's not a complete, chronological history of Africa. The continent's vastness and the sheer immensity of varied peoples who have lived there since the dawn of humanity means this: if such a task could even be completed properly – every society, event and noteworthy individual given due attention – it would probably take several lifetimes.

More importantly, historical chronologies are not how many African peoples have understood and continue to understand their past. For us, there is little distinction between past and present. What, to others, happened in the 'past' is, to us, still happening. People who, to others, lived and died two hundred years ago are, to us, still alive. We continue to communicate with them and invite and welcome them to contemporary gatherings and celebrations. Festivals that, to others, are five hundred years old, to us might as well have been created this morning, so little have their meaning, purpose and process changed.

This perspective of the past gave me no small difficulty in the writing of this book. Often, I found that cultural features I intended to describe as historical still existed as they always had done. Internally, I continuously debated whether to write of them in the past or present tense and sometimes struggled to identify how they might have evolved, if indeed they had.

So, I settled on a thematic approach for the book. Each of its ten chapters focuses on a cultural or historical aspect that has been and continues to be integral to African identity. These include ancestral veneration, music, dancing, oral histories and storytelling, as well as resource wealth, migration, the Transatlantic Slave Trade and racism.

In each chapter, I tell stories that I believe not only highlight its theme but also that I've found the most engaging. In particular, it was either the fascinating characters or the intriguing beliefs and rituals that drew me to them. Also, to emphasise the African conception of a fluid relationship between past and present, I tell contemporary as well as 'historical' stories (some of them personal) and draw connections between them throughout the book.

Crucially, and unlike many other histories of Africa and its peoples, I've avoided concentrating solely on the Transatlantic Slave Trade, colonialism and racism, and amplifying their importance. Instead, I place them in their proper context – a mere three hundred years (albeit dark and significant) at the tail end of a history stretching back hundreds of thousands.

Additionally, where I *have* written about the Transatlantic Slave Trade, colonialism and racism, I've avoided characterising Africans as solely their inevitable, unwitting and hapless victims. I've attempted to demonstrate how these aspects came about not necessarily because of a belief in Africans' natural inferiority, but rather because of a few individuals' avarice and greed for power and position. I've also tried to show how Africans themselves rejected, put a stop to, were sometimes unaffected by, and even contributed to, these aspects.

This book, then, is a physical representation of my personal journey through the African past; a journey that started over a decade ago, has continued to this day and will go on for the rest of my life. In reading it, I hope you not only learn about African identity but also find themes and stories with which you connect. Perhaps you might find parallels or noticeable differences between elements of certain African cultures and those of your own. However you read, and whatever you take away from this literary adventure, it's a pleasure to have you along for the ride.

Luke Pepera, April 2024

1

OUR LOST MILLENNIA

We have a warped understanding of Africa's past. The last three hundred years encompassing the Transatlantic Slave Trade and colonialism are magnified at the expense of everything that came before. We're unable to appreciate fully just how far back in time the earliest African cultures existed, the diversity of these cultures, and their people's achievements up to and including the modern day.

Because human beings first emerged in Africa, any discussion of Africa's past can begin at the very beginning of our species. This gives a sense of just how deep the histories of African peoples are.

Then, to demonstrate just how much they've achieved in all the time they've been on Earth, there are too many examples to choose from. Here, I've explored the wealth, influence and worldliness of two medieval West African civilisations – the Mali Empire and the Songhay Empire that succeeded it.

So, let's first go back about 200,000 years to East Africa. Here, after gradual evolution, we – that is, *Homo sapiens* (our species) with the anatomy we still have – emerged. The earliest fossil evidence for anatomically modern *sapiens* has been found in the east African country of Ethiopia. These are the remains of skeletons from two sites – Omo Kibish and Herto. Those from Omo Kibish date to around 200,000 years ago. Those from Herto to around 160,000 years ago. Genetic evidence shows that the last common ancestor of *every* current human being lived in Africa around 150,000 years ago. Scientists dubbed her 'Eve'.

Potentially, our earliest ancestor is *Sahelanthropus tchadensis*. Its name means 'Sahel man of Chad', where its remains were first found. It lived in Africa about seven million years ago.

Until the emergence of *Homo erectus* about five million years later, early humans lived *only* in Africa. That's because some *erectus* migrated to Asia.

In Africa, by about 800,000 years ago, *erectus* had evolved into *Homo heidelbergensis*.

Between about 700,000 and 500,000 years ago, some *heidelbergensis* migrated to Europe. Adapting to its colder environment, they evolved into Neanderthals.

Meanwhile, by about 300,000 years ago, African *heidelbergensis* had evolved into a more modern-looking ancestor that some scientists call *Homo helmei*. *Helmei* remains have been found in Ethiopia, Kenya and South Africa. A skull found in the South African site of Florisbad dates to around 250,000 years old.

By about 150,000 years ago, *helmei* had evolved into anatomically modern *sapiens*.

Other scientists call *helmei* by different names. To some, *helmei* isn't a species distinct from *sapiens* but rather an early form of it. Thus, they call *helmei* 'late archaic *Homo sapiens*'. To others, even *heidelbergensis* is also an early form of *sapiens*. They call it 'early archaic *Homo sapiens*'.

To all these scientists, our brain size relative to that of our body defines our humanity. Our brain size rapidly increased and became close to what it is now around 400,000 years ago – the time of *heidelbergensis* and *helmei*. Therefore, *this* is when we became '*sapiens*'.

To yet other scientists, because *sapiens* evolved in Africa, *all* early human fossils found there should be classified as '*sapiens*'. '*Sapiens*' might then have emerged as far back as between 300,000 and 800,000 years ago. Perhaps even further back. Some scholars identify 500,000 years ago as the date when *sapiens* emerged.

One reason why this emergence date is difficult to pinpoint is that '*sapiens*' fossils all look so different from each other.

Each is a distinct blend of older and more modern features. *Helmei* specimens found in Jebel Irhoud, Morocco, dating between 350,000 and 160,000 years ago, have modern faces but skull shapes more like those of *heidelbergensis*. Anatomically modern *sapiens* specimens found in Border Cave, South Africa, dating to around 200,000 years ago, have modern skull shapes but brow ridges more like Neanderthals'.

More confusingly, even fossils dating to the *same time* look different from each other.

Even more confusingly, some more recent *sapiens* fossils look *less* like us than older ones. Specimens found in Klasies River Mouth, South Africa, dating from between 110,000 and 60,000 years ago, have jaws that look *less* like ours than the 160,000-year-old Herto (i.e. Ethiopian) specimen. A specimen found in east Turkana, Kenya, dating to about 300,000 years ago, looks a lot more like us than it does *helmei*. It's difficult to tell when the traits that define us emerged.

One explanation for this diversity is that, across time, in various parts of Africa, there lived different-looking early human populations that periodically intermixed.

Africa is large and has extraordinary environmental diversity. Early human populations could live and grow here much more easily than anywhere else. In Europe, where the climate is more temperate, large areas became frozen during very cold periods, making them uninhabitable and impassable for early humans. Conversely, in Africa, even during very cold periods, there were always places where early humans could live, or through which they could travel.

Early human populations adapted to the diverse environments of these places, and so developed different physical traits and behaviours. When they migrated and mixed, some of these were passed down. Eventually, such mixing resulted in the suite of traits that define *us*.

Millions of years ago is when, potentially, not just our earliest ancestors but also the earliest Africans emerged. Before they'd even reached any other continent, over millions of years, these Africans developed physically, socially, culturally and technologically. They practised everything we do today that we consider essential to humanity. They worshipped spirits, crafted tools and made art. A lot more is lost to us than we've discovered. But considering how long Africans have existed, how many populations of them lived in different African environments, and so developed differently, and how much they exchanged not just genes, but ideas, skills and technologies, it's easy to imagine just how many kinds of *things* – from belief systems to hunting technologies – they created over time. All this, whether we know it or not, is African history. This history didn't begin when medieval Europeans reached Africa. It is arguably the deepest, richest and most varied one on Earth.

However, we've so far recovered only a relatively small amount of disparate archaeological material relating to this very deep past. So, to get a better feel for exactly the kinds of things Africans were doing, innovating and achieving, it makes more sense to look at examples from the much more recent past.

Out of all the African civilisations I could have picked, I chose Mali and Songhay for three reasons. First, their citizens' achievements are indisputably world-class. Together, the citizens of both Mali and Songhay created an institution that was respected, innovative and famous not only in its day but even now. Second, their citizens' actions, and, particularly, those of their emperors, had a global impact and helped for ever change the world. And third, these emperors have associated with them some of the most fascinating stories in African history.

It's with the story of one of these emperors that the next section begins.

*

Let's fast-forward now to 1307 AD in Mali, West Africa. This was the year this famous emperor was born. His name was Kanku Musa Keita. He was Mandingo – one of the ethnic groups that live in the western part of the Sahel. The Sahel is the African region between the Sahara to the north and the coastal African countries to the south. Its western part is also known as the 'Sudan', and its inhabitants as 'Sudanese'.

Musa's grand-uncle, the Mandingo prince Sundiata Keita, founded Mali in 1235. It was a massive empire, which stretched over modern-day Mali, Mauritania, Senegal and Guinea.

To establish it, Sundiata had to defeat and conquer the territories of Soumaoro Kanté, king of Sosso, the most powerful kingdom in the Sahel at that time.

When he'd defeated Kanté, Sundiata and his generals – the chiefs of other peoples living in the Sudan – gathered on a plain called Kouroukan Fouga. Here, the generals proclaimed Sundiata emperor. He instituted Mali's – and one of history's – earliest constitutions, which he named after the plain.

According to al-Makrizi, a fourteenth-century Egyptian historian, Musa grew up to become, 'a young man with a brown skin, a pleasant face and good figure'.[1]

He became emperor – or, in Mandingo, *mansa* – of Mali in 1312, essentially by accident.

Musa recounted how he became emperor to the Syrian historian al-Umari, who wrote it down. Musa had met al-Umari probably in 1324 in Cairo, Egypt.

According to Musa, his father Abu Bakr II had wanted to know what lay beyond the Atlantic Ocean. He'd put together a fleet of four hundred boats. Two hundred of these he'd filled with sailors, the other two hundred with several years' worth of gold, food and water. He'd told the fleet's admiral not to return until they either found land or ran out of supplies.

They'd set out and were gone for a long time. Eventually,

only one boat had returned. In an audience with Abu Bakr and his dignitaries, Musa himself had asked what had happened.

The captain had replied, "'Prince, we . . . navigated for a long time, until we saw in the midst of the ocean as if a big river was flowing violently. My boat was the last one; others were ahead of me. As soon as any of them reached this place, [they] drowned in the whirlpool and never came out. I sailed backwards to escape this current.'"[2]

Abu Bakr hadn't believed him. He'd decided he'd lead another expedition himself. He'd assembled a fleet of three *thousand* boats – two thousand for himself and his men, the remainder for supplies. He'd made Musa regent and left. He was never seen again. Some scholars suggest he succeeded in reaching the Americas, a full two hundred years before Columbus.

Musa was very devout. Like all of Mali's rulers since the eleventh century AD, he was Muslim. Islam had entered West African kingdoms in about the eighth or ninth centuries AD. Via trade routes stretching across the Sahara, Arab and African merchants travelled to and traded in each other's cities. As well as bringing goods, like silk, to their African partners, Arab traders brought their religion. To improve their relationship with their Arab counterparts, African merchants and rulers had adopted it.

Before Musa, though Malian rulers had made Islam their religion – which had helped their politics and diplomacy with other Muslim rulers – they'd stopped short of declaring Mali a Muslim state. They, like all Malians, still held on tightly to their traditional belief systems. For those who primarily controlled access to the empire's gold reserves, this was especially true. Malian rulers' wealth relied in large part on the tribute these mine owners paid. They did all they could not to alienate them. So, although, to improve his standing among Muslim rulers, Musa made Islam Mali's official religion, he didn't impose it fanatically. If people didn't want to convert, they didn't have to. He also continued to perform traditional Mandingo rituals.

One day, Musa accidentally killed his mother. We don't know how. He was distraught. He felt he'd seriously wronged Allah. He called in his Islamic scholars and asked them how he might earn Allah's forgiveness. They told him he should visit the Prophet Muhammad's tomb in Medina (modern-day Saudi Arabia) and pray there that Muhammad would ask Allah's forgiveness on his behalf.

Musa called in the governor of Niani, Mali's capital city, and asked his advice on the best day to begin a pilgrimage to Mecca. Musa hadn't yet completed this. But it's a requirement for every Muslim to do so at least once in their lifetime. It seems Musa thought that since he had to travel to Medina, which is close to Mecca, anyway, he might as well visit both.

The fifteenth-century Songhay scholar Mahmud Kati gives us the governor's reply. The Songhay are an ethnic group that live mainly in today's Niger. The Songhay Empire is named after them. The governor said, "'You have to start your journey on a Saturday falling on the twelfth of the month, and you will not die until you get back home safe, if God wishes.'"[3]

Such a Saturday was nine months later. Meanwhile, Musa called on his subjects to contribute whatever goods they could for the journey.

Musa's pilgrimage would go down in history as one of the most magnificent anyone had ever undertaken. He gathered over sixty thousand of his subjects (including five hundred servants), and a hundred camels. All these subjects wore Persian silk and carried gold bars. Each of the servants also carried a gold staff weighing about 3kg. Each camel carried a load of gold weighing about 135kg. Musa himself travelled on horseback at the back of the train, the five hundred servants just in front of him. The train was so long that, when it set out, while those at its front reached the empire's eastern part, Musa was still in Niani, hundreds of kilometres away. He ordered that everywhere the train stopped on a Friday, a mosque be built. He desired to raise his and Mali's prestige in the kingdoms through which he passed.

In July 1324, eight months after they had set off, Musa and his train arrived in Egypt. They camped near the Pyramids of Giza. The largeness of their camp created a stir. Three days later, al-Malik al-Nasir, the Sultan of Egypt, sent an official to meet the train.

"'In all my life I have never seen anything like this,'" said the official. "'Why, this caravan competes in glittering glory with the African sun itself!'"⁴ On behalf of his sultan, he invited the Mandingo to stay in a palace in Cairo. Al-Makrizi described Musa's entrance: 'He appeared amidst his companions magnificently dressed and mounted, and surrounded by more than ten thousand of his subjects.'⁵

In Cairo, another official tried to persuade Musa to greet al-Nasir. Musa refused.

"'I came for the Pilgrimage and nothing else,'" he told this official through an interpreter, according to al-Umari. "'I do not wish to mix anything else with [it].'"⁶ This was just an excuse. Musa knew that, in an audience with the sultan, he'd have to kiss the ground before him, and his hand. One reason for his grand pilgrimage was to raise his prestige. He didn't want to submit himself to another ruler.

"'I continued to cajole him, and he continued to make excuses,'" said the official, who told the story to al-Umari. "'[But] the sultan's protocol demanded that I should bring him into the royal presence, so I kept on at him till he agreed.'"⁷

Even in al-Nasir's presence, Musa refused to submit himself. "'We said to him: 'Kiss the ground!' but he refused outright, saying: 'How may this be?''" said the official. "'Then an intelligent man who was with him whispered to him something we could not understand, and he said: 'I make obeisance to God who created me!' then he prostrated himself and went forward to the sultan.'"⁸

Musa's astute adviser had told him that, instead of kissing the ground in submission to al-Nasir, he should do it in submission to *Allah*. As a Muslim himself, al-Nasir wouldn't dispute this. True to the adviser's word, he wasn't offended at all. "'The sultan half rose to greet [Musa] and sat him by his side,'" said the official. "'They conversed together for a long time, then ... Musa went out. The sultan sent to him several complete suits of honour for himself, his courtiers, and all those who had come with him, and saddled and bridled horses for himself and his chief courtiers.'"[9]

The Mandingo stayed in Cairo for three months, waiting for the season of Muslim pilgrimage to begin. Compared to the amount of gifts Musa gave the Egyptians, al-Nasir's gifts were nothing. Musa was extraordinarily wealthy. His wealth has been estimated to be over £300 billion in today's money. Along with other goods, he brought fifteen tons of gold. 'He brought gifts and presents that amazed the eye with their beauty and splendour,'[10] wrote al-Makrizi. Many of these he gave to al-Nasir's officials. "'[He] flooded Cairo with his benefactions,'" the Egyptian official told al-Umari. "'[H]e forwarded to the royal treasury many loads of unworked native gold and other valuables ... He left no court emir nor holder of a royal office without the gift of a load of gold.'"[11]

The variety of goods on sale in Cairo amazed the Mandingo. They spent lavishly. Musa was a generous tipper. He gave away twenty *thousand* gold pieces. He also bought property – houses in which Mandingo could stay on their way to Mecca. To profit off the Mandingo as much as possible, Cairene merchants increased their prices. "'The Cairenes made incalculable profits out of [Musa] and his suite in buying and selling and giving and taking,'"[12] the Egyptian official told al-Umari. '[Indeed],' wrote al-Umari, '[m]erchants of Cairo ... have told me the profits which they made from the Africans, saying that one of them might buy a shirt or cloak or robe or other garment for five dinars when it was not worth one. Such was [the Mandingo's] simplicity and truthfulness that it was possible to practise any deception on them.'[13] Musa ended up spending almost all the money he'd brought. So much gold entered the Egyptian economy, that its value, and price, fell. The price of goods gold was used to buy shot up. To have money to spend on the rest of his journey, Musa borrowed large sums from Cairo's richest merchants. Seeing another opportunity to profit, these merchants charged him very high interest rates. The value of gold recovered.

Medina and Mecca were the meeting places of some of the greatest Islamic minds. In both, Musa recruited talented professionals of various kinds, including academics, lawyers and architects to help him further develop Mali. He also bought thousands of books on different subjects, including medicine and astronomy.

While Musa was away, Saran Mandian, his top general, had expanded Mali by conquering territories in the east. This included the important city of Timbuktu. Initially, an Amazigh woman called Buktu had founded Timbuktu in about the twelfth century as a rest stop for traders and pilgrims crossing the Sahara. The Amazigh are an indigenous people of North Africa. Buktu gave Timbuktu its name. In Tamasheq, an Amazigh language, *tin Buktu* means 'Buktu's well'. It was a place you could stop to rest and Buktu would look after you. Because Timbuktu was favourably located on the fertile plains of the Niger River and had many surrounding waterways which could be used to transport goods easily, many people stopped there. Soon, the rest stop developed into a town, then a city. By the time Saran Mandian conquered it, many Sahelian trader-scholars lived there permanently.

In Mecca, Musa heard from a Malian messenger about Saran Mandian's conquests. He decided to visit them on his way back to Niani. In Timbuktu, he put the professionals he'd recruited to work. He charged one, an Andalusian (i.e. Muslim Spanish) architect called al-Sahili, with building the Djinguereber and Sankoré mosques, as well as an audience chamber in Niani. This chamber was 'a wonderful edifice', wrote Ibn Khaldun, a fourteenth-century Arab sociologist. He continued, '[it was a] square room surmounted by a cupola . . . covered . . . with plaster and decorated . . . with arabesques in dazzling colours'.[14]

Under Musa's orders, other mosques, as well as libraries, were built around Sankoré. He filled them with scholars and books, making them into madrassas – Muslim schools. He thus effec-tively created a university – one of the world's first. By his death in 1337, Sankoré alone was capable of housing 25,000 students and had a library of between 400,000 and 700,000 books.

Sankoré was turning out world-class engineers, architects, judges and priests. It had exchange programmes with prominent universities of other Muslim states, including Morocco, Tunisia and Egypt. In the same way, Musa developed other universities in Timbuktu. By the end of the fourteenth century, Timbuktu had 180 madrassas. The city became one of the most significant learn-ing centres in Africa, the Islamic world and the world in general.

In 1325, when he'd returned to Niani, Musa paid back in one lump sum all the money he'd borrowed from the Cairene mer-chants, *plus* interest. Gold once more flooded Cairo's market. Its value reduced drastically. Its abundance put the lenders out of business, and again destabilised the Egyptian economy. Musa was an individual who was *so* wealthy that souvenir shopping could cause him to crash, stabilise, and crash again an entire currency. This affected not just Egypt, but the gold markets of the rest of Africa, the Middle East and Europe. When al-Umari visited Egypt *over a decade* after Musa's visit, its economy still hadn't recovered. 'Gold was at a high price in Egypt until [the Mandingo] came in [1324],' he wrote. 'The *mithqal* [Arabic gold coin] did not go below 25 *dirhams* [Arabic silver coin] and was generally above, but from that time its value fell, and it cheapened in price and has remained cheap till now. The *mithqal* does not exceed 22 *dirhams* or less. This has been the state of affairs for about twelve years until this day by reason of the large amount of gold which [the Mandingo] brought into Egypt and spent there.'[15]

Musa's pilgrimage brought him and his empire international renown. From North Africa and Arabia into and throughout Europe, news of his wealth spread. In 1339, Mali was depicted for the first time on a European map. In 1375, under commission from the French king Charles V, the Spanish mapmaker Abraham Cresques drew the Catalan Atlas – a map of the world, on which he put Mali, Musa and Timbuktu. This is the only visual representation we have of the great *mansa*. On the map, Cresques describes him as 'the noblest and richest king in all the land.'[16] Timbuktu is called 'Tenbuch' and is described as a *'ciutat de Melli'* ('city in Mali')[17]. Rumours swirled that Mali was a place of, according to one source, 'gold-producing plants whose nuggets were harvested like carrots'.[18] Curiosity about it grew. In the next century, beginning with the Portuguese, Europeans attempted to sail there directly. Unwittingly, Musa had ushered in the age of European exploration of Africa, which culminated in its short, but impactful, colonisation.

Now, we've learnt not just Musa's amazing tale but got a sense of his, and the medieval Mandingo's, wealth, sophistication and global influence. However, Musa, though exceptional, wasn't the only impressive Malian ruler. There are others worth noting. Moreover, we're yet to see Songhay and its citizens' similar achievements, including their development and innovation of Timbuktu.

Let's then look at these through the eyes of two famous medieval Muslim Amazigh travellers from Morocco, who described in detail all the wonderful things they saw. Their names were Ibn Battuta, a scholar, and al-Hasan al-Wazzan, a diplomat.

We'll begin with the earlier traveller – Battuta – who visited Mali in 1352, fifteen years after Musa's death.

*

Battuta was born in 1304 in Tangier, Morocco to a Muslim family of lawyers. In Tangier, Battuta himself studied law. Because of its location, Tangier was cosmopolitan. Lying at the crossroads between the rest of Africa, Europe and Arabia, peoples of different professions, like traders and soldiers, from each of these places travelled through and lived in it. A young Battuta was exposed to them. He developed an interest in strange lands. As soon as he could, he travelled from Tangier. In 1325, he made his pilgrimage to Mecca. He didn't stop there. By the time he died in 1368, he'd travelled to almost fifty of today's countries, including Turkey, Tanzania, India and China.

When Battuta arrived in Mali, its *mansa* was Musa's brother, Sulayman.

When Musa returned from his pilgrimage, he'd meant to abdicate, make his favourite son, Magha, *mansa* and retire in Mecca. But he died before he could do this. Magha succeeded him. Within a few years, though, he was dead. How is still unknown, though Sulayman is rumoured to have killed his nephew. Certainly, he succeeded him.

Sulayman was miserly. He'd seen his brother as profligate, and the famous pilgrimage he'd undertaken as unnecessarily expensive. '[Sulayman's] not a man from whom one might hope for a rich present,' Battuta wrote.[19] Battuta knew this first-hand. One day, as Battuta was relaxing in his chambers, one of Sulayman's officials, Ibn al-Faqih, burst in.

'"Stand up; here comes the [*mansa's*] stuff and gift to you,"'[20] said al-Faqih.

'So I stood up,' wrote Battuta, 'thinking – since he had called it "stuff" – that it consisted of robes of honour and money, and lo!, it was three cakes of bread, and a piece of beef fried in native oil, and a calabash [that is, a large melon-like fruit, also called a 'gourd'] of sour curds. When I saw this, I burst out laughing, and thought it a most amazing thing that they could . . . make so much of such a paltry matter.'[21]

Though not as generous as his brother, Sulayman was just as wealthy. 'Round his neck hangs a sabre with a gold sheath. He is booted and spurred [and he] holds two short iron-tipped spears, one of silver and the other of gold,' wrote Battuta.[22]

On certain days [he] holds audiences in the palace yard, where there is a platform under a tree, with three steps. This, they call the 'pempi.' It is carpeted with silk and has cushions placed on it. [Over it] is raised . . . a sort of pavilion made of silk, surmounted by a bird in gold, about the size of a falcon. The [mansa] comes out of a door in a corner of the palace, carrying a bow in his hand and a quiver on his back [in Mali, bows and quivers were status symbols identifying members of the nobility]. On his head he has a golden skull-cap, bound with a gold band which has narrow ends shaped like knives . . . [He wears] a velvety red tunic, made of . . . European fabrics . . . On reaching the pempi he stops and looks round the assembly, then ascends it in the sedate manner of a preacher ascending a mosque-pulpit.[23]

Sulayman owned several other quivers of gold and silver, as well as, wrote Battuta, 'swords ornamented with gold and with golden scabbards, gold and silver lances, and crystal maces.'[24]

Sulayman was also just as powerful as Musa. As *mansa*, his people revered him. 'If he summons any of them while he is holding an audience in his pavilion, the person summoned takes off his clothes and puts on worn garments, removes his turban and dons a dirty skullcap, and enters with his garments and trousers raised knee-high,' wrote Battuta.

He goes forward in an attitude of humility and dejection, and knocks the ground hard with his elbows, then stands with bowed head and bent back listening to what he says. If anyone addresses the [mansa] and receives a reply from him, he uncovers his back and throws dust over his head and back . . . like a bather splashing himself with water . . . If the [mansa] delivers any remarks during his audience, those present take off their turbans and put them down, and listen in silence to what he says.[25]

As well as reverent, the Mandingo were noble and just. '[They] have a greater abhorrence of injustice than any other people,' wrote Battuta.

Their [*mansa*] shows no mercy to anyone who is guilty of the least act
of it. There is [therefore] complete security in their country. Neither
traveller nor inhabitant in it has anything to fear from robbers or men of
violence. They do not confiscate the property of any [foreigner] who dies
in their country, even if it be uncounted wealth. On the contrary, they
give it into the charge of some trustworthy person among [the foreigner's
countrymen], until the rightful heir takes possession of it.[26]

The Mandingo were also very pious. 'They are careful to observe
the hours of prayer, and assiduous in attending them in con-
gregations, and in bringing up their children to them,' wrote
Battuta.

On Fridays, if a man does not go early to the mosque, he cannot find a
corner to pray in, on account of the crowd. It is a custom of theirs to send
each man his boy [to the mosque] with his prayer mat; the boy spreads
it out for his master in a place befitting him [and remains on it] until he
comes to the mosque.[27]

The Mandingo also had, wrote Battuta, '[a] zeal for learning the
Qur'an by heart. They put their children in chains if they show
any backwardness in memorising it, and they are not set free
until they have [learnt] it by heart. I [one day] visited the *qadi* [an
Islamic judge] in his house . . . His children were chained up, so I
said to him, "Will you not let them loose?" He replied, "I shall not
do so until they learn the Qur'an by heart."'[28]

There were only a few, minor things Battuta disliked about the
Mandingo. '[One] reprehensible practice among many of them
is the eating of carrion, dogs and asses,' he wrote. '[Also, the]
women servants, slave-girls, and young girls go about in front of
everyone naked, without a stitch of clothing on them. Women go
into [even] the [*mansa's*] presence naked and without coverings,
and his daughters also go about naked.'[29] Probably, Battuta exag-
gerates this 'nakedness'. He was a Muslim perhaps even stricter

than the Mandingo, for whom women showing any kind of flesh would've been 'nakedness'.

Battuta has enriched our picture of Mali. He's shown us in greater detail its splendour, as well as its citizens' admirable or intriguing traits. He's helped really drive home the impressiveness and uniqueness of this Mandingo society.

Now, let's move 150 years into the future to join al-Wazzan on his travels to, and through, Songhay.

*

To many, al-Wazzan is better known as 'Leo Africanus'. In 1518, Knights of the Order of St John – a Christian military group – captured a boat heading from Turkey to Morocco that al-Wazzan happened to be on. The captors took him to the then Pope, Leo X, in Rome. Leo hoped the Muslim traveller would be a useful source of information about his enemies, the Muslim Ottomans. He freed al-Wazzan, gave him an ample pension, and persuaded him to be baptised. As part of the baptism, Leo renamed al-Wazzan after himself. This, in combination with his travels in, and famous writings about, Africa, gave al-Wazzan his nickname.

Al-Wazzan was born in 1488 in Granada, southern Spain. He belonged to a wealthy, upper-middle-class family of civil servants. At the time of his birth, south Spain was just barely still under Muslim control. It had been so since the eighth century AD. But the Christians had now almost reconquered it. Fearing religious persecution if they succeeded, many Muslims fled to North Africa.

Just after al-Wazzan was born, this is exactly what his own family did.

They entered and stayed in Fez, Morocco. They'd left just before the Christians took over Granada and had been able to take much of their property. Al-Wazzan's father and uncle then secured themselves respectable posts in the Moroccan sultan's government. His father earned extra money buying up, and renting out, properties near Fez.

In Morocco, al-Wazzan received an excellent education. He attended local madrassas, and then the famous University of al-Qarawiyyin, one of the world's oldest. While a student, he worked for two years as a secretary at the Maristane, then an important and influential psychiatric hospital. Working there seems to have been a rite of passage for al-Qarawiyyin students. Possibly, al-Wazzan also wanted to earn extra money. After graduating, he became a diplomat like his uncle.

Al-Wazzan, accompanying his uncle on a diplomatic mission, first visited Songhay in about 1510. The Songhay Empire was founded in the fifteenth century by two men – Sunni Madawu, the ruler of Gao (one of the territories Mali had conquered), and his son, Sunni Ali. Since Musa's and Sulayman's deaths, Mali had been beset by civil wars. It had weakened. Some Amazigh had smelt blood. They'd attacked and conquered some of Mali's cities and significant trade routes. Mali had weakened further. Rulers of some of its territories had rebelled, gaining independence. Mali had weakened further still. In the early fifteenth century, Sunni Madawu attacked and defeated Mali. He sacked Niani. In the late fifteenth century, Sunni Ali conquered almost all the territories that had become independent. This was how Songhay was founded. In 1492, Ali died. His son, Sunni Baare, succeeded him.

However, just a year later, Muhammad Ture, a Muslim Soninke from Gao, and governor of Bandiagara (a town in southern Mali), deposed Baare, and seized Songhay. The Soninke are a Sudanese people of primarily today's Mali. Like the Mandingo, to whom they are related, they speak a 'Mandé' language, and so are considered a Mandé people. Muhammad took the title *askiya*, becoming Askiya Muhammad. The original meaning of '*askiya*' has been lost to time and is unknown. Possibly, it comes from a Songhay expression.

Songhay, which, since Sunni Ali's conquests had controlled

Timbuktu, was a powerful state which exerted a lot of influence over trans-Saharan trade. It not only had access to goods that were in great demand abroad, like gold, but its citizens were avid consumers of foreign luxuries, like exquisite cloths and books. It was therefore crucial for foreign merchants to visit, and for foreign kings to stay on their good side – especially those from countries plugged into the trans-Saharan trade network, like Morocco.

Al-Wazzan's uncle was sent to Songhay essentially to pay homage to Askiya Muhammad on behalf of the Moroccan sultan and keep relations sweet. During this visit, Al-Wazzan didn't get to meet the great emperor but he did get to meet the governor of Timbuktu.

Al-Wazzan loved the city so much that, in 1512, he went there again, alone, purely for fun. He then travelled to other important West African towns, including Djenné (in south Mali), Bornu (in Nigeria), and Agadez (in Niger). 'I myself saw fifteen [African] kingdoms [but] there are many more, which although I saw not with mine own eyes, yet [they] are . . . by the [Africans] sufficiently known and frequented,'[30] he wrote.

[In Timbuktu,] there is a very stately mosque, with walls made of stone and mortar, and [a] magnificent palace, which was built by an excellent builder from Granada in Spain (see page 10) . . . [T]here are [also] many shops belonging to craftsmen and merchants, and particularly to the men who weave linen and cotton cloth. European cloth is brought here by Moroccan traders . . . The inhabitants . . . are very rich . . . There are many wells which provide good water . . . There is plenty of corn, cattle, milk and butter . . . The [emperor] is very rich and owns many things made of gold. He lives in a very magnificent way . . . When he travels, he rides a camel which is led by his noblemen. He goes to war in the same way, while all his solders ride horses . . . There are always 3,000 horsemen ready to serve the [emperor], and [numerous] foot soldiers who shoot poisoned arrows . . . The people are kind and happy. They spend much of the night singing and dancing through the streets of the city.[31]

Askiya Muhammad had further developed Timbuktu. Like Musa, he was devout. He also saw great value in scholars. He surrounded himself with them, asking their advice on moral and legal matters. 'In Timbuktu, there are many teachers, judges, imams and other learned men who live at the [emperor's] expense,'[32] wrote al-Wazzan. Muhammad endowed the scholars' learning institutions, donating to Sankoré two gorgeous copies of the Qur'an. He raised Timbuktu's scholarly reputation even higher than Musa had done. Before Muhammad, Timbuktu's scholars had studied mainly books that had been imported from other centres of Islamic scholarship, like Cairo. Under Muhammad, however, Timbuktu's scholars began to write more of their own, and export them.

It's thanks largely to Muhammad that such a rich collection of books from Timbuktu exists. About one million have survived. They date to between the eleventh and twentieth centuries. They come from all over the place: from Timbuktu itself, to North Africa, Iraq, and Spain. They are loose sheets of paper imported from Europe housed in wood or leather covers. The ink with which they're written came from vegetable dyes, taken from mainly Arabic gum trees. Added to this ink were ground and burnt horns and hooves. They made the ink's colours shine more. The books are written in a variety of languages. Arabic's the main one. Some are written in the Songhay languages. Others, in Tamasheq. They're written in a variety of styles: essays, poems, letters. They cover an astonishing range of subjects: medicine, law, philosophy, grammar, calligraphy. One manuscript is a novel about the life of Alexander the Great. Another, an essay about the virtues of dogs. One seventeenth-century poem about giving up earthly desires to lead a more fulfilling life reads:

> Renounce this world; you'll be at ease,
> Only a fool it seeks to please,
> Gather from it only the least,
> 'Cos at the end, it turns to beast . . .

The ignorant are deceived by its beauty,
Until he tastes its veiled cruelty . . .

The joy of this life is followed by misery,
And its charm is brewed with agony.
Like a trip, brief! It never last,
Who yearns for it remains in lust . . .

Refrain from it! With your body and soul,
Abstain from its amity on the whole.'[33]

In Timbuktu, books were considered the most precious items. Owning and donating them became the most prestigious thing you could do – even more prestigious than refurbishing mosques. Timbuktu's scholars were utter book lovers. When any stranger came to the city, they accosted and flattered them in the hopes that they'd give or sell them what books they had. '[In Timbuktu], hand-written books [from North Africa] . . . are more expensive than any other article of trade,'[34] wrote al-Wazzan. Scholars amassed extensive private libraries, and often lent books to one another. In the margins of many are notes and comments in different handwriting. Some are supplementary information to the main text, for instance, dates or biographical details of people mentioned in it. Others are reflections on the text's arguments. Ahmad Baba, a sixteenth-century scholar who wrote more than sixty books on subjects ranging from historical biographies to grammar, had 1,600 books. '[And this was] the smallest library of any of my kin,'[35] he said. Another sixteenth-century scholar, al-Wangari, lent his books so freely to whoever asked for them, and often forgot to get them back, that he accidentally gave away nearly his entire library! Today, arguably the largest library of Timbuktu manuscripts is Mali's Mamma Haidara Commemorative Library. It has 5,000 books dating as far back as the sixteenth century. Abdel Kader Haidara, the founder of this library, is a descendant of Ahmad Baba. Very likely, some of Baba's own books now form part of this library. As one famous Sudanese proverb goes, 'Salt comes from the north, gold from the south, and silver from the country of the white men, but the word of God and the treasures of wisdom are only to be found in Timbuktu.'[36]

By far, the most revered book in Timbuktu was the Qur'an. Almost every household would have a copy, even if its occupiers hadn't yet learnt to read. In the madrassas, it was this text that was most deeply and frequently taught. Young students were made to recite it. They were also taught how to interpret it, as well as Islamic law. If they could afford to, students then entered a university like Sankoré. University-student life revolved around Sankoré, Djinguereber, and Sidi Yahya universities or mosques. There, students took advanced studies in a range of subjects, including Arabic, Islamic law, various sciences, and commentaries on the Qur'an. To earn extra money, and familiarise themselves with their tutors' teachings, they made copies of their books by hand. This was unfavourably looked-upon work. It didn't pay very much, and took a long time to complete. Depending on how long the book was, and how complex the calligraphy it was written in, it might take a student several weeks or months to write it out. Still, the passionate and determined student got some value out of the practice. Undoubtedly, too, *someone* in Timbuktu would be keen to receive the finished product.

With this chapter and the stories I've told in it, I have aimed to introduce what is essentially the point of the book: the extraordinary breadth and depth of African cultures and histories. They extend all the way back to the beginning of our species, and are represented by diverse societies that were, and are, socially, culturally and economically advanced. If we dig a bit deeper than the last three hundred years of slavery and colonialism and also look a bit wider than these events' impacts on modern African societies, this becomes clear.

Now that we've explored a portion of African societies' historical depth, let's look at a little of their modern cultural breadth. Particularly, let's look at a practice that, though ancient, is just as important to Africans today, and that, though a feature of many African cultures, is done differently in almost all of them: ancestral veneration.

2

HOW THE DEAD STILL LIVE

In many African cultures, just as with past and present, there's little distinction between living and dead. Those who have passed on continue to live in some way and have an active presence in our lives. If they lived particularly well, they inspire us just as though they were with us physically. In Africa, no matter what happens, the community endures.

In July 2013, I was in the town of Abetifi, Ghana, with my family. It was my grandpa's funeral. He was Kwahu. Abetifi is their principal town. It's located in the district called Kwahu. My grandpa was born and grew up there. We stayed in his childhood home. My grandfather had converted to Catholicism. At Abetifi, we performed both Christian and Akan funerary rites. My grandpa was buried in a mausoleum, with a church on top of it. In the church, we held a service in honour of him. Afterwards, the retinue of the *Akyempimhene*, chief of the Akyem (another Akan people), processed to the church steps. The chief had come to pay his respects. He often acts as a representative of the *Asantehene*. The Asante are a major Akan ethnic group, to which I also belong. The *Asantehene* is our king. The *Akyempimhene*'s retinue included trumpeters, singers, and shield-bearers. As they processed, they made music and performed acrobatics.

We stayed in Kwahu for several days. In Ghana, funerals are week-long affairs. At one point, I was shown a significant family heirloom. In the house, there stood the stool of my grandfather's side of my family.

Stools are one of the Akan's most important, widespread, and recognisable cultural artefacts. They've been so for some five hundred years. They're not very big – about fifty centimetres wide, and thirty centimetres tall. They're made of three parts: a base, a middle (the legs), and a top (the seat). These are carved from a soft, white wood called *osese*.

The middle is often carved into the shape of a traditional symbol with which a proverb is associated. One of the most popular of these is the *Gye Nyame* symbol. Nyame is the Akan's Sky-God and supreme deity. One proverb associated with him, and thus his symbol, is '*Obi nkyere akwadaa Nyame*' ('Nobody teaches a child about God'). That is, God is everywhere in our lives to the extent that nobody, even a child, needs to be taught that he exists.

Depending on who they're made for, and belong to, stools serve either practical, everyday functions, or sacred, official ones.

Stools made for the ordinary Akan are used just as their name suggests. They're sat on, for instance, to do the cooking or washing up. When an Akan completes a life ceremony – say, marriage – family members might give them a stool to mark the occasion.

Stools made for, and belonging to, Akan chiefs, on the other hand, are symbols of their royal authority. They are part of their regalia. They're used to swear in successors. These stools are often larger, and more elaborately decorated, than the average Akan's. When an Akan chief dies, a mixture of soot and egg yolk is rubbed on his stool to honour him. These 'black stools' are believed to hold the spirits of the chiefs they belonged to. They're kept in their own special room in the palace. Due to their importance in the stool ritual described above, once upon a time in the Asante Empire, you could be executed for dropping an egg.

The Asante's most important cultural artefact is the *Sika Dwa Kofi* ('Golden Stool'). Forty-six centimetres tall and sixty centimetres wide, it's made of solid gold.

According to Asante tradition, Okomfo ('Priest') Anokye, adviser to the Asante prince Osei Tutu, who founded the Asante Empire in 1701, summoned the Golden Stool from a storm-broken sky. Tutu needed a symbol that would unite several disparate Akan kingdoms into a single state and confirm his rulership over them.

In the late-seventeenth century, Tutu led a coalition of Akan kingdoms against then the most powerful Akan kingdom – Denkyira. Denkyira had grown rich from trade with Europeans including the Dutch, exchanging gold and enslaved Africans for guns. With these, they'd conquered other Akan kingdoms, from whom they'd exacted tribute. This included Kwaman, the Asante's kingdom. Denkyira's increased power had made its leaders tyrannical. Consistently, they'd increased the price of tributes and executed those who couldn't pay.

When Tutu became king of Kwaman in the 1680s, he stopped paying tribute. He also conquered some of the Denkyira's territories. Incensed, Denkyira's ruler, Ntim Gyakari, demanded Tutu bring him gold, a necklace of precious beads, which was a traditional Akan symbol of submission, and his favourite wife. Tutu refused. Gyakari officially declared war on Kwaman. Tutu recruited Akan leaders also sick of Denkyira's tyranny.

In 1701, Tutu's coalition's forces routed the Denkyira, and killed Gyakari. Tutu marched into Denkyira's capital, Abankeseso, sacked, and plundered it. Anokye then summoned the Golden Stool. Among a joyous crowd, it fell directly into Tutu's lap. In African cultures (as in many others), like past and present, and living and dead, the distinction between myth and historical fact is blurred.

The Golden Stool is the soul of the Asante nation. It's believed to contain the souls of deceased Asante. It's kept in a secret, sacred grove. It's lain down, always on its side, so that these souls do not spill towards Nyame in the sky. To touch it is forbidden. For it to touch the ground is forbidden. It's seen and treated as a living creature. At festivals throughout the year, it's 'fed' – that is, sacrificed to. It's used to swear in Asante kings. Several other Akan chiefs lift him up and down over the stool three times. Each time, the Asantehene's right-hand chief, the Mamponghene, says, "'We place you on the Golden Stool of Asante with our united blessing.'" If left 'hungry', turned upright, or taken from the Asante, it's believed the Asante nation itself will die.

The stool in my grandfather's childhood home is believed to contain his dead relatives' souls. In it, they continue to live. When he died, his soul, too, entered it. When I touched it, I felt his presence.

Now, let's look at some other examples of how, in Africa, death is not the end of life.

*

Let's begin with the modern-day Dagara. They are a people of primarily northern Ghana. As we'll see with the Dagara (and this chapter's other examples), in African cultures where the dead continue to live, they cannot do so without their mortal community members' or relatives' help. In many cases, they continue to live only because of the centuries-old and diverse funerary rituals these members perform after they die.

Preparing a dead Dagara for burial involves first cleaning the body. At the deceased's house, old Dagara women shave it with a sharp knife. They rub it down with pomade – an oil- or water-based wax. Dagara men dress it in a rich, vibrant smock. They bend and extend its limbs to loosen up its joints. This is for an important, later ritual. One of them leaves the house. He cries and wails loudly. He might also play a xylophone or fire a gun. Usually, this happens if the deceased had been important or wealthy. Others in the community learn that the funeral is about to begin. They also start to cry and wail.

The other men bring the deceased's body outside. They seat it against the house. Elders – senior members of the deceased person's family – summon the chief gravedigger. The gravedigger is an expert in burial customs. They give him axes, hoes and cutlasses with which he and his assistants dig the grave. With his assistants' help, the chief gravedigger also makes what's known as the funeral stand. Meanwhile, mourners chant, musicians play xylophones, and the deceased's relatives throw money at the gravediggers. This is their payment.

The stand is a wooden platform on four long, wooden legs. It is made of wood from *dawadawa* trees. On the platform, the gravediggers build a canopy. Over its roof, they lay vibrant cloths. They place the deceased on the platform. They have to position the body in a specific way, depending on the deceased's sex. The earlier loosening of its joints makes this easier. They have to arrange deceased men cross-legged, facing east, and deceased women, with legs outstretched, arms crossed upon their laps, facing west. These represent men's and women's distinct roles in Dagara society. When, in the east, the sun rises, a male Dagara wakes, gets up, and begins his farm work. When, in the west, the sun sets, a female Dagara, awaiting her husband's return, prepares food for her family.

For several hours, while the mourners' chants and xylophone playing continue, the body remains on the platform. The gravediggers then surround the stand. One stands in front of it, facing away. Two more climb the stand. They lift the body and lower it onto the first digger's shoulders. He then *sprints* to the dug grave. The Dagara believe that the unburied deceased can kill mortals. They must be put in the ground quickly. To prevent the deceased from killing their colleague, the other gravediggers distract them by running about and shouting.

When he reaches the grave, the gravedigger lays down the body. He takes from his pockets a knife, white straw and shea tree leaves. These continue to protect him from the deceased's attacks. He leaps into the grave. The others lift the body and hand it to him. He gently lays it in the earth. The deceased's relatives now arrive. They inspect the grave. If nothing is out of order, they give the signal for the gravediggers to cover the body with gravel.

All pre-burial rituals complete, the deceased's soul begins their journey to *Dapar* – the spirit world. Like many other African peoples, the Dagara believe that death is simply an individual's transition from the visible, physical world to the invisible, spirit world. When they make this transition, they cease to be members of the 'living' and become members of the 'living dead' instead. The spirit world is not separated from the physical world. It rests upon it, like an invisible cloth upon a table. In its nature, it's almost exactly like the physical world. Everything that exists in the physical world also exists in the spirit world. In the latter, the living dead live and behave just like they did in the former. Like mortals, they have senses and emotions. They even continue to practise the trades and professions they did when living. They can communicate with each other, as well as with their physical, mortal relatives.

However, the spirit world, and everything in it, is invisible to the living. It's impossible for them to enter it. Mortals see the living dead only if the living dead purposefully make themselves known to them. The only way for mortals to enter the spirit world is to die and be buried – that is, to transition themselves from living to living dead.

The deceased Dagara's soul reaches the realm between the physical world and *Dapar*. It's a ghostly forest. Separated from their living relatives, and not yet with their living dead ones, the deceased Dagara is a *nyaakpiin* ('ghost'). Some living dead have journeyed here to meet the deceased. They tie them to the top of a tree. The deceased must be purified before they enter *Dapar*. This is done by their mortal relatives' completion of the post-burial ritual. It involves the brewing of two kinds of beer for the living dead. The first is the *koda tuo* ('bitter funeral beer'). It is left in large, clay pots outside the deceased's home for the living dead to drink. When it is brewed, the living dead untie the deceased from the tree and sit them under it. They shave the deceased's head, and then come and drink the *koda tuo*. A hair found in a pot the day after they were laid out confirms this. Three weeks later, the living relatives brew the *koda maar* ('cool funeral beer'). The living dead come and drink this, too, after which they lead the deceased to *Dapar*.

Let's look now at our second example – the Kasena, a people also of modern-day Ghana. As with the Dagara, it's the rituals the deceased Kasena's living relatives complete that enable them to live on in the spirit world. In this case, though, by, for instance, completing the same rituals as when a baby is born, these relatives metaphorically transform the deceased Kasena *themselves* into a newborn baby, such that they can be 'reborn' into the spirit world.

As happens with a newborn baby, with hot water and herbs, a dead Kasena man's sons and brothers wash his corpse. (The only time they don't do this is during the rainy season, as it is feared a washed corpse in the ground might cause too much rainfall). They then dress him. With black string, they tie around his mouth a black cloth called *kyira-ngwana* ('spirit rope'). They wrap him in a *sara* – a mat made of elephant grass – leaving his head uncovered. For dead Kasena women, daughters and sisters do the same.

In the *lua-songo* ('funeral house', i.e. the deceased's house), a male corpse is kept in his widow's, or, if he died unmarried, his grandmother's, room. It's laid on its back. On the other hand, a female corpse is kept in her mother-in-law's room, or in her own. It's laid on its side. Some Kasena families have a special room in which all corpses are kept.

Elderly Kasena often wear talismans, which, when they die, must be removed before they're mourned and buried. Such talismans include *jom* ('protecting amulet') and *tamgom-kwara* ('grove horn'). To remove them, the *tigatu* ('owner of the land') performs various rituals. The one to remove the horn requires a fresh calabash and a small chicken. The *tigatu* enters the room with the corpse, and gently rubs a chicken against it several times – three for a man, four for a woman. As he does so, he says,

"*Kwara kam mo a wora a lia.*" ("It is the horn I am removing.")[2] He sacrifices the chicken and slips off the object. He receives as payment a sheep and a chicken from the deceased's family, and leaves.

The deceased's male relatives also exit the house and gather in the *minchongo* ('front yard'). When a baby is about to be born, they do the same, while the women assist with the birthing. To start the mourning period, the deceased's eldest brother, or son, faces the granary, and wails. Inside, on hearing him, the women, sitting round the corpse, also wail. Mourning is at least three days long. But it can last months, even years.

If the deceased is male, for three days, the men periodically sing funeral songs and perform war dances. If female, they do these for four. If the deceased is an elder, neighbouring clans send dancers and drummers, and the women inside laugh and sing. In many African cultures, living to old age, and thus having had a full life, is something to be celebrated. Near the corpse, the women have placed a pot of shea-nut oil. Periodically, they rub it on the deceased.

Meanwhile, alerted by the wailing, the deceased's extended family and friends visit the funeral house, pay their respects, and offer consolations. It's not too dissimilar to the way in which they greet newborn babies. To the deceased, they give speeches, recounting the history of their relationship, and expressing their feelings about their passing. To the women, they give gifts of kola nuts and drinks.

Now, the *kwobia* – '(community) elders' – take over the funeral proceedings.

They ask the family where the dead person should be buried.

Depending on their status in life, deceased Kasena are buried in one of four places: the *didongo* ('old rooms', i.e. family crypt), the *kunkolo* ('courtyard'), the *naboo* ('cattle yard'), or also within the farmyard in front of the house. Usually, the *songo-tu* ('house owner') is buried in the cattle yard, close to his granary. The *diga-tu* ('senior woman of the household') is ordinarily buried in the courtyard.

From the family, the elders receive two calabashes, a digging stick, a hoe and an axe.

The elders give these to a chief *bayaa* ('funeral expert') and ask him to prepare the grave. Funeral experts have been initiated into a guild called *bayaaro* ('dealing with the dead'). It's an honour for them to dig the grave. As a midwife specialises in bringing a soul from the spirit to the mortal world, so the funeral expert does in returning it.

First, the chief funeral expert completes a certain ritual. Through it, he asks the permission of We (the Kasena's god), the Earth Mother Katiga (We's wife), and the spirits for the deceased to be buried near them.

He puts one of the calabashes face down and calls over two of his attendants. They each carry pebbles – three if the dead person's a man, four if a woman. They stand against the calabash and take turns throwing the pebbles at it.

When they've thrown them all, the chief picks up the calabash. He points it north, south, east and west. He taps it, face down, against the ground – three times for a man, four for a woman.

After the final tap, he traces round it with the digging stick. Here, exactly, is where the grave should be dug.

To do so takes about three days. Funeral experts make them a particular shape, with a narrow entrance and a wide base, such that they resemble the womb. Customarily, the grave (or, for that matter, the corpse) should never be left unattended. The attendant ordered to dig the grave eats, and even sleeps, at the gravesite. Often, friends of the deceased visit him and give him gifts.

Once dug, he sets alight a special powder and tosses it in the grave to smoke it out. He also *boone-yeerem* ('jeers at the hole'). After five or so minutes, when the smoke clears, the other attendants join him. They also shout and jeer at the hole. One of them gathers white elephant grass and ash. He places the grass across the grave's mouth and spreads the ash around it. The grave is considered the dead person's new home, and this ritual is to shoo away all the other spirits potentially occupying it.

Once informed that the grave is ready, the chief expert sends two attendants to tell the elders the same.

The elders tell the family.

The family inspects the grave.

If satisfied, they give the expert who dug it gifts, including groundnuts, fowls (i.e. domestic birds, like hens), kola nuts, tobacco and drinks. They head home to pay their final respects to the deceased. The experts follow them.

Now, any curses that the deceased put upon their children in life must be undone. This is so that these children can attend the funeral (i.e. burial), as, ordinarily, children whose angry parents have cursed them can't. To remove the curse, one of the funeral experts takes a young, slain chicken, and goes with the cursed child to the deceased's body. "'You were wrong to have cursed your son,'" the expert says. "'Your father never cursed you, nor did he chase you away, or prevent you from celebrating his funeral, and for that reason you cannot forbid your son from your funeral by a curse. That is why your son is here today to take part in your funeral celebrations: to show that he has a father. Here is a chicken for you to retract your curse.'"[3] The expert puts the chicken in the deceased's hand. He still holds it himself. He asks the child to take hold of it, too, and pull. The chicken is torn in half. The expert picks up the two halves, leaves, and buries them.

When he returns, he and the other attendants wrap up the corpse in another mat. Heading to the gravesite, they carry it out of the house, head-first, just as babies are born. The family, dancers and drummers follow them. The elders remain behind.

When they reach the gravesite, everyone but the family and experts leaves.

The experts lay the corpse by the grave, its head pointing towards the hole.

One expert stands in the grave. Another picks up the corpse and lowers it to him, feet-first. It is as though the deceased is being returned to Katiga's womb.

The expert in the grave puts the body in the foetal position. Male corpses are positioned facing east, females facing west.

He climbs out. One last time, the family inspects the grave. If they approve, the expert re-enters it, removes the outer mat, and unties the spirit rope. He places the rope and string in front of the corpse.

When he's climbed out again, he and the other attendants cover the body with broken pot pieces and soil. If it is the dry season, they burn the outer mat. If the wet one, they bury it in a valley.

At the graveyard, the experts who carried the corpse and performed the burial wash themselves. Two go to tell the elders that all tasks have been completed. The elders thank the experts and give them even more gifts: tobacco, hoes, millet, and groundnuts.

When the family returns home, the elders ask them whether anything else needs to be done. If the answer is no, they say goodbye and leave.

The women, and mourners not part of the immediate family, go inside. The mourners have brought home-cooked food. For the deceased's family, cooking when mourning is forbidden. The male family members go back to the front yard. For three days, if the deceased was male, they grieve. Four if she was female.

We've seen a little of how, in Africa, in different ways, the dead continue to live. For the Akan, they remain alive in stools as spirits. For the Dagara, they remain alive in their spirit world of *Dapar*. For the Kasena, they are reborn into the spirit world.

Moreover, it's possible for their mortal relatives to communicate with them, ask their advice, and even welcome them back into the physical world to help them. Let's look at some examples.

*

Our main example is the modern-day Yoruba, a people primarily of Nigeria. Welcoming back into the mortal world their living dead relatives is an essential part of their relationship with them. They believe in *atunwa* ('reincarnation'). A child born soon after a Yoruba died is believed to be their reincarnation. If the child is the same sex as the recently deceased, this is especially so. The family confirms the reincarnation, looking for similarities between the new child and the deceased relative – for example, a similar scar in a similar place, or, in slightly older children, the remembrance of events only the deceased experienced. Such children are given names like Babatunde ('the father has come again') or Sehinde ('come again').

In one significant festival, the Yoruba purposefully reincarnate important *ancestors*. This festival is called *Egungun*. In Yoruba, *'Egun'* means 'ancestors'. The festival takes place once a year, sometime between July and December, and lasts two weeks.

Ancestors are a special kind of living dead. Many African people believe that a hierarchy of invisible and visible beings inhabits the universe. At the top of this hierarchy is God. God is all-knowing, all-powerful, and the creator of everything else in the universe. The Yoruba's God is Olodumare. Below God are slightly less powerful deities. They oversee aspects of the human condition, for example, war, love and disease. They're like the deities in the Egyptian, Greek, or Mesopotamian pantheons. Below them are the ancestors. Then, there are the living dead. Then mortals, animals, plants, and the earth's minerals.

To become an ancestor after death, an individual must have lived either an exemplary or extraordinary life. In Africa, where family and community are of paramount importance, this involves having acted in ways that benefitted both. Having completed the rituals that mark important life transitions, like puberty and getting married, is essential. Such rituals are an important part of the tradition that the founders of the community created and passed down. Completing them is a sign of respect for these founders, and the community. It also encourages the community's young people to do the same. This ensures the survival of the tradition, and thus, the community. It's for this reason that, to become an ancestor, an individual must have lived into old age. Elders are more likely than not to have completed these rituals.

Having had children is also essential. It increases the number of people that contribute to the community. So, too, is having behaved socially. For instance, respecting, being kind to, and helping others. Also, avoiding gossiping, indulging in vices, like gambling, and committing crimes, like theft.

There are both personal and community ancestors. The first are progenitors of a nuclear family. For instance, a father or grandmother. The second are believed to be progenitors of an entire clan or ethnic group. Often, they lived and died in time out of mind.

The *Orisha* – deities of the Yoruba pantheon – were once personal, and then community, ancestors. Historically, they were accomplished and deeply admired rulers, warriors and healers. Their descendants held them in such exceptionally high esteem that they began to think of them as deities. Mythologically, *Orisha* didn't die like other human beings. They walked directly into *Orunrere* ('Heaven') through a cave or turned into stone sculptures. Their deity status was cemented.

In Yoruba belief, *Orisha* help create human beings.

To the Yoruba, the human being is made up of three parts: *ara* ('body'), *emi* ('life-force' or 'breath'), and *ori* (personality).

Of the three, *ori* is arguably the most important. Sometimes called the 'inner head', the Yoruba conceive of it as a head *inside* the physical head. For the Yoruba, the head, being home to four out of five of the senses, is the most important part of the body. The *ori* determines a person's personality and the course of their life. In other words, the *ori* a person receives from the *Orisha* pre-ordains everything they'll see, do, and how lucky, rich, or successful they'll be. Sometimes, the Yoruba think of it as a guardian angel, guiding its container to make decisions that will lead them to their destiny. Some *ori* might have abysmal destinies, but great personalities. For the Yoruba, the latter counts much more than, and can help their possessor overcome, the former. An unlucky, but hardworking, kind and respectful, person can achieve much more than a terribly lucky, but lazy, greedy and rude one.

Before a person is born, Obatala, *Orisha* of peace and purity, creates their *ara*. Olodumare, who gave Obatala that job, breathes *emi* into it. The person is then sent to a workshop, where hundreds of *ori*, resembling head sculptures, line rows upon rows of shelves.

This workshop belongs to the *Orisha* Ajala. Unlike most *Orisha*, the Yoruba have little reverence for him. He's a skilled craftsman, who creates *ori*. But he's also lazy, careless, a drunkard, a bit of a coward, and always in debt. The *ori* he crafts all *look* the same. However, some determine great destinies, which would lead their owner to happiness, fame and fortune. Others, well, do the opposite. Only Ajala can tell the difference.

Yet, when the person enters his workshop, Ajala is nowhere to be seen. Usually, he's hiding in the rafters from his creditors. He makes no effort to help the person choose their *ori*. The only way, potentially, that the person can get him to come down is to offer to pay his debts.

When they pick their *ori*, the person is shown their destiny. Now, they can't pick another.

They go to the gates between Heaven and Earth. To the gate-keeper, they relay the destiny they've chosen. The gatekeeper seals it. He shows them through, and they're born into the world. They forget completely what their destiny has in store for them.

As African peoples, we often communicate with our ancestors. Death doesn't sever the relationships we have with our deceased relatives. The living dead continue to participate in our lives just as much as the living. In many instances, we can, and do, speak to them as though they were still in the physical world.

'You, [father], your junior [relative] is ill,' a Suku elder would say at his father's grave. The Suku are a people of Congo. 'We do not know why, we do not know who is responsible. If it is you, if you are angry, we ask for forgiveness. If we have done wrong, pardon us. Do not let him die. Other lineages are prospering, and our people are dying ... Why do you not look after us properly?'[4]

We get in touch with our ancestors often because we need their help. We go to *them*, rather than other living dead, because we respect them the most. They're our society's perfect role models. Also, they're the most able of all the spirit-world beings to help us. The Supreme Being is often aloof. They don't concern themselves with the petty tribulations of mere mortals. We dare not approach the deities because of their immense power and temperamentality. Ancestors are far more approachable and personable. They're close enough to the Supreme Being in the universal hierarchy to have received some of Their mystical powers. Ancestors are more influential than the ordinary living dead. They can use these powers for our benefit.

Or our destruction. Only ancestors we honour are willing to help us. Otherwise, they punish us. Such honouring is known as ancestral veneration. It's the foundation of our relationship with our ancestors. Veneration involves appeasing our ancestors in various ways as often as we can. This could be taking care of their resting place. Or it could be presenting to them at this place offerings, such as food, including honey, fruit, kola nuts and alcohol. Or, especially for community ancestors, it could be putting on festivals that celebrate them.

Commonly, veneration is practised through the performance of the libation ritual. This involves the pouring of an alcoholic drink on the ground while a prayer in honour of the ancestors is said.

'"Supreme God, who is alone great, upon whom men lean and do not fall, receive this wine and drink,"' goes an Akan libation prayer. '"Earth goddess, whose day of worship is Thursday, receive this wine and drink. Spirits of our ancestors, receive this wine and drink."[5]

When venerated, our ancestors bless us. They make us luckier and more prosperous. They increase rainfall, and our crop yields. They tilt circumstances in our favour so that we achieve our ambitions. They keep us in good health. They keep us happy. They come to us in dreams, or as certain types of animals, like birds, and give us advice or guidance.

If ignored, they curse us. Not often actively. They simply withdraw their blessings and protection. We become unlucky. We become ill. We suffer droughts and famine.

The Mbeere, a people of Kenya, believe that, if neglected, their ancestors, called *ngoma* ('shades'), actively harm them. *Ngoma* are like shadows in form and nature. They can't be grasped. It's impossible to capture them. When chased, they always remain just out of reach. They're said to live in natural formations just outside human settlements, like mountains, forests, rivers, and caves. In daylight, they stay in these places. At night-time, they visit their neglectful living relatives. You know an *ngoma*'s nearby when, out of the blue, you hear spooky singing. They make the neglectful living ill. Or they throttle them to death. Or they kill their livestock.

To appease a wrathful *ngoma*, an Mbeere performs a libation. They pour beer, first around the outside of their home, and then outwards to the edge of the settlement. The *ngoma* is appeased by this alcoholic offering. They're also led away from the afflicted household back to their natural dwellings. They cease disturbing their descendant.

Egungun – the Yoruba reincarnation festival mentioned earlier (see page 34) – is for the veneration of community ancestors.

It begins when the *Egungun* cult chooses a skilled dancer. This cult is made up exclusively of men. They handle the festival's proceedings.

By putting on a special costume called *eku*, the dancer will transform into the ancestor. The costume will cover him from head to toe. It's made of cloth and leather. It's variously and brightly coloured. It may be blue, white, and yellow. Ancestors have their preferred colours. Shango, the *Orisha* of war, likes red, whereas Orunmila, the *Orisha* of wisdom, likes white. The *eku* is also decorated with beads, shells and animal skulls that dangle from metallic threads. The more beautiful the costume, and the greater the presence of the ancestor's favourite colours, the happier they'll be. The happier the ancestor, the more blessings they'll give the living community.

The cult members pay the dancer, either in money or cloth. At shrines or in sacred groves, the cult leaders hold an all-night feast. The dancer is also present. They chant. They recite incantations. They pour libations with gin. They might sacrifice an animal, like a goat. The dancer might step on or drink its blood. They thus welcome the ancestor from the spirit world to our own.

The dancer puts on the costume. As soon as he does, he ceases to be himself. He becomes an empty vessel which the ancestor enters. Now, he *is* the ancestor. Some of the previous rituals had been performed partly for his protection. Without them, when the ancestor's spirit entered him, he would've died. The costume is not only a gateway between the physical and spirit worlds. The ancestors' spirits dwell within it. It is sacred, powerful and dangerous. It can be used only for *Egungun*. When not in use, it's kept in a shrine. Like the Golden Stool, it's cared for like a living person. It's 'fed' with the blood of ritually sacrificed animals. Goats, cocks and pigeons are cut. Their blood is poured onto the costume. The ancestors are appeased. The costume's spiritual power is renewed.

The ancestor leaves the grove or shrine. He dances into town. The cult leaders, as well as drummers, singing women and children, follow him. When the ancestor reaches the square, he dances for the crowd's entertainment. His moves are delightful – organic, fluid steps interspersed with energetic bursts of movement.

On the festival's final day, the ancestor is led back to the spirit world. At dusk, the cult members take the ancestor around town. They sing farewell songs. They head to the grove. Rituals similar to those performed at the festival's start are again performed. The ancestor returns to the spirit world. The dancer's transformation is undone. He comes back to himself. Thankfully, he's well.

Just by being in the physical world, ancestors aid their descendants. Their presence keeps at bay misfortune, danger and evil intentions. Some offer more active protection. They take part in rituals meant to rid the community of witchcraft and disease. They act as judges to resolve family or community disputes. They recite proverbs to ridicule and warn those who've behaved anti-socially. They ensure the Yorubas' well-being.

Now, we've seen a little of what ancestors are in the African context, how Africans relate to and communicate with them, and what ancestors and their mortal relatives do for each other.

I mentioned earlier how someone becomes an ancestor by having lived an exemplary life. Next, I want to look at a specific, very intriguing example of this. Intriguing because of how recent it was, and how it demonstrated that African-descent people all over the world, even if they weren't raised in a solely African culture, have a pervasive sense of ancestral veneration.

*

The American actor Chadwick Boseman depicted American, and, particularly, African American ancestors, like James Brown. When he died, he was himself also considered an ancestor. In large part, this was because of how successfully he'd played said ancestors, and his determination not to play Africans solely as victims. But it was also because of his personality – his drive, persistence and humility – that many admired. Boseman had Yoruba ancestry. Obviously, he'd chosen a good *ori*.

Chadwick Aaron Boseman was born on 29 November 1976 in

Anderson, South Carolina. His mother was a nurse. His father worked at a textile factory. He never intended to be an actor.

His first love was art. He drew a lot. He wanted to become an architect.

Then it was basketball. He was good at it, too. College coaches were prepared to give him scholarships. One day, he might have made the NBA.

But one of his school teammates was shot dead. Boseman was distraught. To process his grief, he wrote and directed a play called *Crossroads*. He realised he wanted to tell stories. 'I just had a feeling that this was something that was calling me,' he said. 'Suddenly, playing basketball wasn't as important.'[6]

Boseman applied to Howard, the traditionally African American university, where he majored in directing. He became immersed in African American and African histories and cultures. He met and mixed with Africans from all over the world. He worked in an African bookstore. He visited Africa for the first time when he went with a friend to Ghana. They performed traditional rituals. He later called this, 'one of the most significant learning experiences of my life.'[7] 'At a historically black college, you're getting turned on to all these things – the pantheon of our culture,' said Boseman. 'It's John Coltrane, it's James Baldwin. And it's *Black Panther*.'[8]

Sometimes, Boseman acted. But only because he thought it would make him a better director. 'I felt like I needed to understand what the actors were doing and their process so that I could better guide them,'[9] he said.

Yet, Phylicia Rashad, his acting tutor, recognised his talent and persuaded him to act more and to take it seriously. Rashad is best known for having starred as Clair Huxtable in the 1980s and '90s classic sitcom, *The Cosby Show*. She told Boseman about the British American Drama Academy's Midsummer in Oxford Program. For a month, at Oxford University, American students study British drama. It was a wonderful opportunity. But

Boseman, fearing he'd be rejected, was reluctant to apply. Only with Rashad's support did he do so. 'She basically talked me into auditioning for that program,'[10] he said.

Along with some classmates, Boseman was accepted.

But they'd miscalculated their budget. '[They said,] "We want you to know that we auditioned . . . and we got in!"' said Rashad. 'And I said, "Well that's great!" And they said, "But we're not going to go." And I asked why not. And they said, "Because we don't have the money to go. We can't afford it." And I said, " . . . [Y]ou're going. Pack your bags and be ready. You're going."'[11]

She made some calls and raised the money. 'She essentially got some celebrity friends to pay for us to go,'[12] said Boseman. Later, Boseman revealed that his sponsor was the Hollywood star, Denzel Washington. When Washington received the American Film Institute's Life Achievement Award, Boseman said this in his speech: 'Imagine receiving a letter that your tuition for that summer was paid for, and that your benefactor was none other than the dopest actor on the planet . . . There is no *Black Panther* without Denzel Washington.'[13]

At Oxford, Boseman studied playwrights including Shakespeare, Samuel Beckett, and Harold Pinter. He got turned on to acting. 'When I came back, I began to feel like, "Oh, now I know what it means to be an actor,"' said Boseman. '"There's a difference between being able to do it and *being* it."'[14]

After graduating from Howard, Boseman moved to New York. He pretty much only wrote, directed and auditioned for plays. He barely even saw his family and friends. Each project he worked on had to be meaningful. 'Because that's how it started,'[15] he said.

His career took off. His plays were staged. He got work as a director. In the first play he auditioned for, he got the lead role. His performance got him an agent – Michael Greene. Greene helped him get his first TV job, on the soap opera *All My Children*. 'I was on a roll,' said Boseman. 'With this . . . gig, I was already promised to make six figures. More money than I had ever seen.'[16]

But, when he got the script, Boseman wasn't happy. 'The role wasn't necessarily stereotypical,' he said. 'A young man in his formative years with a violent streak pulled into the allure of gang involvement. That's somebody's real story ... I was conflicted because this role seemed to be wrapped up in assumptions about us as Black folk ... There was barely a glimpse of positivity or talent in the character, barely a glimpse of hope ... Howard had instilled in me a certain amount of pride and for my tastes this role didn't live up to those standards.'[17]

On his third day, two producers called Boseman into their office. He'd already filmed two episodes. They said they loved his performance and wanted him to stick around. If there was anything he needed, he should just ask.

"'Where's [my character's] father?'"[18] said Boseman.

"'Well, he left when [he was] younger,'"[19] said one of the producers.

"'OK,'" said Boseman. "'In this script, it alluded to [my character's] mother not being equipped to operate as a good parent. Why exactly would [his] little brother and [him] have to go into foster care?'"[20]

"'Well of course, she's on heroin,'"[21] said the same producer.

"'If we're around here assuming that the black characters in the show are criminals, on drugs, and deadbeat parents, then that would probably be stereotypical, wouldn't it?'"[22]

The room was silent. The producer Boseman had been talking to picked up and studied his CV.

The other producer smiled awkwardly. Then, she said, "'As you have seen, things move really fast around here. But we are more than happy to connect you with the writers if you have suggestions.'"[23]

"'That would be great,'" said Boseman. "'I didn't know if you guys had decided on all the facts but maybe there's some things that we could come up with, some talent or gift that we could build. Maybe he's really good at math or something. He has to be active. I'm doing my best not to play this character like a victim–"'[24]

"'So you went to Howard University, huh?'"[25] said the producer with his CV.

"'Yes,'"[26] said Boseman.

"'Thank you for your concerns,'" he said, putting the CV back in his desk. "'We'll be watching you.'"[27]

Boseman left. He filmed that day's episode, then went home.

The next day, he was sacked.

"'They decided to go another way,'"[28] Greene told him.

Rumours spread that Boseman was 'difficult'. While his writing was praised, and he was asked plenty to direct, the acting jobs dried up. It would be a while, Greene said, before he got another.

But Boseman didn't give up. He moved to Los Angeles and got small roles in TV shows like *Law & Order*, *CSI: NY* and *Cold Case*. Ten years passed, and he still felt nowhere near his big break. '[E]very pilot I went in for, it was like, "You're gonna test for it and then somebody else will get it,"' said Boseman. 'For some reason, I couldn't get anything.'[29]

One night, Boseman was in a New York bar with some friends. They were drinking, chatting and watching the baseball World Series on TV. Boseman had been directing a play Off Broadway. Its run had just ended, and he was celebrating next door.

Not long before, he'd auditioned for a role in *Django Unchained*. He hadn't got it, but its casting director had passed on his name to Brian Helgeland, a filmmaker working on a Jackie Robinson biopic. Helgeland had told Greene he wanted to see Boseman. Greene had told Boseman.

'I ended up meeting Brian . . . and I think, to some degree, we hit it off because of our working styles,' said Boseman. 'He told me why he wanted to do the film – we met for [about] an hour – and I didn't really think that much of [the] meeting . . . You have auditions all the time where you think you're going to get it and you don't, so I just let it go.'[30]

Boseman had also heard nothing from Greene to indicate how the audition had gone. 'Nobody had called me. Nobody had told me anything,' said Boseman. 'I had gone in for it 100 percent, but there was no reason for me to think I'd done well.'[31]

Still, something had just *felt* right about the whole audition process. 'The Cardinals were playing the Texas Rangers,' said Boseman. 'I was watching the Cardinals celebrate, and I had this feeling that I was gonna get the role. I nudged a friend of mine and said, "Hey, I think I'm gonna get this role playing Jackie Robinson." He said, "What, are you serious?" I said, "Yeah, I just auditioned for it when I was in LA." He nudged my other friend and said, "Let's toast [to] this." So, we toasted to me getting the role before I actually got it.'[32]

The following week, when Boseman was back in LA, his phone rang.

'"I just want to know if you want to play Jackie Robinson,"'[33] said Helgeland.

'"What do you mean?"'[34] said Boseman.

He thought Helgeland was testing him – like, if he *really* wanted the part, he'd have to try even harder. As a formality, Helgeland called him in for a second audition. 'I could sort of tell during that meeting that again, our working styles were vibing together,' said Boseman. 'I did the baseball try-out, and the rest is history.'[35]

The film 42 made Boseman a star. He became known as an actor who could accurately, and deftly, portray the complex characters of African American icons. When director Tate Taylor was looking for a lead for his James Brown biopic, Boseman was his top choice. 'I said, "I need the best fucking actor I can find,"'[36] said Taylor. He'd been pressured to cast a rapper – 'all the usual stunt crap,' he said. '[But] I just had this suspicion [about Boseman]. And he nailed it.'[37] After that, Boseman played Thurgood Marshall, the first African American Supreme Court Justice. His reputation as an icon avatar was cemented. 'In different projects . . . we've had very extensive searches where we'll see literally thousands of people for a role,' said Sarah Halley Finn, Marvel's casting director. 'But when it came to casting *Black Panther*, it was unanimous. We all were in absolute agreement immediately that [Chadwick] was the person to play this part.'[38]

For a while, Boseman had been interested in playing the superhero. Since 2012, he'd kept a journal with notes about him. 'As an actor . . . you walk around saying, 'Hey I could play this guy, I could play that guy, I could do this type of movie, that type of movie, this type of story," said Boseman. 'So Black Panther was on my radar as a dream, as something that would be cool to do and I'm a fan of it, but not like . . . where it would sort of take over your consciousness as something that you're actually going to do.'[39]

In 2014, Boseman was in Australia filming *Gods of Egypt*. The film had been criticised for casting few African actors. Boseman had felt the same, which is why he'd agreed to play Thoth, god of writing, magic and wisdom.

On set, he met a bodyguard called Charles Carter. They hit it off. They shared an interest in, and talked about, martial arts, boxing especially. They quickly became good friends.

One day, Carter, an avid comic-book fan, asked Boseman what he knew about *Black Panther*. Not much, said Boseman. That was pretty much the end of the conversation.

But when Boseman got back to his trailer, he saw an original copy of the 1977 *Black Panther* first issue, which Carter had bought as a child. On it, Carter had written this note: 'You're going to get this role.'[40]

'If they ever do a Black Panther movie, that comic book will be worth a lot,'[41] Boseman later told Carter.

'No, it's a good luck charm to stay with you for ever,' said Carter. 'Just don't forget me when you're a superstar!'[42]

'There was no sign that Marvel was even going to do a Black Panther movie or even bring the [Black Panther] into the [Marvel]

Universe,' said Boseman. '[But] it just sorta became this thing that built in my head, "Maybe this could happen." I started researching the character more.'[43]

Later that year, Boseman was in Zurich, on the red carpet for *Get On Up* – the James Brown film. He got a call from Greene.

'"Marvel wants to talk to you."'[44]

'"Really?"'[45] said Boseman.

'"Yeah,"'[46] said Greene.

'"I'm on the red carpet."'[47]

'"Well, get off the red carpet 'cause they want to talk to you!"'[48]

'And the weird thing about [that] call is that I didn't even have an international plan on my phone until that day,' said Boseman. 'That day I woke up and something said – I guess God – said, 'You need international on your phone. You never know who might call you,' and I put it on my phone that day.'[49]

When he'd walked the carpet, he got in a car to take the call. 'Marvel [are] really secret about everything,'[50] he said.

'"Hey, we heard there's this character that you're interested in,"' said the Marvel representative, as Boseman was driven around. '"If it's the character we think you're interested in, would you be interested in playing it?"'[51]

Boseman was stunned. Generally, he was private and non-talkative. He'd never publicly mentioned his desire to play the character. 'Heard from who, you know?'[52] he said.

'"If it's the character I think you're talking about: Yes,"' replied Boseman. '"Anything you do I'm good with."'[53]

'It was definitely one of those eerie blessings,' said Boseman. 'There's a casting director by the name of Sarah [Halley] Finn and I think she had a sense of it somehow.'[54]

Even weirder, while Boseman was on the call, the car stopped in front of an antique shop, and in the window, facing him, were panther statues.

After Marvel announced *Black Panther*, and Boseman told this story, journalists approached Carter. He declined to be interviewed. 'I'm obviously not responsible for Chad and *Black Panther*,' he said. 'Chad did it. It was all his merit, his skill, his beauty, his amazing talent. He did it all and I didn't want him to think I was trying to take credit just by giving him a gift.'[55]

Nine days before the *Black Panther* premiere, Boseman texted Carter. '"I know it's last minute,"' he said. '"The tickets are hard to come by for this premiere, even for me. If you happen to be on [the West Coast] on the 29 [November,] I have one for you."'[56] Luckily, Carter was on a job in Las Vegas. He went to the LA premiere, then the afterparty, where he met Boseman's family and the other cast members.

When preparing for his role as T'Challa, i.e. The Black Panther, the first thing Boseman did was to ask his father to take a DNA test. 'AfricanAncestry.com. They get specific about what ethnic group you come from, as opposed to just what country,'[57] said Boseman. Boseman learnt that, as well as being Yoruba, he was Limba – a people of Sierra Leone, Menda – also a people of Sierra Leone, and Jola – a people of Guinea-Bissau. 'One of the key factors [when I got the *Black Panther* lead] was me getting a sense of my background,'[58] said Boseman. 'All African Americans, unless they have some direct connection [to Africa], have been severed from that past. There's things that cannot be tracked. You were a product, sold. So it's very difficult as an African American to connect at some points directly to Africa. I have made that part of my search in my life. So those things were already there when I got the role.'[59]

Boseman, and the film's director, Ryan Coogler, made research trips to Africa, including South Africa, Kenya, and Lesotho. 'What we had to do was ground it in an authenticity that is African,' said Boseman. 'So, for me, I am Yoruba, so what is ... particular [about that]? Also, that I'm Limba ... What does that mean to me? How can I bring that to the film ... Because you can bring all of [this stuff] into [Wakanda –] this place that [is] supposed to be

fictitious . . . There are South African references. [There are] references to the Dogon in Mali. All of those were . . . Ryan's research,
my research, the designers' research, and everybody who played
a character. You picked something that you loved and brought it
to the film.'[60]

In Cape Town, a street musician gave Boseman the name
Mxolisi, meaning 'Peacemaker' in Xhosa – an ancient, traditional
language widely spoken in South Africa. 'I think it was his way
of saying, 'As an African American, I know you're disconnected
from your ancestors . . . culture and . . . traditions. Here's my way
of welcoming you back,'[61] said Boseman.

'[Chad and I] would often speak about heritage and what it
means to be African,' said Coogler. 'While filming the movie, we
would meet at the office or at my rental home in Atlanta to discuss
lines and different ways to add depth to each scene. We talked cos-
tumes, military practices . . . [Chad] would ponder every decision,
every choice, not just for how it would reflect on himself, but how
those choices could reverberate . . . He said to me, "Wakandans
have to dance during the coronations. If they just stand there with
spears, what separates them from [the] Romans?"'[62]

Shaka Zulu, Patrice Lumumba (former prime minister of the
Democratic Republic of the Congo), Nelson Mandela, Fela Kuti
(the father of modern Afrobeats), Masai warfare, the practices
of *babalawo* (Yoruba traditional priests and doctors), Dambe
boxing, Zulu stick-fighting, Angolan *capoeira* (dance-fighting),
Xhosa, and a South African accent were just a few of the things
Boseman brought to T'Challa and Wakanda. For him, the last
two especially were essential in portraying the Wakandans as a
distinctly African people whom Europeans had never conquered.
'I had to push for [those],' said Boseman. 'I felt there was no way
in the world I could do the movie without an accent. But I had
to convince [Marvel] it was something we couldn't be afraid of.
My argument was that we train the audience's ear in the first
five minutes – give them subtitles . . . whatever they need – and I

believe they'll follow it the same way they'll follow an Irish ... or a Cockney accent.'[63]

On the set of *Captain America: Civil War* – the MCU (Marvel Cinematic Universe) film T'Challa first appears in – Boseman had asked the South African actor John Kani to teach him some Xhosa. Kani was playing T'Chaka, T'Challa's father. Spontaneously, when filming one scene, they'd done a take entirely in Xhosa. Because Boseman had demonstrated he could learn the language quickly, Marvel had agreed on its use. Incidentally, that take is what convinced Coogler to direct *Black Panther* later. 'I'll never forget, sitting in an editorial suite on the Disney Lot and watching [Chad's] scenes,' said Coogler. 'His first with Scarlett Johansson as [the character] Black Widow, then, with ... John Kani ... It was at that moment I knew I wanted to make [*Black Panther*]. After Scarlett's character leaves them, Chad and John began conversing in a language I had never heard before. It sounded familiar, full of the same clicks and smacks that young black children would make in the States ... But, it had a musicality to it that felt ancient, powerful, and African.'[64]

Boseman anticipated *Black Panther*'s impact. '"They['re] not ready for this, what [we're] doing ... This is *Star Wars*, this is *Lord of the Rings*, but for us ... and bigger!" [Chad] would say this to me while we were struggling to finish a dramatic scene, stretching into double overtime,' said Coogler. 'Or while he was covered in body paint, doing his own stunts. Or crashing into frigid water, and foam landing pads. I would nod and smile, but I didn't believe him. I had no idea if the film would work. I wasn't sure I knew what I was doing. But I look back and realise that Chad knew something we all didn't. He was playing the long game. All while putting in the work. And work he did.'[65] That Boseman was a dedicated actor is an understatement. 'He was incredibly detailed and thoughtful and spent months and months preparing [for *Black Panther*] and continued that training all the way through the shoot,'[66] said Halley Finn. For *Get On Up*, Boseman worked with a dance instructor *eight hours* a day. He only had six weeks to learn *all* the Godfather of Soul's dance moves. 'I would be with friends, just talking, and . . . still be moving,'[67] he said. '[On *42*,] I did some takes . . . fifty times. Then again, I did the splits ninety-six times one day on *Get On Up*. But I didn't give out then.'[68]

'We all knew [*Black Panther*] was unique,' Boseman said. 'You're not thinking: 'Don't screw it up,' exactly. It's more positive than that. It's more like: 'Seize it. Enjoy it.' . . . Other things will undoubtedly happen because of what we've done.'[69] At the world-wide box office, *Black Panther* grossed $1.3 billion. It was nominated for seven Oscars, including Best Picture, and won three, including Best Music, Production, and Costume Design.

Chadwick Boseman died on 28 August 2020 from colon cancer. He'd had it since 2016. He was 43.

The news shocked everyone. Not only was Boseman quite young but also, few knew he was even sick, or that, while making films including *Black Panther*, he'd been battling the illness. '[Chadwick] brought you many of the films you have come to love so much,' said a statement posted to his X account. 'From *Marshall* to *Da 5 Bloods* . . . *Ma Rainey's Black Bottom* and several more, all were filmed during and between countless surgeries and chemotherapy. It was the honor of his career to bring King T'Challa to life in *Black Panther*.'[70]

The tributes came thick and fast, from fans, colleagues and even politicians. ABC did a special feature on Boseman's life. On social media, pictures of children doing the Wakanda salute next to their Black Panther action figures were widely shared. So, too, were stills and clips of the *Black Panther* scene where T'Challa visits the ancestors in the spirit world and talks to the recently deceased T'Chaka. In the captions of many, Boseman was said to have joined, and himself become one of, the ancestors. 'I remember [he was] offered a movie, it was about two slaves, and he was like, "I do not want to perpetuate slavery,"' said Greene, his agent. 'It was like, "We're not going to keep perpetuating the stereotypes," and that's why he wanted to show men of strength and of character. It was always about bringing light.'[71]

'We were in Atlanta, in an abandoned warehouse, with bluescreens, and massive movie lights, but Chad's performance made it feel real,' said Coogler of filming the spirit world scene. 'I think it was because from the time that I met him, the ancestors spoke through him. It's no secret to me now how he was able to skilfully portray some of our most notable ones. I had no doubt that he would live on and continue to bless us with more. But it is with a heavy heart and a sense of deep gratitude to have ever been in his presence, that I have to reckon with the fact that Chad is an ancestor now. And I know that he will watch over us, until we meet again.'[72]

In the films he was in and helped create, and in the inspiration with which he left certain people, Boseman, like the Dagara living dead in Dapar or the Akan spirits in a stool, continues to live on. Put simply, he left a legacy. Like the ancestors of plenty of African cultures, he lived a life many would consider imitable. Like Yoruba do their *egun*, perhaps they'd ask him for strength or advice when attempting to accomplish something in the field he excelled in – acting. For instance, they might ask for his help in succeeding at an audition. To them, he's truly a modern-day ancestor.

We've now explored a little of ancestral veneration – one of the most integral features of African identity. We've seen how the dead continue to live, how the relationship between mortals and spirits operates, and how death doesn't sever the bonds between living and deceased family members. We've also seen what ancestors are, how to become one, and what they do for the living.

Next, I want us to explore another cultural feature integral to many African cultures, and African identity: female-led societies.

3

QUEENMOTHERS AND WARRIOR-QUEENS

As shown in the previous chapter, family and community (whether living or dead) are critical to African peoples, and our cultures. The bonds we forge with others are the foundation for everything we do in life. So, women – from whom every family and community member is born – are particularly revered in much of Africa. Where they are revered, they are given treatment, position and status befitting this reverence. In some cultures, a woman is its *de facto* ruler and most important personage. In others, she rules autocratically. Yet, in others, women rule alongside their male counterparts. Crucially, this is *not* because it's believed women can't rule alone, but because it's thought that a balance in government – whether of sex or wealth or class – is essential to good governance.

The three examples of African female-led societies I listed above aren't mutually exclusive. For instance, in some African cultures, a woman might be both the most important person *and* rule alongside men.

Now, let's look at some examples – both contemporary and historical – of African female-led societies. We'll begin with the present-day Asante of Ghana, where women have long been of paramount importance, and rule alongside, and sometimes instead of, men.

For at least five centuries, the Asante have been both matrilineal and matriarchal. We believe we're all descendants of ancient ancestresses. A newborn Asante belongs to their mother's family. Wealth and titles are inherited through the female line. The eldest daughter – or, at least, her children – gets everything. Only when no female descendants remain do men get a look in.

In Asante, the most important person is the *ohemmaa* ('female ruler'), better known as the 'Queenmother'. She occupies *okonua panyin* – the most senior stool. She's a female royal family member – usually, the Asante king's mother. She lives in her own palace called the *nkotimse* with attendants, servants, and other royal family members.

The *Abusua Tiri* ('Council of the Royal Clan') and the elders elect her. Both are comprised of men and women. When elected, a date is set for when the new Queenmother will be introduced to her people. On that day, she's carried on a sedan chair around Asanteland. She waves in greeting and thanks to cheering spectators.

Ultimately, the Queenmother elects the Asante king. In Asante, it is not the former king's eldest son that necessarily inherits the royal stool – that is, the throne. The new king is chosen from among a group of eligible candidates, usually the former king's adult male relatives. The Queenmother begins by summoning other important members of the royal family to a secret meeting. They discuss the candidates' suitability. When the Queenmother has decided on the one she wants, she officially nominates him. She informs the elders of the other significant families of her choice. They themselves discuss his suitability. However, they very rarely reject him. Anyone the Queenmother thinks *isn't* good for the role can't become king. Once these elders have inevitably agreed, the Queenmother announces her nominee to the Asante people.

The Queenmother presides over the new king's enstoolment – that is, his coronation. In front of all present, including royal family members, she tells him he must rule fairly, warns him against corruption and gives him tips on good kingship.

As a member of the Asanteman, the Supreme State Council of Asante, the Queenmother attends the king's court daily, and guides him. She sits on his left, slightly behind him. This is so that, if anyone threatens her life, the king can step in to intercept it. Customarily, she gives her advice subtly and quietly, talking softly into his ear. Her opinion and judgement are valued above everyone else's. She most influences the king's decisions. She also accompanies him on tours of his kingdom.

She alone can, with impunity, publicly criticise the king, or any of his officials. She selects his senior wife, whom she calls *ba* – 'my child'. In turn, this wife calls her *ena* – 'mother'.

'[The Queenmother] is surrounded by the greatest luxury imaginable,' wrote the nineteenth-century French explorer Bonnat, who visited Asante. 'Everything the king possesses she has in abundance.'[1]

The king is seen as the nation's 'father'. The Queenmother is seen as its 'mother'. The king looks out for primarily Asante men's interests. The Queenmother looks out mainly for women's interests.

To help her, she has her own government, made up exclusively of women. It mirrors perfectly the king's government. They have the same titles, purviews and powers as the king's officials. The Queenmother also has her own legal court. It is just as, if not more, influential than the king's.

The Queenmother attends and presides over girls' puberty rituals. When a legal case involving women, including adultery, domestic violence, or sexual assault, is heard in the king's court, the Queenmother is present. She ensures the woman's side of the story is heard, and her rights are protected. Often, such cases are transferred or first brought to her own court.

The only thing the Queenmother didn't really take part in was warfare. The king led the army against the enemy. The Queenmother ruled Asante in his absence. However, there were exceptions. Arguably, the most famous Asante Queenmother is Yaa Asantewaa. Partly, this is because, when the men refused to, she led the Asante against the British in the War of the Golden Stool in 1900.

Now, let's look briefly at a historical example of an African culture where women, though not necessarily the most important people, still ruled equally with men.

*

This example concerns the nineteenth-century Igbo, a people of what is now Nigeria.

Some Igbo had two monarchs – the male *obi* ('father'), and the female *omu* ('mother').

The *obi* was seen as the community's father. The *omu* was seen as its mother.

They were elected, and not necessarily related.

Both led their own councils of twelve elders. The *obi*'s was called the *onotu*. The *omu*'s was called the *ilogo*. Except that all the *onotu*'s elders were male, and all the *ilogo*'s female, they were exactly the same. Their members had the same titles, powers and responsibilities. The councils were as powerful as each other. The *onotu* could challenge decisions the *ilogo* made, and vice versa. Often, they worked together to ensure the harmonious operation of their community. Seemingly, they succeeded. There's no record of any conflict between an *obi* and an *omu*.

Yet, whereas the *obi* was given special charge over, and mainly concerned himself with, men's affairs, the *omu* did the same for women.

She looked out for women's rights, safety and happiness.

She supervised female customs, like initiation rituals, and institutions, even including secret societies.

Every four days, the community market was opened. Completely, it was women's domain. They sold their husbands' extra farm produce. The *omu* and *ilogo* set, and altered, the market's rules and regulations. They presided over the market, watched for fairness and punished those who broke these rules.

If a woman needed advice, or desired to bring a case against anyone, she went to the *omu*. If a man wanted help with any of his female family members, he often went to her, too. Usually, in cases involving a man and a woman, the *omu* consulted the *obi* and his *onotu*. Above all, a just, fair and conciliatory resolution had to be reached.

Before the *omu* agreed to any major community changes, like a new law, she consulted, and gained the approval of, the *ikporo ani*. The *ikporo ani* was an informal female council drawn from each section of society. Women of different ages, professions and marital statuses were represented. Members of the *ikporo ani* were chosen because of their skills, including intelligence and public speaking, and achievements. When these members heard the new proposal, they discussed it in a general meeting with the rest of the women. They presented any concerns, or suggested changes, to the *omu*. Like this, back and forth they went, till both sides were satisfied.

It's almost incredible just how long female-led societies have existed in Africa, and how long some African cultures have been female-led. To give a sense of the former, I want to share an example of an African female-led society from even further back in time. Arguably, it's the oldest African female-led society we have on record. Here, women were not only seen as important, and ruled alongside men, but, at one point, became absolute rulers.

*

The society I'm talking about is best known as Nubia, or Kush. It's named after the ancient region in which it once existed, which, today, is south Egypt and northern Sudan.

The first Nubian kingdom, Kerma, existed from about 3000 to 1500 BC. This kingdom was centred around, and named after, its capital city of Kerma. In 1500 BC, the Egyptians conquered, and ruled, not just Kerma, but a large part of Nubia. They introduced into its society elements of their culture, including language, religion, and some art and architectural styles. However, Nubia was too big, and its society too complex, for the Egyptians to administer it without local help. So, Nubian elites struck a deal with them, agreeing to govern Nubia on their behalf in exchange for a great deal of autonomy, such that they were essentially sovereign. As part of their nominal conquest of Nubia, the Egyptians called it Kush, which is how this region and its society got their second name. To refer to this region, its society and its people, scholars use Nubia and Kush practically interchangeably.

In 1000 BC, the Nubians regained full independence. In 800 BC, they made Napata, a city just south of Kerma, their new capital. They created a new kingdom, based at, and named after, Napata, which existed until about 300 BC.

In 300 BC, they made Meroë, a city even further south than Napata, their new capital, and the centre of a new kingdom which they named after it. They moved their capital a second time for several reasons. First, the Egyptians were still a threat – they even briefly captured Napata in 591 BC – and the Nubians wanted to get as far away from them as possible. Second, by the sixth century BC, the soil around Napata was already eroding because the Nubians were overgrazing it with their cattle. By the fourth century BC, they needed to find fresh pastures, and, though cattle were the backbone of their economy, to diversify. Meroë, and the land around it, got much higher levels of rainfall than Napata, which allowed the Nubians to grow crops including barley, wheat, lentils, melons, cucumbers and grapes. Third, Meroë was in a much better position for regional and international trade than Napata, lying at the crossroads of the caravan trade between the African interior, north Africa, and Arabia. On their way to Egypt or Yemen, caravans carrying gold, incense and ivory from the African heartland often started from, or stopped off at, Meroë. These goods were then transported as far afield as the Mediterranean.

Meroë existed until about 350 AD, when the Axumite kingdom,

which extended over what's now northern Ethiopia, Eritrea, and eastern Sudan, supplanted it.

Women, and particularly royal women, were always important in Nubia. In Kerma, royal women were priestesses who performed rituals that deepened the Nubian king's connection with the gods, enhancing his religious, and thus political, legitimacy. In honour of this role, when royal women died, they were buried in big, treasure-filled graves next to those of dead kings in the latter's personal cemetery.

The Nubian king, Alara, who founded Napata, increased largely royal women's importance in Nubia.

Sometime between 780 and 760 BC, he adopted the Egyptian cult of the Sun god Amun. Amun was arguably Egypt's most important and revered god. His cult's leaders wielded a large amount of social, cultural and political power. In Egypt, royal women had an integral role in the cult, playing sistra in important ceremonies. Sistra is the plural of 'sistrum'. A sistrum is a rattle-like instrument made of metal or ceramic.

Alara's successors continued what he started. When his brother, Kashta, conquered Egypt in around 750 BC, ushering in its twenty-fifth dynasty, he adopted the institution of the 'God's Wife of Amun'. Crucially, he also increased the power of the female figure at its heart.

The God's Wife of Amun was one of Egypt's most powerful figures. She essentially ruled about half of the country. She was a royal woman based at the Karnak Temple in Thebes, a city in south Egypt. As this temple's leader, she was the pharaoh's religious other half. She did for him what the royal women of Kerma did for the Nubian king, performing rituals that improved his religious, and so political, standing. She had her own administration and controlled the temple's resources.

When Kashta became king of Napata, the God's Wife of Amun was an Egyptian princess called Shepenwepet I. The position of God's Wife was passed down from mother to daughter. But if a God's Wife had no biological daughter, she could nominate another royal woman as her successor by adopting her. Usually, she adopted a blood relative.

When he conquered Egypt, Kashta made Shepenwepet adopt *his* daughter, Amenirdis I. (Some scholars argue that it was instead Kashta's son, Piankhy, who made Shepenwepet adopt Amenirdis, i.e. his sister). Amenirdis's other titles included 'Chief Prophetess of Amun' and 'Mistress of Egypt'. There was also another high priestess at Napata, one of whose titles was 'Mistress of Nubia'.

Amenirdis's biological daughter, Shepenwepet II, succeeded her. During the twenty-fifth Dynasty, the God's Wife pretty much independently ruled Egypt. Nubian kings remained at, and ruled the rest of the kingdom from, Napata.

Alara had also made royal women a crucial part of succession.

He enhanced his sisters' status, raising them to an official, important position called 'king's sisters'. Nubian kingship became elective. Like the queen's sons, all the king's sisters' sons – in short, the king's nephews – had equal claim to the throne. A group of high-ranking officials, including generals, senior civil servants and clan leaders, chose the most virtuous among them as their next king. The woman whose son was chosen became 'Queenmother'. Like in Asante, the incumbent Queenmother – that is, the mother of the king who'd just died – had a decisive say in who was elected. Pre-election, she was also responsible for looking after her grandsons who lived together in the king's palace. They were closest to her, and she had a lot of influence over them. Through them, she also had a lot of influence over Nubia.

However, the crown passed to the younger generation only when all the eligible princes of the previous generation had died. In other words, when a king died, an election was held amongst his eligible surviving brothers and male cousins. Only when *they* all died, would an election be held amongst their sons.

In both Napata and Meroë, the Queenmother became instrumental in the elected prince's coronation.

At certain important rituals, both she and the electee's wife shook sistra, poured libations, and sang both his and the gods' praises. They affirmed the prince's connection to the gods, enhancing his legitimacy and status. In Egypt, only the pharaoh, as master of the ritual, was allowed to pour libations. In Nubia, royal women, as priestesses of Amun, had this privilege.

The electee then toured Amun's temples, which stood in important cities around Nubia, namely Napata, Kawa, and Pnubs. Two Napatan kings also decided to visit the goddess Bastet's temple in the city of Tele. At each temple, the Nubians held a week-long festival in Amun's honour. They carried a statue of Amun through the town. In being carried around as part of this ritual, the statue 'gave' the electee Amun's blessing to rule. 'The people take as . . . king the one whom the god chooses as he [the god] is carried round in procession,' wrote Diodorus Siculus, a first-century BC Greek historian who witnessed this ritual. 'Straightaway they address and honour him as if he were a god since the kingdom was entrusted to him by the will of [Amun].'²

The electee then sat on a throne in the temple. The Queenmother arrived at whichever city her son was in shortly after the festival. She stood next to him and made a speech, in which she asked Amun to confirm him as the rightful ruler of Napata (or Meroë). Officially, the electee was transformed from earthly prince to godly king.

Nubian kings commissioned artworks of their coronations. None exists without a representation of the Queenmother and the queen. They carry the sistra in their left hands. In their right, they carry vases, from which they pour the libations. Deceased royal women were buried in the kings' cemeteries – El Kurru and Nuri. Apart from the king, royal men didn't enjoy the same privilege. In Napata, at least at Nuri, Queenmothers had the largest tombs.

Given royal women's fundamental importance to Nubia's

power structure, it's unsurprising that they eventually became its pinnacle. At least since Napata, royal women had had governing roles (for instance, as God's Wife of Amun), elected the next Nubian king, and performed the necessary ritual to confirm his kingship. In Meroë, some of these women became independent (or mostly independent) rulers who remain well-known leaders in Nubian history. They are called the Kandakes. In the next section, we'll look a little at who they were, what they did and why they're important.

*

For reasons that soon will become apparent, perhaps the best-known Kandake is Amanirenas, who ruled Meroë in the late first-century BC. She was, wrote Strabo, a first-century BC Greek geographer, 'a masculine sort of woman . . . mutilated in one eye'.[3]

Since 30 BC, the Romans had controlled Egypt. They'd stationed there 15,000 soldiers. They intended to conquer Nubia, and south Arabia.

Not long after Rome's conquest of Egypt, the Egyptians rebelled against them. Rome had increased their taxes. The Nubians backed the rebels. The Romans threatened their northern boundary, and they wanted to push them back.

Cornelius Gallus, Roman prefect of Egypt, crushed the rebels. He also conquered northern Nubia. Here, he installed a Nubian viceroy, but its citizens became Roman vassals.

In around 25 BC, Augustus Caesar, Roman Emperor, ordered Cornelius to kill himself. Why is unclear. Cornelius might have conquered northern Nubia against Caesar's orders. Or, in conquering it, he'd accrued too much power for Caesar's liking. Whatever the case, Caesar then made a man called Aelius Gallus prefect of Egypt.

Aelius invaded Arabia. He took almost half of the 15,000 soldiers. A man called Gaius Petronius was made prefect in his place.

The other half of the soldiers were to be used in the invasion of Nubia.

Seeing half the Roman's forces were gone, the northern Nubians rebelled, marching into Egypt.

News of the rebellion reached Meroë. Teriteqas, Meroë's king and Amanirenas's husband, led an army north to support the rebels. Amanirenas marched alongside him. In the summer of 25 BC, the Nubian force sacked southern Roman Egyptian cities. They captured soldiers, enslaved citizens and looted statues of Augustus. In the early twentieth century, archaeologists found the head of one of these statues, taken from the city of Aswan, underneath the entrance of a Meroë palace.

Petronius counter-attacked, pushing back the Nubians to their city of Pselchis. Seemingly, in the battle, Teriteqas was killed. Amanirenas succeeded him.

Petronius demanded the Nubians surrender. The Nubians didn't respond. Petronius attacked again and, wrote Strabo, 'quickly turned [the Nubians] ... Some were driven together into the city [while] others fled into the desert[. Yet] others went onto the neighbouring islands. [Petronius] captured all of them alive, sailing after them in rafts and ships, and immediately sent them ... to [Egypt].'[4]

'He also went against Pselchis and took it,' Strabo continued. 'From Pselchis he went to [Qasr Ibrim], a fortified city. He attacked and took the fortress in the onslaught ... [Afterwards, he] set forth for Napata. This was the royal residence of [Amanirenas], and her son [Akinidad] was there. She was located at a nearby palace, and ... sent ambassadors for friendship.'[5]

Petronius rejected her peace offer. '[He] attacked and took Napata, from which her son had fled,' wrote Strabo. '[He] razed it to the ground. He enslaved its inhabitants and turned back again with the booty, having decided that to go farther would be a difficult journey. He [better] fortified [Qasr Ibrim with] a garrison of four hundred men [and] supplies for two years ... [He] set out for Alexandria . . . 1000 [captives] were sent to Caesar.'⁶ Here, it's worth noting that scholars disagree as to whether Petronius truly sacked Napata. Some argue that its addition to Petronius's list of victories was merely Roman propaganda. Meroitic, the Nubian's language, is still largely undeciphered, so we only really have the Romans' side of the story.

In 22 BC, after waiting till its supplies had run out, Amanirenas marched against Qasr Ibrim with a large army.

News of the march reached Petronius, who rushed to Qasr Ibrim. He managed to beat Amanirenas there. When Amanirenas arrived, she and Petronius agreed on peace. Both sides were exhausted, the Romans especially.

In the winter of 21 BC, Nubian ambassadors travelled to Samos, an island in the Aegean Sea, off Greece's eastern coast. Petronius had given them escorts. Caesar was on the island on his way to Syria. Amanirenas hadn't bothered to go.

The Nubian ambassadors negotiated, drew up and signed a treaty with Caesar. The *northernmost* part of north Nubia (the latter of which Cornelius had conquered) became officially Roman. It was to be a buffer zone between themselves and Nubia. But Nubian elites were to govern it. Nubia was also to control the rest of this territory. Additionally, the Romans agreed to lift taxes from north Nubia and withdraw their forces from Qasr Ibrim. The Nubians, wrote Strabo, 'obtained everything that they needed'.⁷

Amanirenas is best remembered for preventing Rome's conquest of Nubia and securing a favourable peace deal with them. She was one of at least five Kandakes.

'Kandake', the name given to the Nubian royal women who ruled Meroë either absolutely, or almost absolutely, derives from the royal title '*Kdke*' that most of these women held. In Meroitic, '*kdke*' (also rendered as '*ktke*' or '*kentake*') means 'queenmother'. The Kandakes were the first to adopt this word as an official royal title, emphasising the Queenmother's importance.

The other four Kandakes were Shanakdakhete, Nawidemak,

Amanishakheto, and Amanitore. Including Amanirenas, they ruled Meroë between about 200 BC and 50 AD. They were instrumental in developing the kingdom.

Three of these Kandakes – Amanirenas, Amanishakheto, and Amanitore – held the *Kdke* title. They ruled Meroë, but a king was also in the picture.

Three – Amanirenas, Nawidemak, and Amanishakheto – held the title '*qore*' – 'ruler'. Only Meroë's absolute ruler held it. For a time at least, these women ruled autocratically.

As can be seen above, two Kandakes – Amanirenas and Amanishakheto – held both the *Kdke* and *qore* titles. Seemingly, they were, at one time, mothers of young, newly chosen kings, who ruled Meroë absolutely until their sons came of age. Amanirenas must've taken the *qore* title when she became Meroë's ruler after Teriteqas, her husband, died. Then, when their infant son (Akinidad) was elected Meroë's next king, she must've taken the *Kdke* title. Conversely, Amanitore's husband, Natakamani, ruled alongside her.

Whatever the case, during their reigns, Kandakes were the most important persons in Nubia. They ran the government, conducted trade and diplomacy, led the army, and fought wars. They also commissioned the building of magnificent monuments, palaces and tombs.

They had artworks made that showed off their importance. In carvings on stelae or temple walls, they're depicted as large women, sometimes with long fingernails. They could afford all the food they needed, and then some, and never did manual labour. They're shown wearing jewel-encrusted bracelets, rings and earrings. Amanishakheto is shown smiting enemies, an ancient Egyptian motif demonstrating power, which was usually reserved for the depiction of pharaohs.

Kandakes are often depicted alone, but sometimes with a king. In the latter case, they're often drawn as bigger, or the same size, as the king. They're also often positioned in front of him.

Though it's one of the earliest, Nubia isn't the only African society that had a female-led autocracy. Throughout African history, there have been numerous independent female leaders who governed, developed their societies, and led their citizens in wars against enemies, often in the protection of their society's sovereignty. That the Kandakes and even Amanirenas aren't anomalies demonstrates the extent to which the reverence of women is a part of many African cultures.

One such culture is that of the Mbundu, a people of Angola. Traditionally, in Mbundu, women had been seen, and treated, as important. In the culture's founding traditions, they feature as significant ancestresses. In contrast to many cultures in the ancient and medieval eras, when Mbundu women married, they weren't considered their husband's property, and could leave him whenever, however, and for whatever reason they wished. When they did so, they were ordinarily accepted back into their father's family, and could – though weren't obliged to – choose another husband. Royal Mbundu women wielded a great deal of power in court. They took part in official discussions of state and had privileged access to the king. It's unsurprising, then, that this culture gave birth to one of the most resolute female autocrats in African history: Njinga Mbande, an early seventeenth-century queen of Ndongo, a kingdom once in Angola. It's her story that we're going to look at next.

*

Njinga was born in 1582, feet first, with her mother's umbilical cord wrapped around her neck. To the Mbundu, this unusual birth position was a good omen. It meant that Njinga was destined for greatness. Those at her birth gazed at her in wonder, and shouted, '*mà mà, o aoè aoè!*'[8] ('Oh! My mother!') – the traditional Mbundu equivalent of 'Wow!'

Njinga was an exceptionally strong and intelligent child. She could throw a battle-axe – the symbol of Ndongo's royals – better than any of the other royal children. She was the favourite of her father, Mbande a Ngola. He invited her to council meetings with his advisers, diplomats and generals. He even took her on military campaigns. By the time she was in her late teens, she'd developed a reputation as a skilled warrior and diplomat. Her brother, Ngola Mbande, was sickeningly jealous.

The Portuguese had been in West-Central Africa since the fifteenth century. They'd first established contact with Kongo, a kingdom south of Ndongo. In the mid-sixteenth century, they'd established contact with Ndongo. Kongo's leaders allowed them to build their own permanent settlement – Luanda, now Angola's capital.

The Portuguese wanted complete control over Europe's West African trade. In 1571, Sebastião I, Portugal's king, ordered diplomat Paulo Dias de Novais to colonise Ndongo. De Novais had led the first Portuguese mission to Ndongo about ten years earlier.

In 1575, de Novais arrived in Luanda with nine battleships, a thousand soldiers, and cannons. He held the presumptuous title of 'first governor and captain-general of the conquered Kingdom of Angola'. Originally, 'Angola', from which the modern country's name derives, is what the Portuguese and Kongolese called Ndongo. It derived from the title 'Angola Inene' that Ndongo's ruler held.

Over the next fifteen years, de Novais rampaged over the kingdom, burning villages, forcing *sobas* – Mbundu's landowning nobles – to submit, taking control of their lands, and enslaving tens of thousands, who were trafficked to Brazilian sugar plantations.

Ngola Kilombo kia Kasenda, Ndongo's king and Njinga's grandfather, couldn't stop him. 'In three months, [de Novais] has won three wars against the king of Angola, killing and capturing infinite numbers of people,'[9] wrote a Portuguese priest to Sebastião. In just one campaign, Kasenda reportedly lost *40,000* soldiers. The Portuguese cut off the noses of slain Mbundu and sent them as trophies to their camps.

Depressed, Kasenda gave up fighting and retreated to his palace in Kabasa, Ndongo's capital.

De Novais died in 1589. The Portuguese government took over the territory he'd conquered and named it the 'Kingdom of Angola'.

Kasenda died three years later.

Njinga was just ten years old.

Under Mbande a Ngola, Njinga's father, who succeeded Kasenda, Portuguese victories, conquests and enslavement continued. The king lost his nobles' support and trust. Some *sobas* exploited Ndongo's chaos to seize more power for themselves. In 1617, some of the king's inner circle convinced him to send reinforcements against these rebelling *sobas*. Believing victory would restore his damaged reputation, Mbande a Ngola decided to lead them himself. When he reached the given location, the men he'd travelled with turned on him and stabbed him to death.

That same year – that is, 1617 – Ngola Mbande, Njinga's brother, brutally seized the throne. Njinga was now thirty-five years old and had had a son with her favourite male concubine, Kia Ituxi. Mbande had his own half-brother, that brother's mother, her siblings, and even Njinga's infant son murdered. He had a boiling mixture of herbs poured onto the stomachs of Njinga, and his other sisters, Kambu and Funji, sterilising them. None ever conceived again.

Njinga retired to Matamba, a kingdom northeast of Ndongo.

Meanwhile, the Portuguese recruited the Imbangala. The Imbangala were distinct bands of ethnically diverse mercenaries. Most had once been soldiers. They were feared for their violence, and brutal, cultic practices. They lived by wandering, murdering and pillaging. They intimidated young boys into joining their ranks, killed any children born in their camps, and, reportedly, were cannibals.

In 1618, a force consisting of both Portuguese soldiers and Imbangala sacked Kabasa. Ngola Mbande managed to flee with some of his family and close supporters. In 1620, the force sacked Mkaria ka Matamba, Matamba's capital. Some Imbangala turned back and sacked Kabasa again. When they'd left, Mbande returned to his capital. But, in 1621, when the force sacked Kabasa once more, he fled again. This time, the enemy managed to kill his close supporters and capture his mother, Kambu, and Funji.

Mbande sought peace. He planned to send a delegation to Luanda. He called Njinga back from Matamba and asked her to lead it. He knew that she was exceptionally proud of Ndongo and Mbundu customs, and that, like him, she was keen to protect them. He knew, too, that she was politically astute and experienced. The Mbundu probably loved her more than him.

In late 1621, Njinga, sitting on a chair carried by serfs, travelled the 200 miles from Kabasa to Luanda. This was a chance to raise her, and Ndongo's, prestige. She wore traditional Mbundu dress – colourful cloths, jewellery on her arms and legs, coloured feathers in her hair. Beside her walked guards, her waiting-women (dressed like her), playing musicians, and more serfs carrying presents.

The Portuguese welcomed her with a military salute and playing bands. They escorted her to her lodgings. They said they'd pay all her expenses. They held a feast in her honour, and gave her gifts.

Njinga negotiated directly with the Portuguese governor. The Portuguese liked to humiliate their Mbundu counterparts. While the governor sat on a splendid gold and velvet chair, the Mbundu noble was given only a mat on the floor. Sitting below the governor, looking up at him as they talked, the noble was symbolically lowered, the Portuguese presented as more powerful.

When Njinga saw she had no chair, she ordered an attendant to get down on her hands and knees. Njinga then sat on this attendant's back, eye-to-eye with the governor. For the hours they talked, she stayed like that.

The Portuguese agreed to recall their forces from Ndongo. Kambu and Funji were released. Njinga converted to Christianity. She agreed Ndongo would become Portugal's ally. But, arguing that the Portuguese hadn't conquered Mbande, who remained an independent sovereign, she strongly refused to pay tribute, which would make Ndongo Portugal's vassal.

In late 1622, she returned triumphantly to Kabasa. The governor had promised that a treaty including everything discussed would be sent.

But by 1624, Mbande had killed himself.

The Portuguese couldn't control the Imbangala, who continued to rampage. They were also being slow in putting together the treaty. Mbande, who distrusted them, thought they'd reneged on their peace promise. He became depressed. Njinga exacerbated his distress. Regularly, she publicly scolded Mbande about his military losses, grovelling to the Portuguese, and inability to secure peace. If she'd been in charge, she said, none of this would have happened. Shortly afterwards, Mbande ingested poison.

Mbande had a male heir. But he was only seven. He'd been sent to train under an Imbangala leader called Kasa whom Mbande had once recruited. Openly, Njinga supported the child's becoming king. She made herself merely regent, taking the title 'Mistress of Ndongo'.

In 1625, she approached, and seduced, Kasa, showering him with gifts. Initially, Kasa hadn't wanted to marry her because she was older than him. But he soon acquiesced. He also handed over Mbande's son.

At their wedding in Matamba, as revenge for what Ngola Mbande had done to her own son, Njinga threw her nephew into the Kwanza River. He drowned. She then had any rivals, and potential rivals, murdered. She seized the throne, taking the title 'Lady of Angola'.

She tried to secure the peace with the Portuguese, writing to the governor and reminding him of his promise.

This time, the Portuguese flat-out refused. Hari a Kiluanje, a pro-Portuguese Ndongo noble, and Njinga's distant relative, had rebelled against her. The Portuguese tried to exploit this to conquer Ndongo fully. The governor ordered the conquest of more *sobas*. He recruited more Imbangala. He demanded Njinga pay tribute.

Instead, in 1625, Njinga officially launched a revolution against the Portuguese. She sent messengers into Portuguese-held areas to tell Mbundu that their queen was rebelling, and that they should join her.

Njinga's popularity meant many heeded her call. Whole villages were deserted as hundreds of Mbundu, including *sobas*, went to her. Many were armed and had battle experience. The Portuguese, whose tributes dried up, became afraid.

Shortly afterwards, they proclaimed Hari a Kiluanje as Ndongo's rightful king. In May 1626, they attacked Njinga.

Since returning from Luanda to Ndongo in 1622, Njinga had been based at the Kindonga Islands on the Kwanza River in east Ndongo. It was a highly strategic location. Surrounding the islands were low-lying hills where you could place archers. Njinga was on the central island. She further protected herself by digging trenches and posting Mbundu with rifles on the other islands.

In canoes, Portuguese and conquered *sobas*' troops invaded, firing volleys of musket shot and arrows. By the end of July, they'd surrounded Njinga. But there was an outbreak of smallpox. It floored both the Portuguese, whose supplies had almost run out, and Njinga's troops. Again, the Portuguese demanded Njinga surrender. Instead, she burnt her provisions and the Portuguese's boats, and, with her close supporters, she retreated.

By late 1627, she'd returned to the islands, Hari a Kiluanje was dead and the Portuguese had made the latter's half-brother, Ngola Hari, king of Ndongo. Njinga sent her *mwene lumbo* – prime minister – to the Portuguese to work out a peace agreement. The Portuguese declared him a spy and executed him. The governor then sent this message to Njinga: She should submit herself to him. If she again refused, he'd hunt her down and kill her. Njinga's reply: She'd fight to the death for Ndongo's independence.

In 1629, the Portuguese attacked again. The battle was bloody. Losing, Njinga withdrew. The Portuguese chased her. One night, they camped in the very spot Njinga had camped in the night before.

The next day, as Njinga trekked the edge of a 200-metre-high cliff, enemy Mbundu saw her. Some rushed towards her, lost their footing and fell into the ravine below. Njinga's guards made a wall around her. Njinga grabbed a vine growing from the cliff and abseiled into the ravine. Scared to do the same, the Portuguese looked for a safer way down. By the time they'd found one, Njinga was a day ahead of them.

For days afterwards, the Portuguese searched nearby villages. They failed to find Njinga.

But they came across the camp where Kambu and Funji were staying. They ambushed it, defeated Njinga's troops, and captured her sisters. They stripped them naked and marched them to Luanda. The governor made them vassals and forced them to become Christian.

Weakened, upset that her sisters had again been captured, and in desperate need of reinforcements, Njinga turned to an Imbangala captain called Kasanje.

She married him, then completed the rituals to become an Imbangala captain herself. In the *cuia* – blood oath ceremony – she drank human blood. In the *maji a samba* – 'holy oil' ritual – she crushed a baby in a mortar and smeared her body with its blood (this blood being the so-called '*maji a samba*'). According to Imbangala tradition, Tembo a Ndumbo, their ancestress, had done this to her own son to become the first Imbangala. This ritual had then become the Imbangala's first *kijila* ('law'). Many Imbangala rituals derived from Tembo a Ndumbo's actions. As Njinga had no children of her own, she'd sacrificed the child of a loyal female attendant. She then took a new title: *Ngola Njinga Ngombe e Nga* ('Queen Njinga, Master of Arms and Great Warrior').

In the early 1630s, with an Imbangala army, Njinga defeated, captured and deposed Muongo, Matamba's queen, conquering Matamba. She planned to make Matamba her base from which she could retake Ndongo. In the conflict, her warriors had massacred thousands. Muongo was allowed to rule a less important part of the kingdom, but she died shortly afterwards. Njinga gave her a queen's burial, and adopted her daughter, also called Muongo, who lived with Njinga until the latter died.

Njinga then launched a series of assaults against Ndongo. Her army crushed defector *sobas*, destroyed settlements, and blocked Portuguese trade routes. '[She was] just like the queen of the Amazona [and] she governed the army [like] a warrior female,'[10] wrote a contemporary Portuguese missionary. The Portuguese's revenues dried up. '[T]he country doesn't produce much since markets that were open with lots of slaves are now closed . . . because of armies that Njinga . . . brings into the interior,'[11] wrote a Portuguese official to his king.

The Portuguese worried they couldn't afford to defeat Njinga. To try to appease her, they gave back Kambu. Njinga continued her attacks.

In 1642, the Dutch, who'd recently entered West-Central Africa, attacked and badly defeated the Portuguese. They planned to replace them as Africa's top European power. The next year, as part of a truce, the Portuguese gave them Luanda. While the Portuguese were distracted, Njinga retook parts of Ndongo.

Furious, in 1646, the Portuguese attacked Njinga with all their might. The force they put together was huge – bigger than any Portuguese army Njinga had faced so far. It had 30,000 Mbundu soldiers, 2,000 scouts, 600 Portuguese soldiers, 16 cavalry, cannons, Ngola Hari's troops and Imbangala bands.

The battle between this army and Njinga's lasted seven hours. It was horrendously bloody. The Portuguese broke through Njinga's last line of defence and entered her war camp. Njinga escaped, but they re-captured Kambu. They captured or killed others. They took a rich booty of guns, cloths and jewels. They found letters that Funji had secretly sent Njinga, telling her about Portuguese plans. They set all the buildings on fire and moved out.

Depleted, Njinga became a Dutch ally. They'd work together, their treaty said, '[to] exterminate the Portuguese.'[12]

Njinga also learnt that Funji was dead. As punishment for spying, the Portuguese had drowned her.

In late 1647, Njinga and the Dutch attempted to take Massangano, a Portuguese fort. Since Luanda's loss, it was one of the last Portuguese strongholds. Conquering it would mean the Portuguese would probably have to leave West-Central Africa.

The allies took the lands around the fort, blocking its supply routes. But they lacked the firepower to break through its defences. Frustrated, some of the Dutch retreated to Luanda. Njinga attacked pro-Portuguese *sobas*.

In 1648, a Portuguese fleet of 15 ships, and 900 soldiers, arrived from Brazil. It bombed Luanda, where, because of the attack on Massangano, the Dutch numbered only 250. Salvador Correia de Sa, the incoming Portuguese governor and the fleet's admiral, gave the Dutch three days to surrender.

Ouman, the Dutchman in charge of Luanda, sent letters to Njinga and Pieterszoon, another Dutch official, asking for help. Njinga and Pieterszoon had been about to attack Massangano again.

Ouman tried to drag out the negotiations with the Portuguese. Impatient, Correia de Sa resumed bombing. Ouman surrendered.

Heeding Ouman's earlier call for help, Njinga marched to Luanda's outskirts. Pieterszoon had gone on ahead. She awaited his instructions. When she heard nothing, she marched closer to Luanda. At its fort, São Miguel, she saw the Portuguese flag flying. Pieterszoon had arrived just in time to board one of the Dutch ships fleeing the city. Dejected, Njinga returned to Matamba.

She continued fighting the Portuguese in and around Ndongo. She also sent them peace delegations. The Portuguese in Luanda were enraged about her continued attacks. They asked their king's permission to react. The king consulted his advisers. They suggested he refuse. Njinga was still powerful, and willing to fight. But she was also still open to peace. War with her had brought only expensive bills, death and destruction.

By 1656, Njinga and the Portuguese had exchanged numerous embassies. Back and forth, they'd negotiated. Finally, Njinga's ambassador returned with a draft peace treaty.

Face-to-face with Portuguese diplomats, Njinga and her team scrutinised it. Under its terms, Njinga agreed to leave the Imbangala, make Matamba Catholic and become Portugal's ally. The Portuguese agreed to return almost every part of Ndongo they'd conquered (holding onto only a little of the kingdom's north) and recognise Njinga as Queen of Matamba.

Njinga pointed out a passage in the treaty which said she'd have to pay tribute. 'In regard then to paying the tribute that you claim from me, there is no reason to do so, because having been born to rule my kingdom, I should not obey or recognise another sovereign,' she said. 'If the Portuguese want a gift from me every year, I would give it to them voluntarily as long as they equally give me one so that we both would deal with each other courteously.'[13]

The Portuguese ambassadors removed the clause.

Portuguese officials then released Kambu, escorting her to Matamba.

At her palace, when she saw Kambu, Njinga fell to her knees. She stood up, kissed Kambu's hand, and fell once more. Again, she got up. The two sisters hugged and kissed each other's cheeks for a long time, saying nothing.

Njinga signed the treaty.

In January 1657, to celebrate this signing of the peace agreement with the Portuguese, Njinga led her last military ceremony. She was seventy-five years old. Having first led a campaign against the Portuguese in 1602, she'd been fighting against them, on and off, for over fifty years. During the ceremony, she wore full military dress. In the square before Matamba's main church, she sat on a chair. Her main army – 2,000 troops – marched before her, beating drums and waving banners. She ordered them to do their pre-battle dance.

When they'd finished, and got back into formation, she picked up her bow, and stood on the chair.

"'Who can ever defeat this bow?'"[14] she yelled, thrusting it into the sky.

"'No one! No one!'"[15] shouted her troops.

"'Only Maniputo, King of Portugal can defeat it [...] now I say to all of you that I have just made peace with him, and I do not want to go about in the bush any more as I have done up to now ... [Now] it is the time that I leave this bow.'"[16]

She threw the bow on the ground.

"'I want to live in peace and quiet,'" she continued. "'I am already old and it does not suit me to go about like a vagrant ... I give thanks for all the travails that you have suffered in the wars, and now in [getting back] my sister. She is already with me to keep me company, which is what I desire.'"[17]

Kambu, who'd been watching, ran to Njinga, and threw herself on the ground before her.

In this way was Ndongo saved.

Hopefully, this chapter gives you a sense of how women were traditionally treated in many African cultures. Whether women were seen as their culture's most important figures, like in Asante, ruled alongside men, like in Igbo or Nubia, or ruled alone, as in Nubia and Mbundu, there's no doubting the reverence that their people had for them. These people deeply respected the positions these women held, the rituals they performed and the authority it was felt they wielded. They accepted these women's decisions blindly, obeyed their commands and followed them wherever they went, even if it was into battle. There was little to no question of their fitness to rule – in whatever capacity – because of their sex.

Unfortunately, as the next chapter will demonstrate, some non-African peoples haven't shown similar respect when it comes to discussing Africans' social, political and cultural identities. These individuals have often failed to appreciate Africans' profound and nuanced identities and differences. Instead, they refer to every person with African ancestry simply, and often inaccurately, as 'black', based solely on their perceived skin colour. This is not to say that they necessarily use 'black' derogatorily, but that this term is insufficient to describe accurately many African peoples. In the next chapter, I'll explain why. I'll also dig a little deeper into the history of why exactly some non-African peoples describe Africans mainly as 'black'.

4

WE ARE MORE THAN SKIN COLOUR

In the first instance, 'black' is insufficient to describe many African or African-descent peoples because their African-ness – or, to those who use 'black' as a racial term, their 'blackness' – is not all there is to their identities. In other words, there's so much more to the identities of many African peoples than their African-ness, or their skin colour.

Take Kamala Harris, former Vice President of the United States, for example.

Harris was born in 1964 in California. Her father – Donald – is African Jamaican. Her mother – Shyamala – was Indian, more specifically, Hindu Tamil. When Harris was seven, her parents divorced. She, and her younger sister, Maya, lived with Shyamala.

Shyamala raised them as African Americans. 'She knew that her adopted homeland would see Maya and me as black girls, and she was determined to make sure we would grow into confident, proud black women,'[1] said Harris. 'From almost the moment [my mother] arrived from India, she chose and was welcomed to and enveloped in the [African American] community.'[2] Shyamala and the girls attended an African American church. She took them to civil rights marches. Harris rode the African American school bus. Donald also played his part. He loved jazz and introduced Harris to Thelonious Monk and John Coltrane.

All this impacted Harris. Thurgood Marshall became one of her heroes. She chose to go to the traditionally African American university, Howard, mainly because Marshall had gone there. At Howard, she joined Alpha Kappa Alpha, the US's oldest African

American sorority. '[Being raised African American] affects everything about who I am,'[3] said Harris.

But Shyamala also raised her daughters as Indian. She took them on visits to her homeland of Tamil Nadu. At home, they cooked and ate Indian food. They were encouraged to wear Indian clothes and jewellery. She taught them a little Tamil. '[My mother had a] strong awareness and appreciation for Indian culture,'[4] said Harris. '[And being raised Indian also] has had a great deal of influence on what I do . . . and who I am.'[5]

Harris sees herself as 'dual heritage'. To her, both the African-American and Indian parts of her heritage are equally important. She's been active in both the African American and Indian communities. She's attended Alpha Kappa Alpha alumni events. In a speech at the Democratic National Convention, she used the Tamil word *chithis* ('aunties') when thanking her family for their support. 'I don't have any doubts about who I am ethnically or racially,'[6] she said.

Yet, the press has all too often described Harris as solely 'black'. In 2016, when Harris was elected California's senator, many press outlets said she was only the second 'black' woman to have achieved this, but neglected to mention that she was the *first* South Asian American to have done so. Moreover, when describing the African part of Harris's identity, the press has often used the skin colour term – 'black' – rather than an ethnic, or geographic, one. Conversely, when they *have* mentioned the nuanced, Indian part of her identity, they've often used one or other of the latter two terms. Harris is 'both black and Indian American,'[7] said ABC in 2019. She is a 'black, female . . . Democrat . . . [and] the first South Asian senator',[8] said the *New Yorker*. In 2010, when Harris became Attorney General of California, *The New York Times* said she is 'the daughter of a black economist and an Indian biologist'.[9] Not only does it seem, then, that the press thinks 'black' sufficient to describe Harris's entire identity, *despite* her not being fully African, or even having black skin, but it also seems that they think there is nothing more to being African than having dark (or, as they see it, 'black') skin.

It's not only the press that does this. So many non-African people describe all kinds of people with African heritage as 'black'. Yet, Africans are the most culturally, ethnically, racially, and even skin-colour-diverse people in the world.

In the second instance, 'black' is insufficient to describe many African or African-descent peoples because it fails to account for this almost incredible scale of diversity. First, I'll explain why Africans are the most genetically, and thus racially and skin-colour, diverse people in the world.

*

As we know from the existence of 'Eve' – the last common ancestor of every current human being, who lived in Africa around 150,000 years ago – the population from which every person today is descended (i.e., the 'founder population') lived in Africa.

About 100,000 years ago, some of the founder population's descendants – living probably in Ethiopia – migrated via Egypt to Israel. Some of the Israeli population's descendants then travelled along the coasts of the Indian Ocean and spread themselves across southeast Asia and Oceania. By 60,000 years ago, they'd reached Australia. Around 35,000 years ago, other descendants of the original population migrated from Africa to Europe. With more sophisticated behaviours and technologies, they replaced Neanderthals. By about 15,000 years ago, other descendants had reached the Americas.

The people that moved away formed a genetically less-diverse population than both the founder population and the founder's descendants who never migrated. This is known as the 'founder effect'. When members of a group move away, they take with them only a subset of the overall genetic diversity of the group they moved away from.

Imagine you have a bag of forty marbles. There are ten red marbles, ten green ones, ten blue, and ten yellow. These marbles represent the founder population's descendants who lived probably in Ethiopia over 100,000 years ago. You then reach your hand into the bag, grab a handful of marbles, and put them to one side. The marbles you removed represent those who migrated from this population to Israel. You count these marbles. You find that there are five red marbles, three green ones, only one blue one, and no yellow ones. You bag them up. The marbles you extracted – the group that migrated away – is automatically less diverse than the original bag.

Moreover, the people that moved away from the first migratory group – i.e. those who migrated from the Israeli population to southeast Asia and beyond – formed an even less genetically diverse population than both the founder's descendants in Ethiopia *and* the Israeli population. This is known as the 'serial founder effect'. Imagine you reach your hand into the second bag of marbles, take a handful, and put them aside. The marbles you removed represent those who migrated from the Israeli population to southeast Asia and beyond. You count them. You find that there are three red marbles, one green one, and no blue ones. This group is even less diverse than the first two.

The second and third groups of marbles represent the more recent ancestors of, for instance, Indians, Europeans, and Americans. These populations are less diverse than African ones because their ancestors moved away from the founder population which originated in Africa. Genetically, the oldest and most diverse peoples in Africa, and thus probably the world, are the Khoisan, and the Biaka 'Pygmies' of the Central African Republic. Around 120,000 years ago, the Khoisan's ancestors split from the descendants of the founding population. This split was the first. That African peoples' populations have the most genetic diversity also supports the theory that human beings emerged in Africa before spreading to the rest of the world. As the founder effects demonstrate, the most genetically diverse population is the original, and thus the oldest, one.

As well as being the most genetically diverse peoples in the world, Africans are the most linguistically, and thus ethnically and culturally, diverse peoples in the world. Around 7,000 languages are spoken worldwide, and Africans speak about 2,000 of these.

Most of the languages Africans speak originated in Africa, and only Africans speak them. These languages are divided into four major language groups: Niger-Congo, Afro-Asiatic, Nilo-Saharan, and Khoisan. Each of these major groups consists of various subgroups. And each of these subgroups also consists of subgroups (or sub-subgroups). Each of these sub-subgroups has subgroups of its own. Some originally African languages fit into none of the major groups – for example, Shabo, a niche Ethiopian language, and Dompo, spoken in Ghana. Sadly, some of these independent African languages have gone extinct, or are in danger of doing so.

The rest of the languages Africans speak were brought by peoples from other continents. They include the Indian and Pakistani languages, like Urdu, and the European languages, like Portuguese, of the Indo-European language group that entered Africa from at least the fifteenth century onwards. They also include the languages, like Malagasy, of the Austronesian language group, which entered Africa as far back as 2,000 years ago.

Niger-Congo is the largest language group not just in Africa but the world. It contains nearly 1,500 languages and has over 300 million speakers. These languages are divided into seven subgroups: West Atlantic, Mandé, Gur, Kwa, Congo, Adamawa-Eastern, and Kordofanian. In many African countries, it's languages of the Niger-Congo group that are the most widely spoken. In Senegal, half the population – some nine million people – speaks the Niger-Congo language Wolof. Eighty per cent of Ghanaians – some 26 million people – speak languages of the Kwa subgroup called Akan. The Niger-Congo language group is also very old.

All Niger-Congo languages developed from one spoken as far back as 15,000 years ago.

However, the *oldest* language group in both Africa and the world is Khoisan. Khoisan's thirty-five languages sprung from one spoken about 20,000 years ago. These languages are divided into five subgroups: Hadza, Sandawe, Khoe, Ju, and Tuu. Khoisan speakers are spread across mainly southern Africa. They live in countries like Angola, Namibia, and Botswana. The original Khoisan speakers were based more north-east, in what's now Kenya and Somalia. Eight thousand years ago, some of them moved south, bringing their language, and stone-tool-using, hunter-gatherer lifestyle with them.

The Afro-Asiatic language group has 371 languages, including Amharic, Somali, and Hausa, as well as languages that originated from, and are spoken by, non-African peoples, such as Arabic. These almost 400 languages are divided into six subgroups: Chadic, 'Berber', Egyptian, Semitic, Cushitic, and Omotic. The Afro-Asiatic group is also old, with a 10,000-year-old heritage. Its speakers live mainly in North Africa.

The Nilo-Saharan language group has about 200 languages. These are divided into four subgroups: Songhay, Saharan, Kuliak, and a fourth subgroup so diverse and complex it doesn't have a widely agreed-upon name. We'll call it the 'nameless subgroup'.

The nameless subgroup consists of six subgroups (or, sub-subgroups): Maban, Fur, Central Sudanic, Berta, Kunama, and the 'Core'. The Core consists of four subgroups (or, sub-sub-subgroups): Eastern Sudanic, Koman, Gumuz, and Kadu. Eastern Sudanic consists of two subgroups (or, sub-sub-sub-subgroups): Ek and En. These consist of their own subgroups, which, in turn, have *their* own subgroups.

Almost every major group, and subgroup, of African languages, can be similarly broken down. The diversity of African languages, and those of the ethnic groups and cultures they represent, is mind-boggling.

We've now got a sense of how diverse Africans truly are. As we understand from the founder effects, because the human population we are all descended from originated in Africa, any group of people that moved away from this population's non-migrating descendants became less diverse – not just genetically, but also culturally and ethnically. This is because a small, breakaway group was unlikely to take with them all the genetic and cultural elements that comprised the much larger group they broke away from. As a new population, they went on to form a distinct, but more limited, culture.

But the founder effects are just a part of the explanation of why Africans are so diverse. The rest of it also has to do with the fact that human beings originated in Africa, but considers, too, what was happening both millions of years before, and tens of thousands of years after, the exact population we're all descended from emerged over 150,000 years ago.

We know from the first chapter – Our Lost Millennia – that, over millions of years, separate early human populations lived across Africa. They adapted to the different environments in which they lived, and developed differently. Then, they migrated across Africa, mixing with one another. Some populations even migrated out of Africa, and, generations later, some of their descendants came back and mixed with African populations. Genetic evidence from Central African peoples, including the San of Namibia, reveals that 35,000 years ago, some of our ancestors mixed with an as-yet-unidentified early human population. Similar evidence reveals that, between 3,000 and 11,000 years ago, east and west African *sapiens*, moving back and forth along the Sudanic belt (i.e., the grassy region between the Sahara and Central African forest), mixed with each other quite a lot. Around 30,000 years ago, some *sapiens* moved from Africa into Europe and mixed with Neanderthals. Contemporary humans have traces of Neanderthal DNA. Seven thousand years ago, descendants of *sapiens* who'd moved out of Africa and mixed with Eurasian early humans moved back to Africa. More specifically, they migrated to, and mixed with populations in, West Africa. Consequently, the Yoruba of Nigeria, and the Mossi of Burkina Faso, have Eurasian genes. The Chonyi and Kauma of Kenya, and the Khoisan of South Africa, also have Eurasian genes. They acquired these because of back-into-Africa migrations that occurred over the last four thousand or so years.

Whenever early human populations mixed, they exchanged not just their different genes, but also their different cultural features (like languages) and technologies. Their descendants were a combination of, but also distinct from, all the groups that had come together to produce them. In other words, every time distinct early human populations mixed, a completely new group was brought into being, that then went on to mix with another distinct group, which then created *another* new group, and so on.

Because humans have inhabited Africa the longest, it is in *Africa* that the most migration and mixing has occurred between distinct human populations. In short, it is in Africa that, over time, we've seen the creation of the highest number of distinct human populations. For millions of years, when distinct human populations inhabited only Africa, they were migrating and mixing. Even when some moved out of Africa, those in Africa continued to migrate and mix. The sheer number of distinct populations that came out of this mixing meant that, up to the present day, the diversity of African peoples increased exponentially. It's no wonder Africans are the most diverse people on Earth.

Seemingly, some African populations migrated and mixed a lot more than others, meaning that, genetically, culturally, and technologically, they heavily influenced many more African populations than these others did. This is to the extent that we can even identify their migration and mixing patterns in the archaeological and historical records.

One such group of keen migrators and mixers were the Bantu, who still exist. In actuality, the Bantu have never been just one distinct population. Rather, they've always comprised several distinct populations that have spoken different, but closely related, languages with a common origin. In these languages, also labelled 'Bantu', the word '*bantu*' means 'people'. It was Wilhelm Bleek, a nineteenth-century German philologist, who suggested these languages be named after this word. Then, the people themselves, who are amongst the most numerous in Africa, came to be named after this label given to their languages. It is thanks to the Bantu's extensive migrations and mixing that their languages, numbering over five hundred, are the most widely spoken in Africa. These languages are part of the Niger-Congo language group, the largest in the world. A third of Africans speak at least one Bantu language. In total, the number of Bantu speakers in Africa is about two hundred million.

In about 3,000 BC, some Bantu migrated from their place of origin in what is now Cameroon to the north edge of the Central African forest, about where Gabon now is. Unlike the forest's centre, which comprised thick woodland, this north edge was a savanna.

Why these Bantu moved is unclear. They might have gone in search of more areas of fertile land. Or, they might have been forced out. Around 9,000 BC, the Younger Dryas – a cold, dry and unstable one-thousand-year epoch – ended. The Holocene – a stabler epoch, with warmer and wetter weather, and an atmosphere richer in carbon dioxide – followed it. In the Holocene, plants grew more abundantly, so there was more food, which allowed people to sustain larger populations, which put more pressure on other resources, which led to competition and fighting. Some of those who were defeated chose or were made to leave.

In 500 BC – so, 2,500 years *after* the first set of Bantu reached the Central African forest – their descendants moved further south and east. The reason the first set of Bantu hadn't done this is because, until about 500 BC, the forest's centre had been just too dense for them either to live in or travel through. But, by around

500 BC, the regional climate had warmed, so the Atlantic Ocean's surface temperature had risen. This led to increased rainfall, which eroded the soil at the forest's centre and led to the trees' destruction, transforming this centre into a savanna-land, too.

Some Bantu thus travelled down the Atlantic Coast, stopping in the savannas of south Congo. We'll call them the 'Atlantic Coast Bantu'.

Others rather moved east into the Republic of the Congo, then south along nearby rivers. By 300 BC, they'd reached the Great Lakes – Lake Albert, on the border between the Democratic Republic of Congo and Uganda, and Lake Victoria, spreading across Uganda, Kenya, and Tanzania. Here, they encountered Central Sudanic peoples, i.e. peoples who speak the related Central Sudanic languages.

Unlike the Bantu, who were primarily hunter-gatherers who used stone tools, the Central Sudanic were experienced farmers and ironworkers. Their ancestors had lived in the Sudanic belt, where, by about 2,000 BC, they'd learnt how to farm, and, by about 300 BC, had also learnt how to make iron. Possibly, ironworking knowledge had spread to them from Nubian Meroë, which had expert blacksmiths. Or, it had spread from the Nok civilisation, which, between 1,000 BC and 200 AD, thrived in Nigeria. The Nok were accomplished artists, who made astonishing terracotta sculptures, some as tall as four feet. Iron-smelting furnaces and tools have been found at their sites.

The Bantu that reached the Great Lakes eventually adopted ironworking and farming from the Central Sudanic. They learnt how to rear cows and sheep and used their newly gained iron-working knowledge to create Urewe ware – a distinctive type of pottery, which they decorated with geometric lines and shapes. They became what we'll call the 'Great Lakes Bantu'.

Why exactly those who became the Great Lakes Bantu decided to abandon their hunter-gathering, stone-tool-using ways in favour of ironworking and farming is unknown to us.

But we may hazard a couple of guesses.

Probably, the Central Sudanic outnumbered the Bantu. After all, it's much easier to sustain a larger population when you know how to grow much greater quantities of food than you'd otherwise find by just looking around. Moreover, iron tools, and, crucially, weapons, are much more effective than stone ones. It's possible that the Central Sudanic crushed, and then assimilated, the Bantu that entered their vicinity. Or, the Bantu, seeing the iron-working farmers' knowledge and technology as simply better than their own, willingly utilised them. Most likely, over time, it was some combination of both.

Between 300 and 200 BC, some Great Lakes Bantu migrated west, travelling along the southern edge of the Central African forest into northern Angola. Here, they encountered some Atlantic Coast Bantu, settled nearby in south Congo. By 1 AD, these Atlantic Coast Bantu had adopted from their Great Lakes cousins ironworking and farming, becoming what we'll call the 'Angolan Bantu'. Probably, this occurred in the same way as described above.

Between about 100 and 200 AD, other Great Lakes Bantu migrated from the Great Lakes south and east. They settled in Somalia, Kenya, and Tanzania. Over the next two hundred years, some of *these* settlers moved further south, first into Zambia and Malawi, then into Zimbabwe and South Africa.

Meanwhile, during the same period, some Angolan Bantu moved first deeper into Angola, then spread themselves across much of southwest Africa. Others moved east to, and settled in, Zambia and the Democratic Republic of Congo.

As different Bantu groups migrated across Africa, they encountered not just each other, and groups like the Central Sudanic, but also diverse groups of stone-tool-using hunter-gatherers that had inhabited the continent for millennia – for example, the Khoisan. When Bantu groups who'd become ironworkers and farmers encountered these hunter-gatherers, the latter eventually also adopted these practices. In short, these Bantu did to these hunter-gatherers what the Central Sudanic had done to the Bantu that migrated to the Great Lakes. In this way, ironworking and farming spread to almost every culture on the continent.

But the hunter-gatherers left their mark, too. They might have on the whole been dominated, but they inevitably influenced the Bantu's cultures. To different farming, iron-working Bantu groups, different hunter-gatherer groups contributed different words, practices, technologies, and even genes. These Bantu groups became both distinct from each other, and unique.

We can see from the Bantu example how migration and mixing increased African peoples' diversity exponentially. We began with one Bantu group – those who migrated from Cameroon to the Central African forest. Then, as this group's descendants migrated to different places, and mixed with different people, they became different, meaning we now had multiple groups. And as *these* groups' descendants continued to migrate, and mix and become different, we now had even *more* groups. From the Central African forest Bantu came the Atlantic Coast Bantu, the Great Lakes Bantu, and the Angolan Bantu, to name just a few.

Now that we understand just how diverse African peoples are, and why, it's time to explain why, despite Africans' skin colour, ethnic and cultural diversity, some peoples refer to all of them as only 'black'.

To do so, we might begin in the seventeenth-century American colony of Virginia, where a demographic transformation changed how its inhabitants identified themselves, and the identity markers against which they discriminated each other.

*

In early seventeenth-century Virginia, hardly anyone thought that their race or skin colour was the most important part of their, or another's, identity, and so hardly anyone discriminated against others on the basis of these. To see this, you only have to look at how Africans in this place at this time were treated.

Take Anthony Johnson, an early seventeenth-century African-Virginian landowner, and his family, as an example.

Like most, if not all, of the Africans that lived in early seventeenth-century America, Johnson was a 'Creole'. Creoles were the children (or grandchildren) of Africans, or Africans and Europeans, who from about the sixteenth century onwards lived in West Africa's and Europe's coastal settlements. Here, they were exposed to both African and European customs and became multicultural and worldly, able to conduct themselves well in both European and African society.

Some of the earliest Creoles had gone to the Americas voluntarily. They'd joined the treasure-finding expeditions that in the fifteenth and sixteenth centuries Spain and Portugal had launched there. They'd travelled with the likes of Hernán Cortés, Francisco Pizarro, Hernando de Soto, and even Christopher Columbus.

Others had been trafficked. Ordinarily, this was to the Caribbean. In the fifteenth century, here, unlike in what's now North America, the Spanish had established plantations, and so the demand for labour was greater. The first Creoles to be trafficked to Virginia had not been imported directly from Africa. They'd not been imported at all. Virginian planters were on the whole less well-connected and poorer than their Caribbean counterparts. They couldn't afford the cargoes of mainly male enslaved Africans that came from Africa. Instead, these went to the European planters in the Caribbean. Those Africans in Virginia had been gifted by Caribbean Europeans.

Or, they'd come by accident. In 1619, a Portuguese ship called the *San Juan Bautista* set off from Angola to Mexico. On board were over a hundred African Creoles – probably Mbundus from the kingdom of Ndongo, who'd been converted to Christianity. Within a month of departure, exposed to terrible conditions, dozens of them had died. The trip was taking longer than expected, and so the captain stopped off in Jamaica. There, he unloaded the most ill Creoles, and exchanged twenty-four healthy ones for food and medicine. He resumed his journey, but as he sailed along the Mexican coast to Vera Cruz, two English ships – the *White Lion* and the *Treasurer* – attacked and raided him. They split the sixty or so Africans between them, took them to Virginia, and sold them to wealthy Virginians. These were the first Africans of England's mainland American colonies.

Anthony Johnson had himself been trafficked to Virginia in 1621. Mary, the African woman he married in the 1620s or '30s, had been trafficked the year after. Together, they had at least four children – two boys and two girls.

Initially, Johnson and Mary worked as indentured servants on the plantation of a man called Bennett. An indentured servant was someone who'd signed a contract to work on a colonist's land (usually for five years) in exchange for passage overseas, food and shelter. The Johnsons had been trafficked by Portuguese slave traders, and so hadn't signed a contract. But, in the colony, with the exception that they didn't have to be released after the five-year time limit, they were treated as indentured servants.

Johnson and Mary worked for Bennett for twenty years, when they finally negotiated and paid him for their freedom. With the rest of the money they'd saved, they acquired almost 1,000 acres of land, farm animals, and even two servants of their own: an African man called John Casar in the 1640s; and, in the 1650s, an African woman called Mary Gersheene.

Near the Johnsons lived two European landowning brothers called George and Robert Parker. In need of more workers, the Parkers had for some time been trying to steal Casar.

Casar, meanwhile, wanted to join the Parkers. He had a grudge against Anthony Johnson. He said he'd signed an indentured servitude contract with Johnson, had worked the seven years he'd agreed to, but that Johnson had refused to free him. Johnson said there'd been no such contract, and that Casar was rather due to be his servant for life.

The Parkers backed Casar. They said they could prove he had a contract, which his previous employer held. They threatened Johnson, saying that, if he didn't let Casar go, they'd make it so that he lost his rights to use Casar's cows.

Intimidated by such threats, and persuaded by some of his family members that Casar wasn't worth it, Johnson released him. In 1653, he signed a document discharging Casar from his service, agreeing to give him corn and clothes, and pay his freedom dues – that is, money paid to an ex-indentured servant to help them set themselves up. Casar went to work for the Parkers.

But just two years later, feeling that the Parkers had done him an injustice, Johnson petitioned the Virginian court to have Casar given back. He won. Agreeing that Casar had been unfairly taken away, the judge invalidated the 1653 document. He ordered that Casar be returned to Johnson, and the Parkers pay *all* legal fees. He didn't specify how long Casar would have to serve Johnson, so Casar did so for at least another *seventeen* years, probably until he died. Technically, he was one of the first enslaved Africans in Virginia.

In short, the judge didn't think that the Parkers, as Europeans, were superior to the African Johnson, and so had to win the case. This kind of racial bias hardly existed in early Virginia, and so couldn't have influenced the judge's decision. To the judge, Johnson was simply an independent, respectable, landowning gentleman whom other landowning gentlemen – the Parkers – had wronged, and who thus deserved justice.

Most, if not all, the Johnsons' fellow Virginian citizens, European or otherwise, also viewed the Johnsons as respectable landowners. In 1653, a fire destroyed much of the Johnsons' property. When they asked the court for help, they got it. In 1655, one of Johnson's sons was imprisoned for 'committing the sin of fornication.'[10] He'd allegedly impregnated a European servant called

Hannah Leach. The judge said he'd release this son only if the latter would pay damages, all legal fees, and to support the child. To secure this son's freedom, a European neighbour and friend of the Johnsons agreed to act as his guarantor. Another of Johnson's sons – Richard – married and had children with a European woman. Even the Parkers, who were the Johnsons' only rivals, didn't try to steal Casar because they felt that, as an African, and thus inferior, Johnson didn't deserve him. They simply wanted more workers.

In early seventeenth-century Virginia, the reason why race or skin colour wasn't a big deal, and that people didn't discriminate against each other based on one or either of these, was that the society was mixed in terms of both race and class. In other words, you had both African landowners and servants, as well as European landowners and servants, and even both free and enslaved native Americans. African landowners and European landowners on the one hand, and African servants and European ones on the other, had much the same lives. African and European landowners treated each other roughly the same. They also treated both African and European servants roughly the same. European landowners didn't generally treat African servants worse than European ones because of where they came from and what they looked like. Additionally, there was a lot of mixing, not just between African and European landowners on the one hand, and African and European servants on the other, but between all four groups.

European and African servants had the same rights and privileges. They had weekends to themselves, and holidays. They could leave their masters' homesteads, visit nearby towns, walk their streets, and hang about in their taverns. Their masters were morally and culturally obliged to provide them with decent clothing, shelter and food. They also couldn't punish their servants whenever and however they liked. If they had an issue with a servant's misbehaviour, apart from resolving it peacefully themselves, they had to take them to court. They allowed their servants to work for themselves in their free time. Some Creole indentured servants hunted, fished, gardened, and reared animals. Others crafted goods, which they sold to their fellow workers, their masters, and their masters' neighbours. Others continued to work their master's land in exchange for a wage – usually, an amount of a commodity, like tobacco.

Like the Johnsons did, if a Creole servant saved up enough resources and built up good enough connections with their master or other wealthy and important Virginians, they could acquire their freedom. Many Virginian masters were enthusiastic patrons of Creole entrepreneurs, with whom they willingly entered business partnerships. Some were so enthusiastic that, when asked, they aided the patronised in acquiring their freedom, either by lending them money or persuading their masters to release them.

The arrangement benefitted masters, too. Better treatment often meant that their servants worked better. Also, Creoles were customarily or legally obliged to give a little of what they produced to their master. When Creoles ate the food they'd grown, or wore clothes they'd made, it reduced their master's financial burden.

Rather, to early seventeenth-century Virginians, the most important part of their identity was their *Christianity*. Though their society was racially and socially mixed, it was, on the whole, religiously uniform. Most of the African and European landowners and servants were Christian. Some had been for a while, whereas others – African servants especially – had recently converted, or been converted, by their masters. Thus, in early seventeenth-century Virginia, the major dividing line its 'free' inhabitants drew between themselves and 'others' was on the basis not of race, skin colour, or even wealth, but *religion*. By 'free', I mean those who were entitled to Virginian society's rights and privileges. Whether you were European or African on the one hand, or a landowner or a servant on the other, if you were Christian, you were considered a 'free' Virginian. If you *weren't* Christian, you weren't entitled to 'free' Virginians' rights. In short, you were discriminated against.

For instance, in 1644, Virginia's lawmakers passed a law banning sexual relations between Christians and non-Christians. Moreover, in early seventeenth-century Virginia, unlike Christians, non-Christians were often forced or tricked by their masters into being servants for life – essentially, enslaved. Trafficked Creoles, who weren't only non-Christian, but also might not have signed indentured servitude contracts, were particularly affected by this. As an English colony, Virginia was subject to English laws, one of which banned the effective enslavement of fellow Christians. Therefore, to gain their freedom, one strategy Creoles used was to be baptised, then sue their masters for said freedom in Virginia's courts. As late as 1667, an African in servitude called Fernando attempted this. He said he'd been baptised and had lived in England. Many Creoles didn't succeed in their attempts, but a fair few did. The Lower Norfolk County Court, where Fernando first made his case, threw it out. He appealed to the General Court, but no record of its verdict exists.

However, a relatively racially equal, though religiously bigoted, Virginian society wouldn't last for ever. Why? Because it would soon cease to be mixed in the way it had been. In short, it would become segregated and two-tiered – light-skinned European landowners at the top on the one hand, and dark-skinned *enslaved* – not just indentured servant – Africans at the bottom on the other. For 'free' Virginians, the clear dividing line between themselves and 'others' that was once based on religion would now become based on race and skin colour.

How did Virginia transform from a mixed to a segregated, two-tiered society? Essentially, this occurred because of a change in the Virginian economy, and then in the workforce on which that economy came to rely.

*

In 1610, Virginia's economy was a travesty. In Jamestown, the settlement the English colonists had founded in Virginia, they'd failed to establish themselves. Every industry they'd set up to try to form a stable economy had faltered. The gold they'd mined and sent to England had turned out to be 'fool's gold'. The cedar logs, soap ashes, and glass beads in relative abundance around them just weren't popular in their mother country. Supplies had run out, and hundreds had died.

That same year, an Englishman called John Rolfe arrived in Jamestown. Seeing its pitiful state, he set out to save it. He saw that the tobacco the Spanish grew in the Caribbean was loved in England. He asked a ship's captain to bring him some of its seeds from Trinidad, where the best-regarded tobacco was grown. Over 1611 and 1612, he planted the seeds, grew the plants, stripped off their leaves, and cured them. He sent a shipment of a few hundred pounds to England and waited.

A few months later, he got the news he was anxiously hoping to hear.

His tobacco was a hit.

It became known as 'sweet-scented' tobacco. The expert buyers in London couldn't get enough of it.

News of Rolfe's success spread round the colony. Over the next few years, the Virginians transformed huge tracts of forestland into tobacco farms. Everybody turned to tobacco farming. In 1617 – little more than five years after Rolfe had created his tobacco – the Virginians shipped 20,000 pounds of it across the Atlantic. The year after that, they shipped 40,000 pounds. By the 1620s, the size of their tobacco shipments was well into the *hundreds* of thousands of pounds. By the second half of the 1630s, they were shipping over a million pounds of the stuff *each year*.

Tobacco became essential to the colony. It was even used as currency. When some young women were brought to the colony to marry planters, tobacco was used to pay the transportation costs.

To meet demand, the Virginians needed more workers. Indentured servants were no good because after a few years, you ordinarily had to release them. They often set up tobacco farms of their own, becoming your competitors.

Around the Virginians lived tens of thousands of native Americans belonging to groups like the Powhatan. Between the 1610s and 1640s, the Virginians fought several wars against the Powhatan. They enslaved their captives, whom they used on their farms. In 1646, the two groups signed a peace treaty. The Virginians agreed not to enslave any more local native Americans. Some, however, continued the practice. In the mid-to-late seventeenth century, Virginians also employed slave-raiding native American groups like the Westos. The Westos captured and sold into slavery native Americans from Spanish mainland colonies, like Florida. This use of indigenous slave labour was neither new nor unusual. In the previous century, on Hispaniola – a large island in the Caribbean, where Columbus had landed in 1492 – the Spanish had enslaved the Tainos.

But enslaved native Americans were as a workforce no good either. There weren't that many of them to begin with. Also, they didn't live long. For at least 7,000 years, the 'New World', i.e. the Americas, and the 'Old World', i.e. Africa, Europe, and Asia, had been separated. Humans in the Old World had developed agriculture earlier than those in the New. They'd set up and lived in more densely populated permanent settlements, and they reared certain animals. Diseases these animals carried – for instance, smallpox and measles – spread to, and throughout, their populations.

Europeans that arrived in the New World unwittingly carried these diseases. The New Worlders, having never encountered them before, had no immunity, and died in droves. When the Spanish arrived on Hispaniola, the Tainos numbered 500,000. Fifty years later, they'd essentially gone extinct. In 1500, there were about 15 million native Americans in Central Mexico. A century later, only just over one million remained. By 1650, up to *ninety* per cent of the native American population had been wiped out, mainly by these diseases.

For a source of labour, the Virginians would have to look elsewhere. Luckily for them, they wouldn't have to look very far. At the same time as they were establishing their tobacco-plantation economy, the Dutch were establishing a sugar-plantation economy in the Caribbean and helping the French and the English to do the same.

In the 1630s, the Dutch conquered Pernambuco, an important sugar-plantation region in today's Brazil, which had been in Portuguese hands. Continued conflict over Pernambuco between the Dutch and the Portuguese led to a decline in its production. Then, in about the early 1640s, the Portuguese reconquered it. Cutting their losses, in the 1640s and '50s, Dutch planters migrated to and settled on Caribbean islands like Barbados and Martinique. Some English and French planters already lived here, but they weren't growing much sugar, and they weren't rich. They lacked the infrastructure – both the equipment and the workforce – to make sugar farming profitable. Instead, using mainly European indentured servants, they grew and exported mostly tobacco and indigo.

Having once controlled Pernambuco, the Dutch possessed advanced sugar-production equipment and know-how.

But that wasn't all.

While attempting to supplant the Portuguese as European masters of the Atlantic, they obtained something else that both the English and the French on the one hand, and the Virginians on the other, lacked to accelerate the production of their plantation crops. This was a relatively cheap, easily accessible, and reliable workforce.

As we saw in the final section of the last chapter – Queenmothers and Warrior-Queens – the Dutch encroached on Portuguese positions in West and West-Central Africa, seizing them when they could, and deepening their relationships with powerful African monarchs. For instance, in 1638, they captured from the Portuguese São Jorge da Mina – a slaving fort in what is now Ghana. In this way, they gained access to a steady supply of enslaved Africans – a relatively novel workforce as far as the Americas were concerned. However, as an American workforce, enslaved Africans were 'better' than indentured servants and enslaved native Americans for numerous reasons. For example, you didn't have to release them after a set number of years, and, coming from the Old World themselves, they weren't going to die from its diseases.

The Dutch invested heavily in the Caribbean, supplying both their sugar-production equipment and know-how and their workforce of enslaved Africans to the French and the English. Over the next fifty years or so, sugar became the Caribbean's dominant crop. Enslaved Africans replaced European indentured servants as workers. The number, size and output of sugar estates increased at the expense of tobacco and indigo farms. Wealth and power became concentrated in the hands of a landholding, slave-owning elite.

Off the back of sugar profits, France and Britain became rich, imperial powers. Eventually, they competed against the Dutch for the sugar and slave trades. They seized a huge chunk of the latter and introduced tariffs on Dutch imports. By the first half of the eighteenth century, *they* were the European masters of the Atlantic.

To increase the production and profitability of their tobacco farms, the Virginians desired access to the workforce that had accelerated those of the Caribbean sugar plantations. In 1659, Virginia's lawmakers passed a law that financially benefitted transatlantic slave traders. In short, the duties these traders had to pay on goods they brought into Virginia were reduced. The Virginians became some of these traders' most-valued customers, importing from Africa in the second half of the seventeenth century tens of thousands of enslaved Africans. By the eighteenth century, they'd imported some 80,000 of them.

As in the Caribbean, the demographics of Virginia's workforce and society were transformed. No longer were they constituted of different groups. Now, its workforce, which had once been constituted of European servants, African ones, and enslaved native Americans, became constituted of primarily enslaved Africans. Up until at least 1640, Africans in Virginia – enslaved or not – numbered just 150 and made up less than 5 per cent of its population. By 1700, that number, nearly all of whom were enslaved, had shot up to 10,000, and enslaved Africans *alone* made up 22 per cent of the population. Virginian society, which had once been constituted of not just European and African servants, but also free and enslaved native Americans, and African and European landholders, became constituted of primarily enslaved Africans and free European planters. This was also partly because European indentured servants gradually were released, and none were brought in to replace them.

Against their majority enslaved workers, all of whom were African, these planters – essentially, the last remaining 'free' Virginians – began to identify themselves not just by their belief in the same religion, but by their entire 'European-ness'. This included Christianity, but it was arguably their light-coloured skin that became the most important part of their identity. Simply, this is because it was one of, if not the, most obvious difference between themselves and their enslaved workers, and so the most convenient basis for a clear dividing line between said workers and themselves.

Beginning in the late seventeenth century, 'free' Virginians (i.e. European planters) discriminated largely not against non-Christians, but non-*Europeans*. Since, apart from them, the only other major group in Virginia at this time was enslaved, dark-skinned Africans, much of their discrimination targeted specifically these Africans.

When enslaved Africans were trafficked to the colony, European planters stripped them of their names, languages and beliefs, as well as their family members and kinsmen. Those seemingly of the same ethnic group were sent to different plantations where they were banned from practising their traditions, enjoying any free time, pursuing their own crafts and starting their own businesses.

In 1667, Virginia's government passed a law stating that freedom didn't have to be granted to Christian enslaved Africans. In 1669, it passed another law stating that masters who beat their enslaved Africans so badly that these Africans died wouldn't be prosecuted. In 1680, Virginia's government passed a much more comprehensive and discriminatory law. It banned enslaved Africans from both carrying weapons and leaving their masters' plantations without a certificate. It also stated that any such Africans who so much as raised a hand against their master, even just to protect themselves while being beaten, would be punished with whipping. Moreover, it stated that any such Africans who avoided work, and subsequently resisted arrest, may lawfully be killed. This law formed part of the first major slave codes of the early 1680s that discriminated against Africans specifically. '[These codes] would become the model of repression throughout the [US] South for the next 180 years,'[11] wrote one historian. In 1705, Virginia's government passed a long, detailed slave code reiterating previous oppressive laws that discriminated against Africans. It also clearly defined enslaved Africans as property. They were to be considered 'real estate'.[12]

To this day, in North America, race and skin colour, rather than, say, religion, forms the most important part of peoples' identities. To be European, especially having light-coloured, or 'white', skin is to belong to one group of people against others whose recent ancestors came from different continents, and thus whose skin colour might be a different shade. One said group is Africans, with darker-coloured, or 'black', skin. In short, Americans today identify themselves (and others) in much the same way their ancestors did some three hundred years ago, when a demographic change caused the latter to identify themselves by race and skin colour, instead of religion. That's why, despite Kamala Harris's nuanced ancestry and identity, as someone with African ancestry, Americans often call her simply 'black'.

But, as I've shown in this chapter, African peoples are in a multitude of ways far too diverse to be identified by one characteristic, let alone skin colour. We are the most genetically, ethnically, culturally, and skin-colour diverse peoples in the world. Our ancestors' migrating and mixing over millions of years caused a proliferation in the number of distinct populations inhabiting the continent. These populations' identities are just as diverse as the ancestries, cultures and regions that they're based on. Unlike the late seventeenth-century Virginian planters, in describing African peoples, we mustn't then emphasise their race or skin colour at the expense of other aspects of their multi-faceted identities. To do this is to be, at best, inaccurate, and, at worst, offensive.

In the next chapter, we'll continue to explore African peoples' identities. Having looked at how diverse they are, and why, we're now going to look at how the identity of a specific African people was formed. In particular, we're going to look at what ancestral, cultural and regional elements came together to define the Swahili peoples of East Africa.

5

MERCHANTS, TRADERS AND NAVIGATORS

The different elements (or features of specific elements) that come together to make a people who they are don't come from just one source. Rather, they come from a multitude of sources, many of them foreign to the people in question. A people's identity isn't based only on elements and features indigenous to them. Instead, their identity is based on elements they adopted from others through interactions and made their own. In mixing with several other groups, these people might have acquired genes from one group, religion from another, and language from yet another. Together, these elements combined to define the people who adopted them.

A culture, then, isn't created in a vacuum. Its people's interaction with others is crucial to its development. Thus, notions about migration and mixing destroying rather than developing cultures can be argued against. This is not to say that an excess of external influences can't, or doesn't, adversely affect a people. Simply, I want to express what I believe to be a truth that cultures develop through sensibly embracing, rather than rashly being hostile to, other peoples, and the elements and features they might bring.

One example of rash hostility might be the actions that culminated in Britain's Windrush scandal of 2017. In 2012, Home Secretary Theresa May introduced policies making it illegal to provide services, including housing, healthcare and bank accounts to undocumented migrants. For example, as part of the 'Right to Rent' policy, landlords that rented homes to such migrants could be imprisoned. 'The [policies'] aim is to create here in Britain a really hostile environment for illegal migration,'[1] May said. 'What we don't want is a situation where people think that they can come here and overstay because they're able to access everything they need.'[2]

In 2017, it emerged that these policies were unjustly affecting members of the Windrush generation. The Windrush generation are people who migrated to the UK from Caribbean British colonies in the post-war era. They are named after the HMT *Empire Windrush*, the ship which brought the first Caribbean-British subjects in 1948. On 1 January 1973, Britain's 1971 Immigration Act gave all colonial migrants in Britain the right to stay. Windrush members were therefore in Britain legally. Unfortunately, for various reasons, many lacked the documentation to prove this. For example, they'd arrived in the UK as children, travelling on elder relatives' passports, and had never gotten one of their own. Moreover, in 2010, as part of the closure of one of its immigration centres, the Home Office destroyed records of the landing cards issued to Windrush members in the 1950s and '60s. Consequently, though Windrush migrants had lived, worked and paid taxes in the UK for decades, they saw their bank accounts frozen, their benefits stopped, and their houses seized. The UK government told some they had only a few months to leave the country. For weeks, they detained others in immigration centres. Others, they deported.

One victim of this scandal was a fifty-seven-year-old man called Dexter Bristol.

Bristol was born on the Caribbean Island of Grenada in 1961. From the mid-eighteenth century until 1974, Grenada was a British colony. In 1968, he migrated to Britain on his mother's passport. His mother, Sentina D'Artanyan Bristol, was already in the UK, where she'd worked as a seamstress, then a nurse.

Though he'd lived in the UK for over fifty years, Bristol had nothing – not even a passport – proving his right to remain. In the 1970s, Sentina had tried, but failed, to get him a British passport. 'I thought I could sort it out for him later,' she said. 'No one expected [the UK] to turn into what it is now.'[3] For much of his life, Bristol had done odd jobs, and been on benefits. In 2016, he was unemployed. He looked for cleaning work but had no luck. As a victim of the Windrush scandal, he saw his benefits pulled. He was also sacked from a cleaning job he'd secured in 2017.

When Bristol lost his job, he called his mother about his passport. 'I had to say [to him], "Well, you haven't gone one,"'[4] said Sentina. They looked for other documents, asking Jacqueline McKenzie, an immigration lawyer, for help. The search proved difficult. 'There was so little paper trail,'[5] said McKenzie. '[The government] asked for [his] school records, but [Dexter's] a grown man, and we've moved from house to house, we haven't kept those things,'[6] said Sentina. 'Digital national insurance records only go back to 1976,' said McKenzie. '[Dexter's] medical records only started in the 1980s, and the NHS couldn't explain where the earlier ones were – they might have been purged.'[7]

Bristol, who feared being deported, became depressed. 'I would give him £20 when I saw him,' said Sentina. '[Initially,] I didn't realise his benefits had been cut off . . . He was very upset about losing his job – I could see the change in him.'[8] 'I saw him getting more and more upset and stressed by the ongoing process to prove he was a British citizen,'[9] said McKenzie. 'He was prepared to fight but as the months went on and he was required to find more evidence it became very difficult and we saw him just decline into a shadow of himself.'[10] 'This whole thing is making me bitter and hateful and nobody wants to be that way for ever,'[11] Bristol wrote to his mother in December 2017. 'From the day of my birth there has been unstoppable hurt,' he wrote in a note found in his flat. 'I just kept taking the pain, I can't anymore. I have never been alive, just a tragic shell. I'm 56 now and still don't know anything.'[12] 'I became aware he was [a] deeply unhappy and troubled man,' said Bristol's neighbour. 'The walls separating my flat and his were thin. I would often hear him cry loudly.'[13]

In early 2018, outside his home, Bristol suffered heart failure, collapsed, and died. McKenzie had just made a breakthrough in his case. The council of the area Bristol had grown up in had sent her some documents. 'I wrote to him ... to say: we are going to fight this and we are going to win it,' said McKenzie. 'But he died before he got that letter.'[14] '[H]e died being denied an immigration status which was rightfully his.'[15]

On the other hand, an example of a people who have, historically, sensibly embraced other peoples, and the elements and features they bring, is that living on East Africa's coast, whom we know as the Swahili. As will be explained next, the Swahili have not only interacted with peoples from various cultures for millennia but became who they are – that is, Swahili – largely *because* of the elements and features they adopted from these foreign peoples.

*

East Africans have been trading with peoples from Yemen, Oman, Iran, India and China since at least 100 AD. By that time, on the East African coast, Bantu peoples lived in, or had established, settlements. One of the earliest, biggest and most important of these was Rhapta. It was located in Kenya, near the mouth of the Tana River, near the Lamu archipelago. Cushitic – ancient Somali – peoples established it in 100 BC, and it existed until about 200 AD.

Each settlement had its own independent ruler. 'Men of the greatest stature ... inhabit the whole [East African] coast and at each place have set up chiefs,'[16] says *The Periplus of the Erythraean Sea*. Written in 100 AD by an unknown author, *The Periplus* is a guide to Indian Ocean trade. '[The settlements' rulers] were known as *Wafalme*,' wrote al-Mas'udi, a tenth-century Arab historian and geographer. '[*Wafalme*, or *mfalme*,] means [']son of the Great Lord[', that is, 'king'], since he is chosen to govern them justly.'[17] Queens were known as '*malkia*'. 'The [*Wafalme* of Malindi, a settlement in Kenya,] wore a robe ... of damask trimmed with green satin, and a rich [turban],' wrote a fifteenth-century Portuguese sailor. 'He was seated on two cushioned chairs of bronze, beneath a round sunshade of crimson satin attached to a pole. An old man, who attended him as a page, carried a short sword in a silver sheath. There were ... two trumpets of ivory, richly carved, and the size of a man, which were blown from a hole in the side.'[18]

By al-Mas'udi's time at least, these rulers had no real power. They went on diplomatic missions and had some input in trade. For example, during such missions, they signed trade agreements with other rulers. These took the form of blood-brotherhood rituals. The two parties mixed some of their blood with ink, and marked treaties written in Arabic on fine leather. Mostly, though, these rulers were figureheads, whose good health, long lives, and stable reigns made people feel as though their settlements were thriving.

Sheikhs – clan leaders – held the real power. They were heads of merchant families, who largely controlled trade. Each clan lived independently and according to its own laws. But *sheikhs* also often banded together to increase their clan's influence. In that case, they elected one of their own to lead the group. For example, the settlement of Mombasa, in Kenya, had twelve *sheikhs*. They banded together into two separate groups. Six formed one group called *Mvita*. The other six formed another group called *Kilindini*. The members of each group elected one among them *tamim* ('leader'). In this case, the *tamim* of the *Kilindini* group also headed a council of all the twelve *sheikhs*. The *Mvita tamim* was his deputy. 'If [the *Wafalme*] is tyrannical or strays from the truth, [the *sheikhs*] kill him and exclude his seed from the throne; for they consider that in acting wrongfully he forfeits his position as the son of the Lord,'[19] wrote al-Mas'udi.

Between October and March, a wind blows from Asia to Africa. Between April and September, another wind blows in the opposite direction. Traders from Yemen, Oman, Iran, India and China used these winds to sail to the settlements on East Africa's coast, and back home. 'The ships are usually fitted out in the inner [Red Sea] ports,' says *The Periplus*. 'Some make voyages directly to these [East African] market-towns [while] others exchange cargo as they go.'²⁰ 'The pilots of Oman [sail down the East African Coast] to reach the island of [Pemba, near Tanzania],' wrote al-Mas'udi. 'The people of [Iran] also make this voyage.' ²¹ 'We found [in Malindi] four vessels belonging to Indian Christians,' wrote the fifteenth-century Portuguese sailor. 'These Indians are tawny men; they wear but little clothing and have long beards and long hair, which they braid. They told us that they ate no beef.'²²

Between 1417 and 1419, a Chinese treasure fleet used the winter wind to sail to four settlements on East Africa's coast: Mogadishu, Baraawe and Zhubu in Somalia, as well as Malindi. The fleet's admiral was a eunuch called Zheng He. Reportedly, he was 'seven feet tall and had a waist about five feet in circumference. His cheeks and forehead were high, but his nose was small. He had glaring eyes and a voice as loud as a huge bell.'²³

Originally, Zheng He's name was 'Ma He'. He was born in 1371 to a Muslim family in Yunnan, a province in south-west China. He later became Buddhist. When he was ten, the Hongwu Emperor, founder of the Ming Dynasty, conquered Yunnan from the Yuan Dynasty, which the Mongol, Kublai Khan, had founded in the mid-thirteenth century. In the fighting, Ma's father was killed, and he was captured.

After being made a eunuch, he served Hongwu's fourth son, Prince of Yan, who governed Beiping – now Beijing. Together, they fought against the Mongol peoples on Yan's border. Ma's bravery, strength and skill earnt him Yan's confidence.

In 1398, Hongwu died. His eldest son had died six years before. So, that son's eldest son (i.e. Hongwu's grandson), a teenager called Jianwen, became emperor. In 1399, Yan rebelled. Jianwen besieged Beiping. In protecting an important reservoir, Ma let Yan's army counterattack successfully. In 1402, Yan defeated his nephew, and took Nanjing, then the capital city. He was proclaimed the 'Yongle (meaning 'perpetual happiness') Emperor'. In 1404, to commemorate Ma's role in his victory, Yan gave him the noble surname 'Zheng'.

Yongle wanted to expand China's influence in Southeast Asia and the Indian Ocean. He put Zheng in charge of building a massive fleet. Certainly, Zheng had the experience. He'd served as Grand Director of the eunuch Directorate of Palace Servants, responsible for building and maintaining palaces. 'Grand Director' was the highest title a eunuch could hold. The *Mingshi* – an official history of the Ming Dynasty compiled in the seventeenth and eighteenth centuries – refers to Zheng as the 'Grand Director of the Three Treasures'. The 'Three Treasures' are Buddha, Buddhist law, and Buddhist monks.

When completed, the fleet comprised 255 three-masted ships. The sixty-two main ones, which a Chinese observer called 'lofty and majestic in . . . form and appearance,'[24] were as long as 250 feet. According to some historical accounts, they were almost *twice* this size. '[Their] mat . . . [and] cloth sails, anchors, and rudder required 200–300 people to handle them,'[25] said the observer. In total, the fleet's crew numbered about 30,000. Yongle reckoned that when other rulers saw it, China's apparent power would so overawe them that they'd pay tribute.

Between 1405 and 1411, the fleet made three voyages to India. Along the way, it stopped at Vietnam, Indonesia, and Sri Lanka. From 1413 to 1415, it made another voyage, going as far as Hormuz, an island off the southern coast of Iran.

Around the same time – that is, in 1415 – ambassadors from Mogadishu and Malindi used the summer wind to sail to China. They brought presents including frankincense, ivory and live animals, such as leopards, zebras, lions and giraffes. In China, in a special ceremony, Malindi's ambassadors gifted Yongle a giraffe. The creature caused a stir. To flatter Yongle, Chinese officials said it was a *qilin*, an auspicious unicorn, or hooved chimera – part lion, part dragon, part horse – which Yongle's wise governance had made appear. Interestingly, this was not the first giraffe from Malindi Yongle had received. In 1414, the sultan of Bengal, who'd obtained a giraffe from Malindi, gifted it to Yongle, and it caused a similar stir. The intention of China's 1417 voyage to East Africa was to obtain more of this kind of creature.

When the fleet left Malindi on its way back to China, two ships at the back of it crashed into *Mwamba Hassan* – a large rock near Lamu Island, part of the Lamu archipelago. The ships sank. About twenty surviving sailors swam to Lamu. According to tradition, a giant python was terrorising the islanders, who asked for the sailors' help. One of the sailors, a master swordsman, lured the snake from its lair and killed it. Grateful, the islanders welcomed the sailors to stay. They did so, marrying and having children with Lamu women. Over the next few hundred years, some of their descendants migrated to other nearby islands, and perhaps even to mainland Kenya.

Six hundred years later – in 2004 – one of these descendants wrote to the Chinese embassy in Nairobi, saying she was interested in traditional Chinese medicine and wanted to study it in China. Her name is Mwamaka Sharifu. In 1986, she was born in Siyu village, on Pate Island, another of the Lamu archipelago. Her father was a fisherman, and her mother was a housewife. They didn't have much money and had barely afforded to send Mwamaka to high school, let alone university. In 2002, Chinese scientists DNA-tested the family. They'd heard that they looked Chinese and had a family history which said they were descended from a Chinese sailor. The scientists collected strands of Mwamaka's mother's hair and had them tested in China. When they got the results, they told the family their ancestry could be traced to Jiangsu province, east China. 'My grandmother's great grandfather . . . was among the few Chinese sailors who were rescued after their ship hit . . . *Mwamba Hassan* and capsized,'[26] said Mwamaka.

The Chinese government granted Mwamaka's request. They gave her a full scholarship to the Nanjing University of Traditional Chinese Medicine. Over the next seven years, Mwamaka learnt Chinese and qualified as a doctor. 'I . . . can now not only speak and write in [Chinese], but also translate it to Kiswahili or English with ease,' she said. 'I gradually adapted to . . . life [in China] and managed to live almost like the Chinese.'[27] By 2012, Mwamaka was an intern doctor at the Nanjing Municipal Hospital. By 2017, she was studying for a doctorate in Obstetrics and Gynaecology at Tongji Medical College. 'I hope to work in hospitals and universities [in Kenya] from where I will help to increase awareness of the advantages of Chinese medicine,' she said. 'Chinese medicine tends to focus on the whole person and can promote [their] long-term wellbeing.'[28]

To East Africa, traders from Yemen, Oman, and Iran brought both homemade goods and those they'd obtained from Indian and Chinese merchants. '[Aden, in Yemen,] is the port of the Indians, and . . . [t]here are Indian merchants living there,' wrote the fourteenth-century Muslim, Amazigh scholar, Ibn Battuta. '[To] it come large vessels from [Cambay], [Kollam], Calicut, and many other Malabar ports.'[29] Meanwhile, Indian and Chinese merchants brought only the goods of their homelands. 'Into [East Africa's] market-towns are imported the lances made especially for them [in Yemen],' says *The Periplus*. '[Also,] hatchets, swords . . . many kinds of small glass vessels . . . wine and . . . wheat.'[30] Other Yemeni goods brought to East Africa, dating between the tenth and fifteenth centuries, included black-on-yellow ceramics and rose water. Persian goods dating between the eighth and twelfth centuries included Sassanian-Islamic jars containing date syrup, Islamic tin-glazed white bowls, and earthenware jars. Indian goods dating between the eighth and fifteenth centuries included glass and carnelian beads, cloth, rice, wheat, butter, soap, oils and indigo. Chinese goods, similarly dated, included olive-green jars, Qingbai glazed stoneware and Ming Dynasty blue-on-white porcelain.

From East African merchants, Yemeni, Omani, Persian, Indian and Chinese traders took away a variety of goods, including ivory, gold, ambergris, mangrove poles, pearls, rock crystal and animal skins. '[At] Rhapta . . . there is much ivory and tortoise-shell,' says *The Periplus.* 'Much ivory is taken away from [here and the other settlements,] . . . and also rhinoceros horn and tortoise-shell.'[31] 'The best amber is that found on the islands and on the shores of [East Africa],'[32] wrote al-Mas'udi. '[The region also] produces wild leopard skins. The people wear them as clothes or export them to Muslim countries. They are the largest leopard skins and the most beautiful for making saddles . . . [East Africans] also export tortoise-shell for making combs, for which ivory is likewise used . . . [Elephant] tusks weighing fifty pounds and more . . . usually go to Oman, and from there are sent to China and India . . . In China the kings and military and civil officers use ivory palanquins: no officer or notable dares to come into the royal presence in an iron palanquin, and ivory alone can be used . . . [The Chinese] also burn ivory before their idols and cense their altars with it . . . In India ivory is [also] much sought after. It is used for the handles of daggers called . . . *harri* . . . and also for the curved sword-scabbards called *kartal* . . . But the chief use of ivory is making chessmen and backgammon pieces.'[33]

East African merchants had indirectly obtained many of these goods – ivory, especially – from hunter-gatherers living further inland – for instance, in Uganda, central Ethiopia, and Zimbabwe. These hunter-gatherers had these goods in abundance and were willing to trade for them. They knew their sources, and how best to extract them. 'When [the hunter-gatherers] want to catch elephants, [they] throw down the leaves, bark and branches of a certain tree which grows in their country,' wrote al-Mas'udi. '[T]hen they wait in ambush until the elephants come to drink. The water burns them and makes them drunk. They fall down and cannot get up . . . [the hunters then] rush upon them armed with very long spears, and kill them for their ivory.'[34]

However, these hunter-gatherers dealt only with traders from farming communities living between them and the coast. With them, they had longstanding personal and economic relationships.

Before the foreign traders came in the winter, East African merchants sailed to numerous settlements along the coast, where they met the farming community traders. They used vessels they'd made with nearby resources, like coconut-tree wood. The best-known of these is the *mtepe*, a 20-metre-long sewn cargo boat with a square-matting sail. With the farming community traders, East African merchants exchanged goods they'd made with local materials, like shell jewellery and copper tools, for the hunter-gatherers' goods. They then sailed to the main trading – that is, the biggest – coastal settlements, where they stored these, awaiting the foreigners' arrivals.

Between East African and foreign merchants, the actual exchange of goods was highly ritualised. 'When Persian traders wish to enter [the East African coast], they form a caravan of several thousand men and present [East African traders] with strips of cloth,' wrote Tuan Ch'eng-Shih, a ninth-century Chinese scholar. 'All, whether old or young, draw blood and swear an oath, and then only do they trade their goods.'[35]

'[In Mogadishu, when a foreign ship] reaches the port, it is met by . . . small boats, in each of which are a number of young men, each carrying a covered dish containing food,' wrote Ibn Battuta. 'He presents this to one of the merchants on the ship[,] saying[,] "This is my guest," and all the others do the same. Each merchant on disembarking goes only to the house of the young man who is his host . . . The host then sells his goods for him and buys for him, and if anyone buys anything from him at too low a price or sells to him in the absence of his host, the sale is regarded by them as invalid.'[36]

Zheng's 1417 voyage encouraged East African settlements to send more embassies. Between 1416 and 1423, Baraawe and Mogadishu sent four joint ones. Malindi sent at least one, headed by its king. He never got to meet Yongle, having died in the south-eastern province of Fujian on the way to Nanjing. In Fujian, he was buried, and Yongle gave him a memorial title, and decreed that, every year, he be given a sacrifice.

Essentially, for close to two thousand years, this is how East Africans interacted with peoples from Yemen, Oman, Iran, India and China. East African and foreign peoples exchanged not only goods, but also ideas, practices and technologies. For whatever reason, East Africans thought some of the foreigners' practices, and so on, useful, and adopted them. In doing so, they became a *new* people – the Swahili. Now, through mainly the example of Kilwa, one of the most historically important Swahili settlements, located on an island off Tanzania's coast, we're going to look in detail at which elements and features East Africans adopted that made them Swahili.

*

Ibn Battuta visited Kilwa in 1331.

By then, he'd visited many of the settlements on East Africa's coast. After his 1325 pilgrimage, he travelled in Iraq and Iran, before heading back to Saudi Arabia. In 1330, he boarded the ship of an Ethiopian Yemeni, which went to Aden. He didn't at all intend to go to East Africa. But something he heard or saw in Aden convinced him it was worth it. He boarded a ship to Zeila, north Somalia. '[Zeila] is a large city with a great bazaar, but . . . the dirtiest, most abominable, and most stinking town in the world,' wrote Battuta. 'The reason for the stench is the quantity of its fish and the blood of the camels that they slaughter in the streets. When we got there, we chose to spend the night at sea, in spite of its extreme roughness, rather than in the town, because of its filth.'[37]

'[W]e [then] sailed for fifteen days and came to [Mogadishu], which is an enormous town. Its inhabitants are merchants and have many camels.'[38] Being made to understand that Battuta wasn't a trader, but a scholar, the Mogadishi merchants called for the city's *qadi* (judge). '[This *qadi*] came down to the beach with a number of students, and sent one of them to me,' wrote Battuta. 'When I disembarked with my party, I saluted him and his party, and he said[,] "In the name of God, let us go and salute the Shaykh." [That is what] they call the sultan ... I said to him[,] "When I have settled down I shall go to him," and he replied[,] "It is the custom that whenever a theologian, or *sharif* (a descendant of the Prophet Muhammad), or man of religion comes here, he must see the sultan before taking his lodging." So I went to him as they asked.'[39]

Mogadishu's sultan was Abu Bakr. '[He] is of Berberah [– that is, 'negro' –] origin, and he talks in the [Mogadishi – that is, 'Somali' –] language, though he knows Arabic,' wrote Battuta. 'We stayed [with him for] three days, food being brought to us three times a day,'[40]. Battuta feasted on local dishes including chicken stew, fish and vegetables on rice cooked in butter, bananas in fresh milk, and another stew made of sour milk, green ginger, mangoes, pickled lemons and chillies. '[O]n the fourth [day], a Friday, the *qadi* and one of the *viziers* (ministers) brought me a set of garments,' wrote Battuta. 'We then went to the mosque and prayed behind the [sultan's] screen. When [Abu Bakr] came out I greeted him and he bade me welcome ... [We] set out for his palace on foot.'[41] Abu Bakr wore splendid clothes. His attendants were barefoot. 'Over his head were carried four canopies of coloured silk, each surmounted by a golden bird,'[42] wrote Battuta.

Two weeks later, Battuta boarded a ship that stopped for one night at Mombasa. '[Mombasa's] inhabitants are pious, honourable, and upright, and they have well-built wooden mosques,' wrote Battuta. 'They have fruit trees on the island, but no cereals, which have to be brought to them from the [mainland]. Their food consists chiefly of bananas and fish.'[43]

Sailing past the islands of Pemba and Zanzibar, the ship reached Kilwa. By Battuta's arrival, Kilwa was the wealthiest, most important and best-known settlement on the East African coast. 'Kilwa . . . is a large town,' wrote Battuta. 'The majority of its inhabitants are [East Africans], jet-black in colour . . . with tattoo-marks on their faces.'[44]

'[A]ll around [Kilwa] is very luxuriant,' says an early sixteenth-century Portuguese account, 'with many trees and gardens of all sorts of vegetables, citrons, lemons, and the best sweet oranges that were ever seen, sugar canes, figs, pomegranates, and a great abundance of flocks, especially sheep.'[45]

In the late twelfth century, Kilwa had seized the regional gold trade from Mogadishu. It conquered the settlements that gold from further inland was taken to before it was transported to the main trading ones. This included perhaps the most important settlement – Sofala, in Mozambique. The gold taken here came from Great Zimbabwe, a kingdom that existed between 1100 and 1600 AD in Zimbabwe. With two harbours that could dock many large ships, Kilwa became for foreign traders the best place to get gold, as well as ivory.

In the fourteenth century, Great Zimbabwe hit its peak. Kilwan merchants became extremely rich. They imported more Islamic pottery, Indian glass beads and Chinese porcelain and silk than they ever had. With this porcelain, they decorated their tombs. In the fifteenth century, they feasted off it. 'In [Kilwa,] there are rich merchants, and there is much gold and silver and amber and musk and pearls,' wrote a late fifteenth-century Portuguese trav-eller. 'Those of [this] land wear clothes of fine cotton and of silk and many fine things, and they are black men.'[46]

The Kilwans also expanded their city. In the eighth century, they'd made single-floor houses out of red-soil mud and palm tree leaves. Now, they built multi-storey complexes out of stone, around which they built stone walls with guarded metal gates and towers. The inhabitants of Somalia's settlements also built with stone. '[The Mogadishi] pile up stones to make their dwellings,' wrote one of admiral Zheng He's crew. '[At Baraawe, and Zhubu, too,] stones are piled up to make walls and buildings.'[47] These could be up to four or five storeys high.

More specifically, the material the Kilwans and Somalians used to build their buildings was *Porites*, a kind of stony coral. Knowledge of this coral's building properties came from probably Yemenis in the tenth century. Inhabitants of the Lamu archipelago were the first East Africans to build with it. In the town of Shanga, on Pate Island, remains of tenth-century stone mosques have been found. The remains of almost two hundred stone buildings dating to the fourteenth century have also been found. Earlier buildings were made of timber. Either divers collected the coral, or, at low tide, workmen cut it from offshore reefs. When wet, it could be moulded into blocks. Builders also heated it in kilns to make lime mortar to join the bricks.

The stone buildings were expertly made. For the floors, the builders laid down a foundation of tightly packed coral chips, over which they poured a high-quality lime plaster. For the roofs, they laid large, rectangular coral blocks over squared timber beams spanning the house's width. Over these, they poured a thick layer of mixed concrete made from coral chips, sand and lime. When it had dried, they plastered it to make it watertight. They also plastered the ceiling, and all walls, except those of the storage rooms. Every so often, the buildings' owners had these walls re-plastered to keep them looking new. 'Kilwa is one of the most beautiful and well-constructed towns in the world,' wrote Battuta. 'The whole of it is elegantly built.'[48] '[It] is a beautiful country [with] houses . . . high like those of Spain,'[49] wrote the late fifteenth-century Portuguese traveller. '[Kilwa] is of good buildings of stone and mortar with terraces, and the houses have much good works,'[50] says the early sixteenth-century Portuguese account. 'In Kilwa, there are storied houses very stoutly built of masonry and covered with a plaster that has a thousand paintings,'[51] says another. '[The houses have] flat roofs, and at the back, there are orchards planted with fruit trees and palms to give shade,'[52] says one more.

It continues, '[a]t one part of [Kilwa] the king had his palace, built in the style of a fortress, with towers and turrets and every kind of defence.'[53] This 'king' was al-Hasan ibn Sulayman. Battuta met him. '[He is] a man of great humility; he sits with poor brethren, and eats with them, and greatly respects men of religion and noble descent,'[54] wrote Battuta. '[He] was noted for his gifts and generosity. He used to devote the fifth part of the booty made on his expeditions to pious and charitable purposes . . . and I have seen him give the clothes off his back to a mendicant who asked him for them . . . [He is a] liberal and virtuous sultan.'[55]

Ibn Sulayman's 'palace' was called Husuni Kubwa. He built it in 1300 on a hill overlooking the ocean. Undoubtedly, it was Kilwa's most impressive stone building. Surrounded by a high wall and acres of land, it was made up of two sections: a northern, triangular-shaped one, and a southern, square-shaped one.

The triangular-shaped section was where ibn Sulayman lived, and entertained friends. Every one of its buildings was finished with high-quality, decorative stonework. In one room, coral blocks decorated with Arabic writing in black ink were found. The triangular-shaped section's rooms were arranged around a large courtyard, where dance shows and banquets were held. In this courtyard, many fragments of fine, fourteenth-century Chinese porcelain – probably dishes – were found. Flanking the courtyard's sides were lounges, where guests, sitting on cushions, watched these shows, or talked. Through a western corridor, they entered an enclosed square where there was a swimming pool. It was eight metres wide, two metres deep, and shaped like an octagon. On its southern side were more lounges. On its western side was a veranda. A northern corridor took guests to their bedrooms.

The square-shaped section was where business was done. Three rows of rooms separated it from the northern section. Its rooms were arranged around a huge square, where, perhaps, goods were counted, and packed up, ready for transport. Its size suggests this was the trading centre of not just the palace but also of Kilwa. The rooms' walls were un-plastered.

On the southwest corner of Husuni Kubwa was the 'Factor's House'. The Factor was in charge of day-to-day trading activities, like making sure ships were correctly loaded, and collecting custom duties. He did these on the ground floor of his house, which visitors entered through a big forecourt. On the first floor were his living quarters, which he reached via a grand staircase.

At the palace's centre was the uniquely designed 'Pavilion'. Lying between its two sections, and attached to neither of them, this building combined their functions. Here, ibn Sulayman both received guests and negotiated trade deals. '[W]e can picture him sitting on the dais, which would be provided with carpets and cushions,' wrote the British archaeologist Neville Chittick. 'The Pavilion occupies the most favoured position of all the buildings, enjoying a fine view westwards over the coast and the roofs of the buildings beyond to the town and harbour of Kilwa in the distance.'[56]

East of the Pavilion was the chamberlain's house. Attached to this were rooms where guests were made to wait before their audience with ibn Sulayman.

Kilwa's second most impressive building was the Great Mosque. As its name implies, it wasn't Kilwa's only mosque. Husuni Kubwa had one attached to its northern section, which was for ibn Sulayman's exclusive use. Moreover, according to a sixteenth-century Portuguese account, around Kilwa, there were 'many domed mosques ... [with the Great Mosque being] like that of Cordoba.'[57] The Great Mosque was built just before ibn Sulayman's day, sometime between the late twelfth and late thirteenth centuries. It had eighteen domes, and eighteen barrel-vaulted ceilings. Over time, Kilwa's rulers frequently expanded

and renovated it, demonstrating both its and Islam's importance
to them. Arguably, it's the finest medieval mosque in East Africa.

East Africans have been Muslim since the eighth century A D. In
Shanga, remains of a timber mosque dating to 780 A D were found.
Muslim states and merchants were crucial to international trade
networks, especially the Indian Ocean one. People saw Islam as
the 'religion of trade'. To get closer to these big players, early East
African merchants and rulers adopted it. But they didn't all adopt
the same sect at the same time. Over centuries, at different times,
different rulers adopted and abandoned different sects depending
on how influential they were in trade. By 1000 A D, most peoples
on East Africa's coast were Muslim.

The inhabitants of Shanga were Zaidi, a Shi'ite sect. Since the
late eighth century, Zaidis had been living in Yemen. They were
some of the first Muslim traders in East Africa. By the early tenth
century, they'd also converted northern Somalis.

Since the eighth century, the inhabitants of Pemba Island, near
Tanzania, had been Ibadi. Since the late seventh century, an Ibadi
community had flourished in Basra, Iraq. Then, Basra was one
of the Persian Gulf's most important trading towns. In Indian
Ocean trade, Ibadi merchants were huge players. In 750 A D, some
of them tried to conquer Qanbalu, a town on Pemba. Whether
successful or not, they managed to convert some of the islanders.
On Pemba, remains of a tenth-century Ibadi stone mosque were
found. '[Pemba] has a mixed population of [African] Muslims
and ... idolaters,'[58] wrote al-Mas'udi.

In 1000 A D, Shanga Muslims migrated down the coast. They
went to Malindi, Mombasa, and Kilwa, where they introduced
coin-based currency, and new architectural and artistic styles,
including stone-building. They converted the Malindis and
Mombasans, building mosques in their towns, but they failed
with the Kilwans, who continued to practise their traditional religion. Fifty years later, Pemba Ibadis also migrated south, as far as
Kilwa, and failed to convert them.

In around 1280 AD, the Mahdalis, an African family with distant Arab ancestry, migrated from Somalia to Kilwa. They claimed they descended from a Yemeni *sharifian* clan – in other words, that they were descendants of the Prophet Muhammad. The *sharifian* movement was linked to the Shafi'i school of the Sunni Islamic sect. This school had developed in Yemen in the eleventh century. Sunni Islam had been present in East Africa since the tenth or eleventh centuries. In 1050, Pemba Sunnis built a mosque over the tenth-century Ibadi one.

The Mahdalis overthrew Kilwa's rulers. They also established themselves in Baraawe, Lamu, Pate, and Mombasa. Their influence meant that not just Kilwa, but most of the coast, quickly became staunchly Sunni. The Swahili are still Sunni-Shafi'i. '[The Kilwans'] chief qualities are devotion and piety,'[59] wrote Battuta. He prayed in the Great Mosque. 'All persons of quality carry praying beads,'[60] wrote a sixteenth-century Portuguese sailor. At other times, other *sharifian* families also migrated from north to south.

As we've seen above, not just with Kilwa, but other coastal East-African settlements, like Shanga and Baraawe, thanks to their interactions with foreign peoples, East Africans were exposed to new and different ideas and practices, which, for various reasons, they adopted. Examples include stone-building (which elite East Africans adopted to show off their wealth), Islam (which East-African traders adopted to enhance their relationships with their Muslim-Arab or Persian trade partners), speaking Arabic, and feasting off Ming-dynasty porcelain. The Swahili have always identified themselves as trading peoples living on the East African coast who adopted the practices of stone-building and Islam. Foreign peoples, and academics, including anthropologists, archaeologists and historians, also identify them this way. In short, East Africans became 'Swahili' when they began trading internationally, building in stone and practising Islam.

Having said that, many 'Swahili' today don't often call themselves such, preferring to identify themselves with the town they
come from. For example, those from Malindi call themselves
waMalindi – 'people of Malindi town'. 'Swahili', which is derived
from *sawahil*, the Arabic word for 'coast', wasn't used as an ethnic
term until the nineteenth century, when Omani rulers colonised
parts of East Africa's coast, and called the people who lived there
Swahili.

The first East Africans to adopt the practices of stone-building
and Islam – that is, the first East Africans to become 'Swahili' –
were those who from about the eighth century lived in Somalia
and the Lamu archipelago. Being closest to the Middle East, these
settlements were the first to be visited frequently by Yemeni and
Persian traders, who brought their various practices. Consequently,
in Swahili mythology, their birthplace – Shungwaya – is on the
mainland opposite the Lamu archipelago. By the end of the ninth
century, the Somalians' and islanders' transformation was complete. In the tenth century, their descendants migrated south as
far as Mozambique, similarly transforming other East-African
communities. By the eleventh century, the 'Swahili Coast' – a civilisation of related, but distinct and independent, city-states – had
come into being.

Hopefully, this chapter has demonstrated that interaction with
foreign peoples can contribute to the advancement of a culture and
isn't inevitably the cause of its destruction. The Swahili not only
came into being but thrived because of their sensible embrace-
ment of foreign cultural features. It allowed them to become arguably the premier African traders. Conversely, in modern Britain,
arguably, it was not interaction with members of the Windrush
generation that led to tensions which may have destroyed society.
Rather, it was the disappointed reaction to the government's rashly
hostile actions against foreigners which affected these members.
In short, the threat to society came not from interaction with
other peoples, but a failure to embrace them sensibly.

In the next chapter, we'll look in detail at a cultural feature that's almost uniquely African – oral literature. Specifically, I'm going to describe examples of it, explain how some of these have survived across centuries and continents, and tell you about some of its most excellent practitioners.

6

RAPPERS, SINGERS AND STORYTELLERS

In African cultures the world over, there are many forms of oral literature, including epic poems, fables and songs. Worldwide, one of the best-known forms of African (as well as American) oral literature is rap songs. There are various ways in which these are expressed, one of which is the rap battle, where two rappers compete against each other in their use of the form. But rap as we know it hasn't always existed. It has precursors that are both more local and closer in time to it, and those that originated potentially hundreds of years ago in a different part of the world. How rap – and, specifically, the rap battle – might have evolved from these precursors is what we're going to look at now.

Arguably, the rap battle most of us are familiar with was born in December 1981 at the Harlem World Club in New York.

'The World', as its regulars called it, began in the 1970s as a disco club. It had gold shag carpeting, mirrored walls, a lighted dancefloor, and a one-hundred-foot lightning-shaped bar. Its owner, a large African American guy nicknamed 'Fat Man', saw the rising popularity of Hip-Hop, and turned it into a rap club.

By the 1980s, The World was home to some of the biggest and best-loved rap shows in the city and hosted many of the era's top emcees. '[The] World at that time was the hottest club in Manhattan,'[1] said Kool Moe Dee. 'Moe' had come up in the 1970s as a member of The Treacherous Three, a rap group known for its fast, smooth, and witty rhymes. By the 1980s, Moe's reputation as a lyrically gifted rhymer had been established. 'Harlem World around 1980 was the showplace for Hip-Hop groups back in the day . . . [the] one venue that all the [emcee] groups could really get their shine on,'² said Grandmaster Caz. He's an emcee as highly regarded as Kool Moe Dee. He wrote one of the rhymes in The Sugar Hill Gang's 'Rapper's Delight', which, arguably more than any other song, helped make rap mainstream. Unfortunately, he didn't receive any credit for it.³ '[O]f course [the best emcees in the '80s were] Caz, Mo[e] Dee, and Melle Mel,'⁴ said Troy Smith. Smith grew up in Harlem, and personally knew many of Hip-Hop's pioneers. He also put together one of the largest and most important collections of early Hip-Hop tapes. 'But as far as [Harlem], Mo[e] . . . was the top man,'⁵ Smith continued. 'Doug, Spoon[ie Gee], Kool Mo[e] Dee, and the Fearless Four . . . [w]henever they came in they were treated like Royalty.'⁶ '[Moe's] just simply a very cool, down-to-earth brother, with a vicious mic,' said Charlie Rock, who worked at The World in the '80s. 'One thing I can say about [Moe, Caz, and Melle Mel] is that they always walked like they were superstars . . . [T]hey were definitely the kings of the streets.'⁷

Every December, The World held the Christmas Rappers Convention, a two-week-long rap contest. 'Any night that was a holiday [The World] had some type of Hip-Hop show going on,'⁸ said Rock. Back then, rap contests, or battles, were less about rappers battling *each other*, and more about how pumped up they got the crowd. One by one, emcees went on stage and performed their best rhymes over the same beat. The winner was the one the crowd cheered the loudest for. 'I'm not battling against *you*,' said Caz. 'I'm showing what [I] do and you show what you do.'⁹ 'You say a rhyme, I say a rhyme,'¹⁰ he continued, '[and] let [the crowd] judge what they like best.'¹¹ 'Whoever's got the better rhyme win[s].'¹²

In 1981, Moe was hosting this contest. One emcee taking part in it was Busy Bee Starski. 'Busy' had also come up in the '70s. He wasn't ranked with Moe or Caz. He was known for his repetitive and simple, but funny and catchy, rhymes. 'Busy is "Throw your hands in the air!" . . . that kind of [rapper],' said Caz. '[He'd] never said nothing about nobody in his life. Not in a rhyme!'[13] But the crowd loved Busy. They said he really knew how to 'rock the party' and called him 'Chief Rocker Busy Bee.' 'Busy was . . . a crowd mover,'[14] said Rock. '[He was] one of the funniest guys in Hip-Hop without question,'[15] said Moe. He'd won contests all over New York.

Arrogance was part of Busy Bee's 'Chief Rocker' persona. One night when he was scheduled to perform, Busy continuously bragged about his skills and previous wins. He said he was certain to win that year's Christmas Rappers Convention, and crouched next to the trophy, telling people to take pictures. '[He came] in like [Muhammad] Ali used to do at the training camps: "I'm knocking out all bums!"' said Kool Moe Dee. 'It was comical.'[16]

In response to Busy's bragging, someone shouted out from the crowd, '"You can't beat [Kool Moe Dee]."'[17]

'"I don't care who it is. I beat anybody,"' replied Busy. '"I done won 800 of these [contests] in a row . . . Just give me the trophy right now 'cos nobody can beat me. I'm Chief Rocker Busy Bee. I'll be back to claim this [trophy] in about 25 minutes . . . Anybody get in here it's gonna be suicide, that's it. I'm knocking out all bums! I'm knocking out all bums!"'[18]

Busy's reply annoyed Kool Moe Dee. '[Moe was] going around us, like[,] "Yo man, I'm about to get this dude,"' said Caz. 'Busy . . . was winning all the emcee contests [but] it was like, "Wait, hold up man. Alright, you can rock a party man but you ain't no rhymer. You can't out-rhyme nobody. And that's what this [contest] is about."'[19] '[T]he crowd was looking at me like[,] "Oh my goodness do you hear what [Busy's] saying, I know you're gonna say something,"'[20] said Moe. 'I don't even know what I expected [Busy] to do. Was he supposed to turn around and say, "No I can't beat him"? Because that wouldn't . . . work. So [Busy] did what he was supposed to do. But my ego was just outta whack at the time. So I said, "I can't believe he didn't acknowledge that he couldn't beat me in a battle."'[21]

Once he'd finished bragging, Busy performed his party-rocking rap. '[Afterwards,] I . . . chilled out,' said Busy. 'I went . . . to smoke some weed, drink some champagne, chill out with the girls . . . I thought [that night's competition] was over.'[22]

It was far from over. While Busy had been performing, Moe was writing rhymes. 'I was like[,] "Alright, there's one more contestant and that's me,"'[23] said Moe.

"'Put my name on the list,"'[24] he told Charlie Rock.

"'You getting in the battle?"'[25] said Rock.

"'Yeah,'" said Moe. "'And put me on right after Busy Bee.'"[26]

Then, while Busy was chilling, the host that took Kool Moe Dee's place announced, "'We got one more contestant . . . So we going [to] let him rap.'"[27]

Moe got up on stage. "How did people think Busy Bee Starski rocked the house?"[28] he said.

The audience cheered.

"I hear that in the place to be," said Moe. "But if ya'll noticed it or not, I heard a lotta shit, you know. Busy Bee is popping shit saying he'll take out any emcee and all that. I give it to the man, he know how to rock the crowd, but when it come[s] to having rhymes, no way he can fuck around. And I'mma prove that right now . . . One for the treble. Two for the bass. C'mon Easy Lee and let's rock the place!"[29]:

Hold on, Busy Bee, I don't mean to be bold
But put that "ba-ditty-ba" bullshit on hold
We gonna get right down to the nitty-grit
Gonna tell you little somethin' why you ain't shit . . .

And I remember, Busy, from the olden-times
When my man, Spoonie G[ee], used to sell you rhymes
Remember that rhyme called, "Ditty-Ba-Ditty"?
Man, goddamn, that shit was a pity![30]

While Moe was rapping, some of Busy's crew went to find him.

When they did, one of them said, "'Yo Biz! Yo Biz . . . [Moe's] going crazy over you!'"[31]

"'What?! Who?'"[32] said Busy.

"'Kool Moe Dee['s] disrespecting you,'" said another, "'calling you all kinda this [and] saying this and that.'"[33]

"'Yeah?'"[34] said Busy

He rushed upstairs. "Shut up! Shut up!"[35] he shouted at Moe.

Moe's full rap dissing Busy is three verses long. '[Moe] just went after Busy,'[36] said Caz. '[He] kinda took Busy Bee apart,'[37] said the rapper Ice T. 'It was real ugly for Busy that night . . . [He] really got crushed,' said Charlie Rock. 'Moe was definitely a better emcee . . . [He] was a pure emcee . . . better than just about anybody on the solo tip . . . When he said that rhyme about " . . . put that ba-ditty-ba bullshit on hold," the house exploded!'[38] '[T]he crowd lost their minds,'[39] said Moe. '[They were] going berserk because they [were] like, "I can't believe he's attacking [Busy] like this." And it's by surprise. Nobody knew what was gonna happen.'[40] '[Moe's] rant was all truth,'[41] said Caz. 'I was standing in the front with my mouth open like everybody else . . . *I* knew what was gonna happen, but I didn't know . . . the degree.'[42] 'Busy was rocking the crowd,' he continued. 'Moe Dee was rocking Busy.'[43]

'We had recorded that [night's] show live to a high-quality reel-to-reel, so it sounded really clear,' said Rock. 'We stayed up late at night just making tapes, and the next day just walk[ed] around Harlem saying, "Yo, we got the battle, we got the battle[!]" [We sold] the tapes at about $10 a pop. In the early eighties that was a lot of money for a tape . . . [But it] was a famous tape. You could not imagine how many of [them] we sold on the streets . . . We . . . sold so many of those tapes!'[44]

The tape became one of the highest-selling bootleg rap tapes of all time. Rock's convinced that if it'd been a record, it would have gone platinum, maybe even double. 'Everybody had [it], and people would run up to me and be like, "I heard what you did to Busy Bee!"[45] said Moe.

For many, that tape was the first time they'd heard one rapper directly diss another in a battle. Its influence helped transform battles from crowd-pleasing shows of verbal skill to today's one-on-one lyrical duels. '[P]eople [had] had battles but they never really said anything about each other,' said Moe. 'I was one of the first rappers to actually take a rhyme and make it about a [specific] person.'[46] '[Moe] hit [Busy] where he lived. He changed the way people battled,'[47] said Caz. '[After that night, b]attling became a little more personal – man against man . . . [Kool Moe Dee vs. Busy Bee] was really the first definitive [rap] battle – me against you directly. I'm talking about *you* . . . about how you lied about such-and-such and who do you think you are . . . [Moe] was the first cat to really go [in] on somebody like that. So that kinda upped the standard. Now when you battled somebody, you battled *them*.'[48]

Despite what went down that night between Moe and Busy, they were then, and remain, good friends. '[We] homeboys right now. We was then, too,'[49] said Busy. '[W]e're real cool,' said Moe. '[W]e make light of [what happened that night], and we'll probably end up doing something together at some point.'[50]

The rap battle as it's generally known may have come to be on that December night in 1981 when Kool Moe Dee dissed Busy Bee Starski. But Kool Moe Dee invented neither rhymed insults nor the competitive use of insults, rhymed or not. Rather, he introduced rhymed insults into the context of the rap battle, helping to birth a new form of it.

In other words, the modern rap battle developed from earlier forms of oral literature involving rhymed insults and their competitive use. One of these is the Dozens, an early African American rhymed-insult competition, whose features and influence we're now going to look at.

*

This is an example of the Dozens:

[Player A]: '[I]f I was as ugly as you I would kill myself.'
[Player B]: 'You ain't so hot yourself. Your hair looks like a wire fence.'
[Player A]: 'Your paw's hair look like a wire fence[.]'
[Player B]: 'You are my paw.'
[Player A]: 'If I am your paw I must have done it to your maw.'
[Audience]: '[O]h! He told you about your maw. I would not take that if I was you. Go ahead and tell him something back.'[51]

The Dozens is a game where two players take turns insulting each other before an audience. Each time, the players try to make their insult wittier or more damning to win this audience's support. Usually, both the players and audience are teenage, male African Americans. They play the game in the playground or the streets.

Often, the game begins spontaneously. The boys are talking. Then, one of them – the 'instigator' – randomly hurls against another – the 'receiver' – a classic Dozens insult: 'At least my mother ain't no doorknob [where] everybody gets a turn.'[52]

No one knows where such insults came from. They've been passed down generations via word of mouth. In style, form and content, they vary hugely. Some rhyme. Others are puns. Some are one-liners. Others are short stories. Most are general or metaphorical. Some are personal and blunt. Many are sexualised – as is to be expected in a game played usually by teenage boys – and target the opponent's female relatives. Others highlight the opponent's weaknesses. For example, if they are bad at schoolwork, they're creatively called stupid. Rhymed Dozens insults used to be the most common type, but, by the 1960s, they'd largely died out, and unrhymed one-line insults targeting the opponent's mother or weaknesses had replaced them.

In response to the instigator's insult, the audience jeers, which encourages the receiver to launch an insult back: 'Least my mother ain't no cake; everybody get a piece.'⁵³ If he improvised a responding insult, he won even more of the audience's approval.

It's on. The players trade insults back and forth until one of them gets bored and introduces a new topic of conversation. Very rarely, the game ended when one player got so offended by his opponent's insult that he attacked him. Having lost his cool, he was considered the loser.

As for where the Dozens came from, no one knows. In the historical record, it turns up for the first time in Blues songs of the 1910s. In the 1920s, the pianist and singer Speckled Red had a hit song called 'The Dirty Dozen'. He told record-producer Bob Koester that the Dozens was 'a kids' game [where] I insult twelve of your relatives [and] you insult twelve of mine, back and forth[, and the] first guy who throws a punch loses.'⁵⁴ Others suggest that the Dozens came from satirical rhymes based on the hours of the clock. In the United States, by the late nineteenth century, there existed rhyming, clock-based songs that highlighted Christianity's key aspects. Often, their lyrics were swapped out for ruder ones, such as this 1922 example:

I looked at the clock, and the clock struck one.
I said, "Now, Daddy, ain't we got fun[.]"⁵⁵

Probably, the Dozens was played in the neighbourhoods of the southern US decades before these satirical rhymes came into being.

Arguably, rap, and the rap battle, evolved from the Dozens. Certainly, the Dozens is their precursor, and the similarities between it and rap battling in particular are striking. In both, you have two contestants before an audience, trading lines back and forth, trying to impress this audience by making theirs the wittiest and most lyrically impressive. Both Dozens players and rappers use rhymed insults. For both, improvisation is a highly regarded skill. In both, the audience actively participates, hyping up the contestants and deciding the winner with their boos and cheers. Many rappers have admitted to having played the Dozens, from which they learnt some of their craft.

As for the Dozens, *it* arguably evolved from an insult game that teenagers of the Igbo people in Nigeria play called *Ikocha Nkocha* ('Making Disparaging Remarks'). The similarities between the Dozens and *Ikocha Nkocha* (as well as other African word games) are just as striking as those between it and the modern rap battle.

*

This is an example of *Ikocha Nkocha*:

[Player A]: '[L]et us play *Ikocha Nkocha*.'
[Player B]: 'All right, are you ready?'
[Player A]: 'Yes, I am ready, but you start.'
[Player B (to Audience)]: . . . '*Churu m ya*.' [Literally, 'Scare him away for me.' This phrase is meant to attract the audience's attention and be a call for their support.]
[Audience (to Player A)]: . . . '*Cha, cha, cha*.' [The sound made to an animal to scare it away.]
[Player B]: 'Look at him with his ears shaped like the pricked ears of a dog that has just heard the pounding of food in a mortar.'
[Audience (to Player A)]: . . . 'Are you going to let him get away with that?'
[Player A (to Audience)]: . . . '*Churu m ya*.'
[Audience (to Player B)]: . . . '*Cha, cha, cha*.'
[Player A]: 'Look at him with cheeks like those of a child whose mother bore him a junior sibling too early.'
[Audience (to Player B)]: . . . 'He gave you a worse one.'[56]

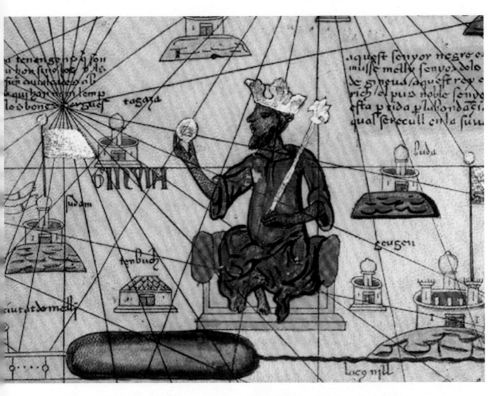

Mansa Musa, depicted on Abraham Cresques's Catalan Atlas.

Nineteenth-century illustration
of Ibn Battuta (right) and his
tour guide in Egypt.

Sixteenth-century portrait
of al-Hasan al-Wazzan.

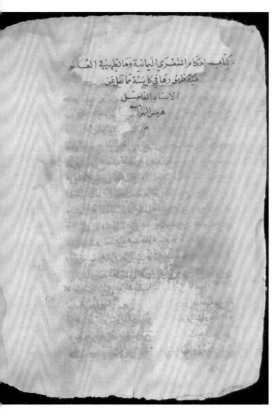

Page from a thirteenth-century astronomy manuscript from the university in Timbuktu.

An *eku*, the costume a dancer wears for the Yoruba *Egungun* festival.

Attendants carry the Golden Stool in procession.

Above The head of a bronze
statue of Augustus found
underneath the entrance
of a Meröe palace.

Above right First-century
AD stela depicting Kandake
Amanishakheto (centre).

Right Nineteenth-century
portrait of Njinga Mbande.

Seventeenth-century engraving depicting Njinga (centre) sitting on her
attendant negotiating with the seated Portuguese governor of Angola.

Fifth-century AD 'Urewe ware' found in eastern South Africa.

A written record of Anthony Johnson's appeal to the Virginian court to have John Casar returned to him as his servant.

Ming dynasty painting of the Malindi giraffe the sultan of Bengal gifted to the Yongle emperor.

Mwamaka Sharifu (front) and other students graduate from the Nanjing University of Chinese Medicine.

Top The ruins of Husuni Kubwa.

Above The Prayer Hall of the Great Mosque of Kilwa.

Left Kool Moe Dee.

Nineteenth-century illustration of Wolof griots holding *xalam* (lutes).

Above Gold head of a staff decorated with an Ananse motif (centre).

Left An eighteenth-century illustration of a Wolof griot (right) playing a *balafon*.

Above The removal of the University of Cape Town's statue of Cecil Rhodes.

Left Sixteenth-century portrait of Alessandro de' Medici.

Ikocha Nkocha is usually played at night, before an audience of family members and friends. Its format is identical to the Dozens'. In both, insults targeting the mother are some of the most common and the worst kind. Lastly, many of the enslaved Africans trafficked to the Americas, and most of those trafficked to Virginia, were Igbo. They might have brought *Ikocha Nkocha* with them, which, in the American environment, evolved into the Dozens.

Seemingly, across Africa, riddling word games are the most common.

African riddles are often short statements that use imagery to try to make the listener think of a specific, real-world thing. This thing is the answer. To get it, the listener needs to think outside the box. For example, take this riddle of the Makua – a Bantu people of Mozambique and Tanzania: Water standing up. Answer: Sugar cane. Or this one of the Tonga – a Bantu people of Zambia and Zimbabwe: Little things that defeat us. Answer: Mosquitoes.

Male teenagers of the Hehe – a Bantu people of mainly Tanzania – play a riddling game similar to the Dozens and *Ikocha Nkocha*. Like the *Ikocha Nkocha* players, they play it at night, after dinner and just before bed. Like with the Dozens, the game often begins spontaneously when, while a group of friends are talking, one says randomly to another a classic riddle. Like Dozens insults, these riddles vary in style, form and content. Improvisation is highly respected. The audience jeers. The receiver says a riddle back. The game enters full swing. The person who answers the least number of riddles loses.

Riddling among the Kgatla people of South Africa and the Akan of Ghana is more like rap battles than the Dozens. It isn't a game between children, but an organised duel between adults. Two contestants take turns either posing classic, or, preferably, improvising increasingly wittier, complex and puzzling riddles. (In the Kgatla's case, these contestants are part of larger teams.)

Often, the riddles are spoken with blistering speed. In the Akan's case, insults are often embedded in them. Again, the player who answers the least number of riddles is the loser. The winner is reckoned to be more intelligent, creative and verbally gifted than them.

We've now witnessed several forms of African oral literature from rap songs to insult, and riddling, games, like the Dozens, *Ikocha Nkocha*, and that which the Hehe play. But these aren't all there is to this literature. As I hinted at right at the start of this chapter, African oral literature is rich. To demonstrate this, we're going to look at another of its forms, present in virtually every African culture: Proverbs.

*

Proverbs are short metaphorical statements that express simple truths. Often, they're expressed verbally. In this case, they're some-times characterised by literary devices, like rhyme or rhythm. This marks them off from everyday speech and conversation. But they may also be expressed visually – for example, via sculpture. Often, the metaphor describes animal or plant behaviour, and the truth is about an aspect of human nature. 'The strength of the crocodile is in the water,' is one proverb of the Tsonga – a Bantu people of southern Africa. What it means is, people who exploit their natural talents are more likely to succeed.

Many African cultures have thousands of proverbs. For instance, about 4000 proverbs of the Rundi – a people of Burundi, in East Africa – have been recorded, and about 2000 of the Hausa – a people of northern Nigeria.

The origins of African proverbs are obscure. Ancestors of the distant, forgotten past are believed to have created them. Thus, proverbs are representative of these ancestors' traditional wisdom and instruction. Combined with their incisiveness, this gives them a sacred, objective, and indisputable quality.

Therefore, Africans often use proverbs to strengthen their argument, or criticise others without offending them. In some African cultures, in traditional courts, people even cited proverbs to bolster their case, just like how lawyers in modern courts cite legal precedents. Because proverbs are considered ancestors' teachings, and, in some cases, direct quotes, they have an otherworldly persuasiveness. And due to both their link to the ancestors and their often metaphorical nature, the person to whom they're directed doesn't take them as personal insults. The critic isn't the proverb's user, but rather the ancestors whose proverb they're quoting. Moreover, that person isn't being criticised specifically. Instead, the user is merely pointing out a universal truth that *everyone* would do well to abide by.

A person – usually, an elder – who not only knows a lot of proverbs to illuminate their points but also when to use which proverb is highly esteemed. 'A person who knows the issues as well as appropriate proverbs is the one who settles society's problems,'[57] say the Yoruba. Conversely, those who know few proverbs, and apply them indiscriminately, are thought of as foolish, childish, and unconvincing. A person would rather not use a proverb at all than use it wrongly.

The Urhobo – a people of southern Nigeria – use proverbs to strengthen their arguments and criticise others without offending them, enabling themselves to resolve disputes peacefully.

When an Urhobo married couple fights, they don't resolve things by themselves. One or other goes to their family's head. Usually, this is the eldest man. They tell him of the dispute, and the issue causing it. Examples include infidelity, financial trouble, sexual problems, or substance abuse. The family head gathers elders from both the husband's and the wife's families. They agree to meet in one of their houses. When the other elders, and the couple, arrive, they're offered drinks and kola nuts.

The host explains that the meeting's purpose is to help the

couple resolve their issue peacefully. Each half will be able to have their say. The elders will give their thoughts, comments and advice, and help them reach a fair and acceptable agreement.

This process is called *erhuere* ('to repair'). Above everything else, the Urhobo value fairness, reconciliation and harmony. *Erhuere's* aim is to ensure a resolution that leaves neither party with even an ounce of resentment. Most of all, what the elders fear is that, if not completely dispelled, such resentment could cause actions that might destroy the entire community.

The elders listen to both halves of the couple equitably. They ensure, through their reactions, that each half will feel that their emotions, thoughts and actions are fairly considered and validated. They speak gently and encourage both halves to do the same. They neither blame nor castigate either half. If one half bears the brunt of the responsibility, they softly encourage, but never force, them to see the error of their ways, and apologise. Here, proverbs are particularly useful.

In one *erhuere*, recorded in 2011, the Urhobo husband and wife were arguing.

The wife sold corn. The couple also owned a poultry farm, which both were supposed to manage.

However, while the wife did so, the husband got a taxi-driving job instead. He spent much time away from home.

One day, he returned home with a seriously injured hand. He couldn't work for two months. His wife helped nurse him.

When he'd recovered, she begged him to help run the farm. It was, after all, what he'd been trained to do.

He refused and went back to driving.

Frustrated, the wife handed the business over to the husband's deadbeat cousin. He knew nothing about chickens and was running the business into the ground.

The husband angrily told his wife to take the business back again, but she refused.

They were now suffering financial problems.

From their families, six elders – four male and two female –
held the *erhuere*.

"'I no longer understand what my husband is doing,'" said the
wife. "'You are all witnesses that he only came home because of
the injury that almost took his life. He has left the care of the
family to me. *[One] finger cannot pick up louse from the head*
[i.e. one person cannot alone do work meant for two, or more].
He spends his time and money on mistresses that are capable of
giving him incurable diseases. I want to know why he neglects the
children and me.

"'I am a woman. Why should I do the work a woman should
do as well as that which a man ought to do? I will not run that
poultry [farm] again.'"[58]

"'Have you ever asked why I had to take up the assistant driver
job?'" said the husband. "*A person who has one finger pointing at
another has three pointing towards himself* [i.e. when something
goes wrong, we're quick to blame others without thinking about,
and realising, our own culpability].'"[59]

"'[Husband], *the hand of the squirrel should not deny one of the
elephant's thigh*[s i.e. be careful not to neglect great opportunities
right in front of you],'" said one elder. "'I do not see the sense in
your neglecting your lucrative poultry business and staying away
from your family for most part of the year. *Husband, do this so
that I do that makes the home peaceful* [i.e. it's the husband's job
to work to provide, and the wife's to keep the home. The wife can
do her job only if the husband does his]. I am not against you,
but remember, *when the roots of a tree begin to decay, it spreads
death to the branches* [i.e. what begins by affecting just one, or
two, family members eventually comes to affect them all. The
elder was reminding the husband of what effect his behaviour,
and his and his wife's arguing, was having on their children].'"[60]

"'My child, your words are hard and are not expected from a
sensible woman like you,'" said another elder to the wife. "'This
is not enough for you to fight over. *If a man sees a snake and*

a woman kills it, it is all right as long as the snake is killed [i.e. sometimes, it's fine for a wife to do a job meant for her husband]. The husband and the children are yours. You should not use your mouth to bring them bad luck. *When the earthworm pays respect to the soil, it opens for it* [i.e. respectful, gentle conversation is best for getting others to see your side of things]."[61]

"'Our people, [the wife] needs to be encouraged here,'" said a third elder. "'Taking care of five children alone is not easy . . . Six months ago the baby had chicken pox and was admitted to a hospital. The doctor and nurses kept asking for the child's father and he never came in spite of several messages sent to him. [The wife] has her goods to sell in addition to running the poultry. *If one cannot help the wife in carrying her load, one should not add to the burden* [i.e. if you can't help, don't hinder]."[62]

"'[Fellow elders], *This is not enough to fight over" makes the fighter angry* [i.e. belittling someone's feelings makes them only angrier],'" said a fourth elder. "'When will [the husband] learn that [the] . . . driver job is dangerous and unprofitable? Whenever the vehicle breaks down on a long trip, you have to spend the night in it instead of the comfort of your bed. The sooner you resign from this job and return, the better for you and your household.

"'I understand the poultry business is lucrative. If properly managed, whatever income realised from it should be enough to maintain your family. *A person carrying an elephant home on his head need not use his toes to dig up cricket[s] on the way* [i.e. someone already with a job that earns them more than enough doesn't need side-hustles]. Come home and take care of your wife and your children. This will please all of us here. *When a child is given what she has been clamouring for, her restlessness disappears* [i.e. the easiest way to appease, and come to terms with, someone is to give them what they want]."[63]

"'My elders, I thank you very much for this meeting,'" said the husband. "'*You need only tell a child a phrase and he completes the sentence* [i.e. to do the right thing, a sensible person needs to be only slightly prompted]. I have heard all you have told me. I promise to give up the job in another two weeks after I have collected this month's salary from the company.'"[64]

We can see that the wife's and elders' adept use of proverbs helped convince the husband to do what they wanted him to do – that is, to quit his taxi-driving job, and pay more attention to the poultry farm and his family.

*

Arguably, Africa's best-known, most versatile and most accomplished practitioners of oral literature are the West-African wordsmiths known as 'griots'. Griots are wordsmiths in the most literal sense. Like a blacksmith crafts metal, or a potter clay, into various forms, griots do the same with words. Often, these are songs or stories.

The griot emerged at least a thousand years ago in the Ghana Empire – a Soninke empire that existed in Mali and Mauritania between about 300 and 1100 AD, and which the Mali Empire replaced. In the Mali Empire, the griot profession flourished, spreading across the Sudan. In different Sudanese cultures, griots go by different names. In Soninke culture, griots are called *jeseré* or *jaaré*. In the culture of the Wolof – a people of primarily Senegal – griots are called *géwél* or *guewel*. These names derive from the Wolof word *géew* – 'circle'. What the griot says is so interesting that people make a circle around them to listen. In Mandingo culture, male griots are called *jali* or *jalike*, and female griots are called *jalimuso*. As this demonstrates, it's not only men that can become griots. Female griots are sometimes called 'griottes'. Except maybe the names, there's little that distinguishes male and female griots. '[T]his [griot] profession, also followed by [Wolof] women, becomes an inherited family tradition,'[65] wrote Anne Raffenel, a nineteenth-century Frenchman who travelled in Senegal and the Gambia. '[G]riot[t]es ... are very numerous,' wrote Silvestre Goldberry, an early nineteenth-century aide to the French governor in Senegal. '[G]riots and griot[t]es are equally . . . musicians and poets.'[66] Lastly, in the culture of the Bamana – a people of primarily Mali, who, like the Mandingo and the Soninke (to whom they're related), speak a Mandé language, griots are called *jeli*, and female griots are called *jelimuso*. As for the word 'griot' itself, no one knows quite where it came from. It might have come from the French word *guiriot*, found in an early seventeenth-century manuscript. Or, it might have come from the Wolof word *gueroual*, or the Amazigh word *iggio*, or the word *criado*, which is Portuguese. Probably, the word 'griot' originated in the Sudan, and connects in some way to the Ghana Empire.

Each Sudanese culture has a griot origin myth. These myths tell remarkably similar stories, suggesting that they derive from the same, older story. It's likely this original story was created also in the Ghana Empire some one thousand years ago.

The Wolof version of the myth begins with two brothers on a long journey.

They'd reached a desert when their food and water ran out.

The younger brother was starving.

The elder brother, pitying the younger, told him not to worry. He – the elder – was a good hunter and would soon find some food.

He told his younger brother to stay put and left.

Some moments later, he returned, carrying a piece of flesh. He cooked it and gave it to his younger brother. When the younger brother insisted on sharing it, the elder told him he'd already eaten his own half.

The younger thanked him and ate. He asked his elder brother how he'd managed to find any game in such a barren place. The elder didn't reply. When the younger had finished eating, they continued walking.

Three days later, the elder brother collapsed and couldn't get up again.

The younger brother inspected him and saw a terrible wound on his leg that had become infected. He asked his elder brother how he had got it.

The elder confessed that, dismayed at seeing his brother starve, he'd cut off some of his own flesh, which is what he'd given him.

The younger was horrified at his own cannibalism. But his elder brother's devotion also moved him deeply.

By then, they were close to their destination. The younger lifted his brother up and carried him for the rest of their journey.

He had his elder brother treated, and wrote a song in his honour, praising his bravery, nobility and selflessness. The elder, pleased, showered him with gifts.

In Wolof and Mandingo society, griots are members of a middle class – between nobles and serfs – that the Mandingo call *nyamakala* ('possessors of occult power'). This class also includes other craftspeople, such as blacksmiths, potters and weavers. Each group of craftspeople is considered a separate caste. Marriage is only between caste members. This is to prevent trade secrets getting out. Among the castes, there is no hierarchy. They're also not ostracised. The castes think of themselves, and nobles and serfs think of them, as guilds. Unlike serfs, craftspeople were completely free. But, unlike nobles, they hadn't much wealth (land, especially), and, generally, couldn't hold important political roles. For their livelihood, they relied on nobles' patronage.

Each noble family had in their service a specific family of every kind of craft. When a noble child was born, a child of the griots serving the newborn's parents was put into their service. In Wolof, this practice is called *géwélu juddu* ('the griot by birth'). The two grew up together, played together, and taught each other many things. In the histories of Sudanese princes, kings and emperors, the intimacy and importance of this relationship is often highlighted. Only members of the Kouyaté griot family served Mali's ruling Keita family. Balla Fasséké Kouyaté had been the griot of Sundiata, founder of the Mali Empire. His family's descendants served Sundiata's, including Musa and Sulayman. 'Each prince has [a griot] attached to his entourage,' wrote René Caillié, a nineteenth-century Frenchman who travelled in Senegal. 'That of Hamet-Dou[, Chief of Brakna, a region in south-west Mauritania,] follows him wherever he goes. Often, seated in his tent, he sings his praises and comes out with the most outrageous flattery.'[67] One of the effects of European colonialism was the almost total destruction of the traditional nobility. Today, griots' patrons tend to be whoever can afford their services. They've also had to find other ways to make money, including performing live shows, teaching, making and selling albums, and tourism-related gigs.

Still, nobles particularly – but serfs, too – fear, revere and resent craftspeople, griots especially. The griot's *nyama* ('power') is contained in their words. With them, they can influence, make and break people. '[Griots] possess to the highest degree the talent of persuasion,' wrote Caillié. '[T]heir [slanders] are so skilful that they always influence the reputation of those against whom they are directed.'[68] Often, even nobles treat griots as the most important people in society. But they also considered them non-human. For nobles, the griots' origin story proved as much. When the younger brother – the first griot, from whom all griots are descended – broke the very serious cannibalism taboo, he, and, by extension, his descendants, became different from everyone else. Thus, nobles discriminated against griots. '[Griots] are so much despised by all other [Sudanese], that they not only account them infamous, but will scarce allow them a grave when they die; believing the earth would never produce any fruit or plants should it be defiled with the dead carcasses,' wrote John Barbot, a seventeenth-century English Royal African Company agent who travelled in Senegal and the Gambia. '[Therefore,] they only thrust them into the hollow trunks or stumps of trees.'[69]

Nearly always, griots accompany their words with instrumental music. The oldest of their instruments are probably the 'lute' and the *balafon*. They date to the time of the Ghana Empire.

The lute is also probably their most commonly played instrument. Made of wood, cowhide, and nylon – traditionally, horsehair – strings, the basic one looks like a banjo. In different Sudanese cultures, its size, shape and number of strings varies. They also call it by different names. In Wolof, it's called a *xalam* (or *xhalam*, or *khalam*). In Mandingo, it's called a *koni* (or *n'koni*, or *ngoni*). In Soninke, it's called a *gambere*. In Songhay, it's called a *molo*.

In some of these cultures, different variants of lute also exist. In Wolof, there are four kinds of *xalam*. Some variants have their own names. In Mandingo, there's the famous *kora* – harp-lute, which looks like this: sticking out of the top of half a calabash are three wooden poles. The middle pole is about two metres long, and the others, about fifty centimetres. The calabash is wrapped in cowhide. Sticking out of its face is a wooden board, about twenty centimetres long. Stretching from the calabash's base, over the board's edge, to the middle pole's top are about twenty nylon – traditionally, rawhide – strings. The griot sits with the strings facing them, holds the outer poles, and plucks the strings with their thumbs and forefingers.

On the other hand, the *balafon* looks like a xylophone. On top of a bamboo frame lie hardwood keys. Under it hang calabashes of various sizes, which act as resonators. The *balafon* is played with rubber-ended hardwood sticks, usually by men. They play it sitting, or hanging the instrument from their shoulder with a cloth strap, standing.

Soumaoro Kanté, early thirteenth-century ruler of the West-African Sosso kingdom, and whom Sundiata eventually defeated, is said to have invented the *balafon*. When Sundiata sent Balla Fasséké to negotiate peace with Soumaoro, Balla played Soumaoro's *balafon* so beautifully that the latter decided to keep Balla as his griot, imprisoning him. Only when Sundiata defeated Soumaoro was Balla freed. Balla then told the Mandingo about the *balafon*, including how to make and play it. From Mali, this knowledge spread throughout the Sudan.

Another important griot instrument is the drums. In Mandingo, there are several kinds, including the *tama* and the *dundun*. The *tama* is small and shaped like an hourglass. It's held under the left armpit and played with a curved stick held in the other hand. The *dundun* is large and cylindrical and played with two sticks. It makes a deeper, bass sound.

The stories griots usually tell are historical epics. These recount the lives of culturally significant figures. Most that have been recorded are about the founders or reformers of the great medieval Sudanese empires including Ghana, Mali, and Songhay. Examples of these historical epics include *The Epic of Sundiata*, *The Epic of Askiya Muhammad*, and the *Epic of Samory Touré*. Touré was the founder of the nineteenth-century Wassoulou Empire, now Guinea.

These epics were created either when their subjects were living or just after they died. Some are so old that the meanings of some of their words have been lost to time. *The Epic of Askiya Muhammad* has nearly one hundred lines of indecipherable words.

The epics are part myth, but mostly historical fact. They contain accurate and valuable information about the culture's origin, development, and most important beliefs, customs and values. In learning, and reciting, them, griots pass this information on, and keep it alive, and connect their people to their ancestors.

Each epic is made up of different 'episodes'. Each kind of episode serves a particular literary purpose. Narratives move the action along, summarising key events in the hero's life. Songs describe in poetic detail, and thus highlight, certain, particularly important events. Praise songs are interludes between, for instance, two narrative episodes, building up, or deflating tension.

A single epic has hundreds, if not thousands, of these episodes. In a single storytelling session, it's impossible for the griot to recite them all, even just the key ones. The amount they decide to do depends largely on their audience. When wanting to entertain, and show off their skills in front of, learned elders, who themselves know the epic quite well, they might include most of the episodes, especially the lesser-known ones. In this instance, it can take them up to *four* hours to recite the entire epic. In front of children, however, they might choose to recite just a few key parts, taking no more than an hour or so.

In each session, then, a griot technically creates a new version of the epic. When they pass an epic down, it might not be the version they learnt from their elders, but one they created. Their student might choose to learn, or use, only some of its episodes. They might meet other griots, from whom they learn new versions. As such, each griot, and griot family, has their own versions of epics.

The songs griots usually sing are praise songs. Praise-singing is what griots do most often and are best known for. For patrons, they compose and recite songs that talk about their good qualities and deeds. This is what, in the origin myth, the younger brother did for the elder, and what Hamet-Dou's griot did for him. '[These praise] songs are martial,' wrote La Courbe, an eighteenth-century Frenchman who lived in Senegal, serving as director of the Senegal Company. '[They say,] as they name you[,] that you are of a great [ancestry] . . . that you overcome all your enemies, that you are generous, and other things of this nature.'[70] '[Their] usual [praise-singing] . . . is no more than this: He is a great man, or a great lord; he is rich, he is powerful, he's generous . . . and much more . . . often repeated,'[71] wrote Barbot. Sometimes, griots compose and recite praise songs about themselves, which are meant to highlight their skills to the audience.

No important person's entourage or celebration, including weddings, coronations and initiations, is complete without griots' singing. Usually, griots are employed to sing the praises of the people at the celebration's centre, and important guests. At coronations, when chiefs arrive, both the griots present, and those of their crew, sing their praises. Sometimes, griots lead the ceremony's proceedings. At initiation ceremonies, they may instruct the initiates. 'The kings and great men of [the Sudan] keep each of them two, three, or more of these [griots], to divert them, and [to] entertain foreigners upon occasion,'[72] wrote Barbot. 'Hamet-Dou is always surrounded by . . . [these] professional itinerant singers,'[73] wrote Caillié.

When the Muslim Amazigh traveller Ibn Battuta was in Mali in the 1350s AD, he met the emperor Sulayman's griot, who was a man called Dugha, and described the latter's praise-singing. 'Dugha stands at the door of the audience chamber wearing splendid robes of [embroidered silk],' wrote Battuta. 'On his head is a turban which has fringes . . . He is girt with a sword whose sheath is of gold, and on his feet are light boots and spurs . . . In his hands there are two small spears, one of gold and one [of] silver with points of iron.'[74]

Battuta continued:

I was [in Mali] during the two festivals of the sacrifice and the fast-breaking. On these days the [mansa] takes his seat on the pempi [the silk-carpeted platform in the palace yard] after the mid-afternoon prayer . . . At his head stand four emirs driving off the flies, having in their hands silver ornaments resembling saddle-stirrups . . . Dugha comes with his four wives and his [concubines], who are about a hundred in number. They are wearing beautiful robes, and on their heads they have gold and silver fillets, with gold and silver balls attached. A chair is placed for Dugha to sit on. He plays on an instrument made of reeds, with some small calabashes at its lower end [(i.e. a balafon)], and chants a poem in praise of the [mansa], recalling his battles and deeds of valour. The women and girls sing along with him and play with bows. Accompanying them are about thirty youths, wearing red woollen tunics and white skull caps; each of them has his drum slung from his shoulder [(i.e. a dundun)] and beats it. Afterwards come his boy pupils who play and turn wheels in the air . . . They show a marvellous nimbleness and agility in these exercises and play most cleverly with swords. Dugha also makes a fine play with the sword. Thereupon the [mansa] orders a gift to be presented to Dugha and he is given a purse containing . . . gold dust, and is informed of the contents of the purse before all the people. The commanders rise and twang their bows in thanks to the [*mansa*]. The next day each one of them gives Dugha a gift, every man according to his rank. Every Friday after . . . prayer, Dugha carries out a similar ceremony to this that we have described.[75]

In Senegal, certain women sponsor griots to write and perform praise songs for them. These women are called *diriyanké* ('[women] living in opulence and elegance'). Married or not, they are wealthy and independent businesswomen, who travel with large entourages made up of their female friends, *góor-jigéen* ('men-women' i.e. male cross-dressers), and griots. When these women's griots perform their praise songs, the former's prestige, and the chances high-quality businesspeople will approach them, are increased.

Political parties also employ griots to write and perform praise songs for their candidates at the latter's rallies. Usually, they perform these before or after the candidates' speeches. The prestige these candidates gained is often given as the reason that they won an election.

Paying griots isn't optional. 'When they get nothing, they say all kinds of idiocies and create for [their patron] an obscure, despised ancestry,'[76] wrote H. de Lavallière, an early twentieth-century French colonial officer who spent three years in Guinea. The traditional rewards of money, precious metals, food, clothes, houses and livestock are still given to griots. However, since the nineteenth century, concubines and prisoners of war are no longer given as rewards. More modern things, like cars and plane tickets (which help griots complete their pilgrimages to Mecca), have replaced them. '[Griots] never forget to ask for something from the princes whose praises they sing, and since they are rarely refused, they all have large herds and good amounts,'[77] wrote Caillié. Though not super rich, as, historically, those who served emperors were, griots today don't do half-badly.

Arguably, the most important part of the praise song is the genealogy. One by one, the griot names their patron's ancestors and their achievements. Surname first, they begin with the earliest one, ending with the patron themselves. Between each name and achievement, they say 'fathered'. As they list each ancestor, they stab their finger in the air. For example, 'So-and-so, who achieved such, fathered so-and-so, who achieved such, fathered so-and-so, who achieved such,' and so on. 'Without hesitation and all at once [griots] can list eighty names in the genealogy of a person,' said de Lavallière. '[T]hey highlight him by recounting the meritorious acts of his ancestors.'[78] Genealogy's repetitive, rhythmic form holds the audience in a trance.

In Wolof, griots also recite genealogies with drums. Each Wolof family has a *bakk* – a percussive rhythmic sequence associated with their surname. When the griot plays the *bakk* of their patron's family, it's clear to all that they're reciting that patron's genealogy. To praise a range of patrons, the griot learns, along with verbal genealogies, a ton of these rhythms.

In medieval Mali, Battuta had the pleasure of also seeing the emperor Sulayman's griots recite their ruler's genealogy. 'Each of [these griots] is inside a figure resembling a thrush, made of feathers, and provided with a wooden head with a red beak, to look like a thrush's head. They stand in front of the [*mansa*] in this ... make-up and recite their [praise songs]. I was told that their [singing includes] a kind of sermonizing in which they say to the [*mansa*]: "This *pempi* which you occupy was that whereon sat this king and that king, and such and such were this one's noble actions and such and such the other's. So do you too do good deeds whose memory will outlive you." ... I was told that this practice is a very old custom amongst them, prior to the introduction of Islam, and that they have kept it up.'[79]

Because of their use of genealogies, praise songs particularly are believed to be full of *nyama* ('power'). By listing his patron's name and achievements alongside those of his ancestors, the griot makes them feel a storm of emotions. For example, the griot makes their patron feel proud and confident, for the latter is both reminded of their esteemed ancestry and is included among them. But the griot also makes their patron feel fearful, anxious, and perhaps even ashamed, because the latter is also reminded that they have a lot to live up to, and that, in comparison to their ancestors, they might have achieved little.

In Bamana, only by mastering genealogies can the griot reach the rank of *nara* or *ngara* ('master griot' or 'Master of the Word').

Because griots most often tell historical epics or praise-sing, they are most commonly described as historians, storytellers or singers.

But their reputation as linguists means people employ them in all sorts of other speech-related jobs. They're asked to craft words into, for instance, political speeches, pieces of sage advice, or exciting announcements of important news. They're employed as mediators, interpreters and 'hype men'.

When something important happens in the community, like a celebration, it's the griot that spreads the news. In celebrations that need news to be shared, a griot is employed to do it. In Mandingo naming ceremonies, when the parents decide on the newborn's name, they whisper it to the griot. The griot announces it to the crowd, saying something like, 'The child will be called so-and-so, like his grandfather.'[80] For that ancestor, the griot sings a praise song.

Related to the griot's roles as historian and storyteller is that of witness. Often, this is for the signing of contracts, agreements and treaties between clans. What the griot records is taken to be the official version of events. If clans argue about an agreement, they seek the griot who witnessed its signing. If this griot isn't alive, they go to one of their descendants, to whom the agreement's details were undoubtedly passed down. 'By their frequent contact with rulers, [griots] have been called to witness by their very own eyes the different events that constitute the history of the country,' wrote de Lavallière. 'They have preserved [their] flavour, and it is from them that one can still find today information that is more or less correct.'[81]

Historically, griots advised their nobles on proper kingship, and crucial decisions. They also taught them about their history, culture, its customs, and their roles in them. Sometimes, they advised quietly, whispering into their patron's ear. Other times, they did so as a shouted command or a praise song. As such, they had quite a lot of influence over the state.

At important negotiations, a griot was without fail at their noble's side. Their diplomacy was also invaluable. By singing their patron's praises, they intimidated the opposite party. By singing those of the opposite party, they flattered them. These helped ensure their patron, and their people, were given a better deal. '[In a negotiation, when I gave their chief gifts, the Wolof griots] shouted themselves hoarse from chanting my praises, accompanying their voices with their three-stringed instrument, on the end of which were attached rattles [i.e. a *xalam*],' wrote the eighteenth-century Frenchman La Courbe. '[The griots] were saying that they could clearly see that I was an important person because of the gifts I had given to their king, that no chief administrator before me had been so generous, and that they hoped that I would be equally generous to them.'[82]

More recently, in Wolof, where wrestling has for centuries been the most popular sport, griots manage wrestlers, advising them on their training, pre-match rituals, and business decisions. They prepare their wrestlers good-luck charms, collect their prize money, and help them spend it wisely.

They also announce their fighters as they step into the ring. During fights, griots stand ringside, cheering on and hyping up their champion with praise songs. '[T]he great satisfaction [wrestlers] have in throwing their [opponents] consists in the [griots] extolling their valour with a loud voice and encouraging them to gain many more such victories,'[83] wrote Barbot, the seventeenth-century Englishman.

Historically, as battlefield musicians, griots also hyped up their soldiers with praise songs. The songs were also meant to intimidate the enemy. 'By these [songs, griots] say in a [happy] and assured manner that [their soldiers] will not fail to match the valour of their ancestors, and that on the contrary, they will surpass them in bravery,'[84] wrote Father Jean-Baptiste Gaby, an early eighteenth-century clergyman. '[I]n spite of many wounds, [griots] persist in exciting the combatants who, in order not to be unworthy of their ancestors, race off to a certain death rather than give way,'[85] wrote de Lavallière.

When individuals, or families, are fighting, they ask griots to help them resolve things. Better than most, griots know how to say things that will reduce tension, foster empathy, and encourage agreement.

Often, griots are also employed as interpreters. Usually, they speak several languages. They're not only linguistically talented and skilled but well-travelled and worldly.

Battuta calls Dugha – Sulayman's griot – 'the interpreter'[86] more than once. As well as several Mandé languages, Dugha spoke Arabic. '"Speak before [the *mansa*] and I will express on your behalf what is necessary,"'[87] he told Battuta. 'He who wants to speak to the [*mansa*] speaks to Dugha,' Battuta explains. 'Dugha speaks [back] to the man who is standing, and [then] speaks to the [*mansa*].'[88]

Griots' prestige means they're often also asked to do non-speech-related duties. These include makeshift doctors, diviners (i.e. those who specialise in spirit world matters), and even executioners. In Mandingo weddings, a *jelimuso* dresses the bride, and a *jeli* carries her on his back over the threshold.

Becoming a 'Master of the Word' is a long and difficult journey.

The griot's first teacher is a family member, usually their parent. But that teacher may also be their grandparent, or even elder sibling.

The parent begins by just generally making their child aware that they belong to a griot family. In Mandingo, when children play by wrestling, the griot child is encouraged to take on a role where they use their words, not their body – for example, referee. At home, the Mandingo griot parent puts their toddler on their lap and teaches them about their instruments and how to play them. When this parent goes to perform, they take their child with them and encourage them to try it out. The young griot then becomes their parent's backup singer. When the parent chants a certain line, the child responds with a previously learnt one. 'When we were very young, our fathers used to make a little [kora] for us, so we could come to understand how the fingers and thumbs are going,' said Jali Nyama Suso, a twentieth-century Mandingo griot from the Gambia. '[Then], you go travelling with your father, and any time he starts to play you join in by tapping out a rhythm on the side of the kora.'[89]

When their child is between seven and ten years old, the parent teaches them in a more structured way how to sing and play their instruments. The child continues to go to performances, supporting their parent both vocally and instrumentally, until their early teens.

Now, a master griot becomes their teacher. Sometimes, it's the same griot that taught their parent. The master takes the apprentice to ceremonies where they're allowed to play centre-stage.

At twenty-one, the griot's formal teaching is more or less complete. Now, they're allowed to set out, and play, on their own. Often, they travel across the Sudan where they meet griots from other families and places, and from whom they learn new techniques and versions of epics. More recently, griots learn such things from listening to other griots on the radio or watching them on TV. Also, there are griot academies where griots of all ages can learn different parts of their craft from master griots. Many come to learn the basics of, for instance, praise-singing, before developing their knowledge elsewhere. Others, somewhat older, come to do the equivalent of a master's or PhD in, for example, reciting historical epics, or *balafon*-playing.

If the young griot's talented and works hard, by the time they're fifty, they're good enough to be recognised as a master griot. They turn their attention more to teaching the next generations.

Usually, griots specialise. For example, they might make their living solely from reciting epics. At different times throughout their life, they might specialise in different things. Having mainly recited epics as a young adult, the griot might decide to learn about, and make their living with, for instance, music performances.

In Wolof, each griot family is known for being good at a particular skill. But the children of those families aren't forced to specialise in the skill their family has traditionally been good at. Rather, they're encouraged to specialise in the one they seem to have a particular interest in, or talent for.

A child born into a praise-singing family who talked a lot, and liked to talk, was encouraged to become a *waxkat* ('person who speaks') – in short, an interpreter or spokesperson. One born into a spokespeople family that liked to sing, and was good at it, was encouraged to become a *woykat* ('person who sings').

In this chapter, we've explored many facets of the nearly uniquely African cultural feature that is oral literature. We've looked at its various forms, from rap, to insult, and riddling, games, to proverbs, historical epics, and songs, and how some of these might have evolved from others. We've looked at the purposes these forms serve, from proving one's verbal skill, to strengthening one's argument, to teaching others about their history and culture. Lastly, we've looked at these forms' practitioners, from male teenagers to elders, and professional wordsmiths. If all of this can't demonstrate the breadth, sophistication, and craft of African oral literature, I don't know what can!

In the next chapter, through the example of *Anansesem* ('spider-stories') – stories mainly about the Akan (i.e. Ghanaian) folklore figure Ananse – we're going to look at how, sometimes, when African oral literature forms were transported from one cultural context to another, their nature and purpose changed.

7

STORY OF THE SPIDER-GOD

Although most Akan, who live mainly in Ghana, but also in Togo and the Ivory Coast, tell *Anansesem* the tradition appears richest in the Akan subgroup the Asante of Ghana. Possibly, Ananse himself, and the best-known *Anansesem*, originated in this culture, from which they spread to other Akan. Still, these other Akan created their own stories, some of which may have fed back into the Asante tradition.

Traditionally, mainly elders told *Anansesem*, and only orally. Usually, this was at night, either in a street with their kinsfolk surrounding them or, if it was raining, in a three-walled room in the grounds of a large house filled with villagers. Such storytelling sessions still take place. But, because, unlike myths, which are considered at least partly historical, *Anansesem* aren't thought of as sacred, or even true, anyone, and not just a restricted group of elderly religious specialists, is allowed to tell them. Nowadays, in schools, teachers and children tell *Anansesem*, and they're even also written down, and read independently.

Because *Anansesem* aren't believed to be true, before telling one, the teller says, "'We do not really mean, we do not really mean (that what we are going to say is true).'"[1] After telling the story, they say, "'Some [of this story] you may take as true, and the rest you may praise me (for the telling of it).'"[2] In other words, I – the storyteller – am not definitely saying that what I told you is true, but you – the listener – can believe whichever parts of the story you want. As for the rest of it, praise me for inventing such interesting things.

Most, but not all, *Anansesem*, feature Ananse. Ananse's full name is Kweku Ananse. In Akan, there are male and female names associated with the days of the week. For example, the male name 'Kofi', and the female name 'Afua', are associated with Friday. An Akan child is given the name associated with the day on which they were born. 'Kweku' is the male name associated with Wednesday, and thus means 'Wednesday-born'.

In *Anansesem*, Ananse is often depicted as a spider. In the Asante language of Twi, Ananse means 'spider'. Sometimes, though, Ananse is depicted as a human-spider hybrid – for instance, with the body of a spider, but a human head, speech and behaviour.

Ananse is the archetypal trickster. He's small, slow and weak, but also intelligent, cunning and brave. In most conflicts with other beings, he's the underdog and must use his latter traits to defeat them. In Asante, the spider, a sophisticated hunter, symbolises wisdom. We sometimes call even our supreme deity, the Sky-God Nyame, 'Ananse Kokuroko' ('The Great Spider', or 'The Wise One'). "'The wisdom of the spider is greater than that of all the world together,"[3] say Akan storytellers.

However, Ananse is also greedy, selfish, vengeful, callous, and rude. He acts largely in his own interests and doesn't care if his actions inconvenience others. "'Woe to one who would put his trust in Ananse – a sly, selfish, and greedy person,"[4] say Akan storytellers. Even Nyame, and Ananse's family members, consisting of his mother (Nsia), wife (Aso), and four sons (Ntikuma, Nyiwankonfwea ['Thin-legs'], Afudotwedotwe ['Belly-fit-to-burst'], and Tikonokono ['Big-big-head']), aren't spared.

Ananse is deeply connected to Nyame. Both are Akan patriarchs possessing mystical powers. In the myths of some Akan, both are gods who together created the universe and everything in it. To other Akan, Ananse is Nyame's son. To yet others, he's the sole supreme being. To others still, he was a mortal many centuries ago who founded the Twi-speaking nations. They call him, 'the father of our grandfathers'.

Whatever the case, it's Ananse that gave humans their traits – for instance, love, jealousy, justice, and storytelling. Whereas Nyame never leaves the sky and is difficult to contact, Ananse moves frequently between Nyame's spirit world, and humans' physical one. As he likes to undermine Nyame's authority, he always seeks to steal these traits the latter created and owns. Sometimes, this is to gift to human beings, but, more often, he wants them for himself, and they end up with humans unintentionally.

Take as examples two of the best-known *Anansesem*.

The first – *How it Came About That the Sky-God's Stories Came to Be Known As 'Spider-Stories'* – is arguably the most famous, and the quintessential, *Anansesem*. It demonstrates Ananse's connection to Nyame, and the former's desire to undermine the latter's authority. It demonstrates Ananse's complex, trickster character as, on the one hand, an admirable genius, and, on the other, a greedy, ruthless troublemaker. It demonstrates Ananse's connections to both the physical and spirit worlds, and his ability to move between them. It demonstrates his possession of mystical powers, but also his humanity. Lastly, it demonstrates his role as the wielder, and bringer, of humans' traits. This is how it goes:

Kweku Ananse, the Spider, once went to [Nyame], the Sky-god, [to] buy the Sky-god's stories.

The Sky-god said, 'Will you be able to buy them?'

The Spider said, 'Rather, I shall be able.'

The Sky-god said, 'Great and powerful towns like Kokofu, Bekwai, [and] Asumengya have come, but they were unable to purchase them, and you who are but a mere masterless man, (you say) you will be able?'

The Spider said, 'What is the price of (the stories)?'

The Sky-god said, 'They cannot be bought for anything except the Onini creature the Python; Osebo, the Leopard; Mmoatia, the Fairy; (and) Mmoboro, the Hornets.'

The Spider said, 'I will bring some of all these things, and (what is more), I'll add my [mother], Nsia . . . to the lot.'

The Sky-god said, 'Go and bring them then.'

The Spider came, and told his mother all about it, saying, 'I wish to buy the stories of the Sky-god, and the Sky-god says I must bring Onini, the Python; Osebo, the Leopard; Mmoatia, a Fairy; and Mmoboro, [the] Hornets; and I said I would add you to the lot and go and give the Sky-god.'

Now[,] the Spider consulted his wife Aso, saying, 'What is to be done that we may get Onini, the Python?'

And Aso said to him, 'You go off and cut a branch of a palm tree, and cut some string creeper as well, and bring them.'

And the Spider came back with them.

And Aso said, 'Take them to the stream.'

And Ananse took them; as he was going along[,] he said, 'It's longer than he is, it's not so long as he; you lie, it's longer than he.' . . .

The Python (who had overheard this imaginary conversation) said, 'What's it all about?'

The Spider said, 'Is it not (my wife) Aso, who is arguing with me that this palm branch is longer than you, and I say she is a liar.'

And Onini, the Python, said, 'Bring it, and come and measure me.'

[Ananse] took the palm branch and laid it along the Python's body. He said, 'Stretch yourself out.' And the Python stretched himself out, and Ananse took the rope-creeper and wound it . . . until he came to the [Python's] head. [He] said, 'Fool, I shall take you to the Sky-god and receive the Sky-god's tales (in exchange).' Ananse took him off to Nyame . . .

The Sky-god said, 'My hand has touched [it], there remains what still remains.'

The Spider returned, and came and told his wife what had happened, saying, 'There remain the Hornets.'

His wife said, 'Look for a gourd, and fill it with water, and go off with it.'

The Spider went along through the bush, when he saw [a swarm of] Hornets hanging there, and he poured out some of the water and sprinkled it on the Hornets. The Spider then poured the remainder upon himself and cut a leaf of the plantain [tree] and covered his head with it.

And now he addressed the Hornets, saying, 'As the rain has come, had you not better come and enter this, my gourd, so that the rain will not beat you; don't you see that I have taken a plantain leaf to cover myself?'

Then the [Hornets] said, 'We thank you . . . we thank you . . . .'

All the Hornets flew, disappearing into the gourd, fom!

Father Spider covered the mouth, and he said, 'Fools, I have got you, and I am taking you to receive the tales of the Sky-god.' And he took the Hornets to the Sky-god.

The Sky-god said, 'My [hand] has touched [it], what remains (still) remains.'

The Spider came back once more, and told his wife, and said, 'There remains Osebo, the Leopard.'

Aso said, 'Go and dig a hole.'

Ananse said, 'That's enough, I understand.'

Then the Spider went off to look for the Leopard's tracks, and (having found them) he dug a very deep pit, and covered it over, and came back home.

Very early [the] next day, when objects began to be visible, the Spider said he would go off, and when he went, (lo) a Leopard [was] lying in the pit.

Ananse said[,] 'Little father's child, little mother's child, I have told you not to get drunk, and now, just as one would expect of you, you have become intoxicated, and that's why you have fallen into the pit; if I were to say I would get you out, [the] next day, if you saw me or likewise any of my children, you would go and catch them.'

The Leopard said, 'O! I could not do such a thing.'

Ananse went and cut two sticks, put one here, and one there. He said, 'Put one of your paws here, and one also of your paws here.' And the Leopard placed them (where he was told).

As he was about to climb up, Ananse lifted . . . his knife, and in a flash it descended on his head, gao! . . . The pit received the Leopard [and] fom! [was the sound of his falling].

Ananse got a ladder to descend into the pit to go and get the Leopard out ... [H]e said, 'Fool, I am taking you to exchange for the stories of the Sky-god.' He lifted ... the Leopard to go and give to Nyame ...

The Sky-god said, 'My hands have touched [it], what remains still remains.'

The Spider came, and he carved an Akua's child (a ... flat-faced wooden doll), and he tapped some sticky [rubber] (from a tree) and plastered the doll's body with it, and he pounded *eto* (mashed yams), and put some in the doll's hand, and he pounded some more and placed it in a brass basin; he tied string round the doll's waist, and went with it and placed it at the foot of an *odum*-tree, the place where the Fairies come to play.

And a Fairy came along. She said, 'Akua, may I eat a little of this mash?'

Ananse tugged at the string, and the doll nodded her head.

The Fairy told one of her sisters, saying, 'She says I may eat some.'

[Her sister] said, 'Eat some, then.'

And [the Fairy] finished eating, and thanked her (the doll). But when she thanked her, she did not answer. And the Fairy said to her sister, 'When I thank her, she does not reply.'

The sister of the ... Fairy said, 'Slap her [face].'

And [the Fairy] slapped [the doll], pa! And her hand stuck there. She said to her sister, 'My hand has stuck there.'

[Her sister] said, 'Take the [hand] that remains and slap her [face] again.'

And [the Fairy] took it and slapped [the doll], pa! and this one, too, stuck fast. And the Fairy told her sister saying, 'My two hands have stuck fast.'

[Her sister] said, 'Push [Akua] with your stomach.'

[The Fairy] pushed [the doll], and her stomach stuck to it. And Ananse came and tied her up, and ... said, 'Fool, I have got you, I shall take you to the Sky-god (in exchange) for his stories.' And he went off home with her.

And Ananse told his mother ... Nsia ... saying, 'Rise up, let us go, for I am taking you along with the Fairy to go and give the Sky-god (in exchange) for his stories.'

He lifted them up, and went off there to where the Sky-god was.

He said, 'Sky-god, here is a Fairy, and my [mother] whom I spoke about, here she is, too.'

Now the Sky-god called (his elders), the Kontire and Akwam chiefs, the Adonten (leader of the main body of the army), the Gyase [chamberlain]; the Oyoko, Ankobea, and Kyidom (leader of the rear-guard). And he put the matter before them, saying, 'Very great kings have come, and were not able to buy the Sky-god's stories, but Kweku Ananse, the Spider, has been able to pay the price; I have received from him Mmoboro, the Hornets; I have received from him Mmoatia, the Fairy; I have received from him Osebo, the Leopard; I have received from him Onini, the Python; and of his own accord, Ananse has added his mother to the lot; all these things lie here . . . Sing his praise.'

'Eee!' (they [all] shouted).

The Sky-god said, 'Kweku Ananse, from today and going on for ever, I take my Sky-god's stories and I present them to you . . . my blessing, blessing, blessing. No more we shall call them the stories of the Sky-god[, that is, *Nyankonsem* ('Sky-god-stories')], but we shall call them [*Anansesem* ('Spider-stories')].'[5]

The second *Anansesem – How it Came About That Wisdom Came Among the Tribe –* demonstrates more clearly how humans' traits came from Ananse unintentionally. This is how it goes:

They say that Kweku, the Spider, was there, and that he swept up all knowledge, gathered it together in one spot, and placed it in a gourd pot . . .

He then declared that he would climb a tree and go and hang [the gourd] on it, so that all [the] wisdom on earth would be finished.

So[,] he took [the gourd] up to go with it, and when he reached beneath the tree where he was going to hang it, he took a string, and tied it to the gourd, and hung it in front of him, and he set himself to climb the tree.

He climbed, and climbed, and climbed; in vain. He strove again, again he made to climb, and climb, and climb; in vain.

Now, his son, Ntikuma, who was standing by, said, 'Oh, your eyes have surely died (for shame), would it not have been better if you had turned round the gourd and put it on your back, then doubtless you would have been able to climb?'

He (the Spider) said, 'Clear out, you and your old-fashioned sayings.'

Then he turned to climb once more as before, but once again, fruitlessly.

Then he considered long, and (finally) took the gourd and put it behind him.

Then he set himself to climb, and mounted swiftly . . .

He reached where the branches began to spread out from the stem, and he said (to himself), 'I, Kweku Ananse . . . might as well be dead, my child who is so small, so small, so small – there was I, I collected all wisdom (so I thought) in one place, yet some remained which even I did not perceive, and lo! my child, this still-sucking infant, has shown it [to] me.'

Then he seized that gourd, and there was a sound of rending . . . and he cast it away, and there was a sound of scattering.

That is how everyone got wisdom; and anyone who did not go there in time (to pick some up) is – excuse my saying so – a fool.[6]

Akan don't tell *Anansesem* just for fun. Rather, doing so is essential to their survival.

Traditional Akan, and particularly Asante, society is very hierarchical. Youngsters are expected to show due reverence and respect to elders. Commoners are expected to do the same to aristocrats. This includes never offending them.

But, like any other person, if someone has wronged them, even if that someone is more senior than them, an Akan can't help feeling resentful and wanting to express this resentment. How then can they do the latter without offending the more senior person in question, which would otherwise lead to tension, conflict, and perhaps the loss of their livelihood or even life?

In short, by telling *Anansesem*. To express their resentment of the senior person who wronged them, the Akan tells an audience an *Anansesem* in which one character – often, an animal, or Ananse – wrongs another exactly how the senior person wronged them. For the first character, which represents the senior person, the Akan chooses an animal whose natural behaviour matches this person's wrong action. For example, if the senior person stole from them, the Akan would make their character a magpie. Also, when playing this character, the Akan mimics the senior person's mannerisms, so that it's clear to the audience, now roaring with laughter, who wronged the Akan. Because the Akan expresses their resentment indirectly through a story, bookends this story with the disclaimers that it isn't true, and tells it at night, which is associated with light-hearted activities, the senior person, who's probably also in the audience themselves, is unlikely to be offended.

Between the seventeenth and nineteenth centuries, the majority of enslaved Asante were trafficked to Jamaica. Asante cultural elements, including *Anansesem* and Akan day-names, came to define Jamaican culture.

But the lives of enslaved Asante in Jamaica were very different from those who remained in Asanteland. Therefore, the former adapted in various ways some of these cultural elements.

Now that we've explored the nature and purpose of *Anansesem* in Asanteland, in the next section, we'll explore why, and how, in Jamaica, these changed.

*

Much more than in Asanteland, poverty, violence and exploitation characterised Asante life in Jamaica. Thus, in Jamaica, Ananse became a wholly earthly being, and much more cynical, selfish, greedy, cunning, lustful, violent and even apathetic than his Asanteland counterpart.

He also acquired many more antagonists, all of whom are strikingly similar to, and so must represent, either the callous Jamaican plantation master or his brutal overseer. These include Ananse's arch-enemy, the tyrannical Tiger (who stands in for

Nyame), Massa, Buckra, King, Preacher, Death and Dry-Bone.

Dry-Bone is the second-worst of the lot. He's depicted as a skeleton, because, for the Jamaican Asante, plantation masters' cruelty stripped away their humanity, as well as being greedy, secretive, sinister and oppressive. For example, he's said to have the power to increase his weight at will, and frequently punishes other characters by sitting on their backs and increasing his weight until they collapse. However, like the plantation master, Dry-Bone often stays in his comfortable home, and, as the former has his overseer, the latter has a cockerel whom he orders to spy on others.

In Jamaica, *Anansesem* were essentially inspirational stories. If Tiger and Dry-Bone and so on were plantation masters and overseers, then the Jamaican Asante themselves were Ananse, and just how Ananse resisted, outsmarted, and avenged himself on his antagonists, the Jamaican Asante felt inspired to do the same. To reduce the productivity of their masters' plantations, they pretended not to know how to work certain machinery, vandalised this machinery, and even purposefully injured themselves or re-opened, and infected, old wounds.

Maroons – runaway enslaved Africans who established their own communities and became freedom fighters – invaded plantations, raided and sabotaged them, and attacked overseers. Often, they defeated much larger, and better-armed, European forces. When British and enslaved African troops patrolled the Maroons' territories, the latter called out to the enslaved Africans, boasting of their free life in the bush, and urging them to join.

In the two Jamaican *Anansesem* below, the antagonistic nature, and inspirational purpose, of the stories, are apparent.

This is how the first one goes:

One great hungry time Ananse couldn't get anything to eat, so he take up his hand-basket an' a big pot an' went down to the seaside to catch fish.

When he reach there, he make up a large fire and put the pot on the fire, an' say, 'Come, big fish!'

He catch some big fish [and] put them aside.

He said, 'Big fish, go, make little fish come!'

He then catch the little fish.

He say, 'Little fish go, make big fish come!' . . .

He then catch the pot full an' his hand-basket.

He [boil] the pot full and sit down and eat it off; he then started [back] home . . . with the pot on his head and the basket.

Reaching a little way, he hide the pot away in the bush an['] take the basket along with him now.

While going along, he meet up Tiger.

Now Tiger is a very rough man an' Ananse 'fraid of him.

Tiger said to him, 'What you have in that basket, sah?' – speak to him very rough.

Ananse speak in a very feeble voice, say, 'Nothing, sah! Nothing, sah!'

So both of them pass each other, an' when they went on a little way, Tiger hide in the bush watching Ananse.

Ananse then sit down underneath a tree, open his basket, take out the fishes one [by] one, and say, 'Pretty little yallah-tail this!' an' put it aside; he take out a snapper an' say, 'Pretty little snapper this!' an' put it one side . . .

Tiger then run up an' say, 'Think you haven't not'ing in that basket, sah!'

Ananse say, 'I jus' going down to the sea [to] have a bathe, sah, an' I catch them few 'itt[l]e fishes.'

Tiger say 'Give it to me here, sah!' – talk in a very rough manner. An' Tiger take it an' eat them all an' spit up the bones.

Ananse then take up the bones an' eat them, an' while eating he grumble . . .

So both of them start to go home now with the empty basket, but this time Ananse was studying for Tiger.

When he reach part of the way, Ananse see a fruit-tree. Ananse say, 'What a pretty fruit-tree!' . . .

Tiger say, 'Climb it, sah!' (in a rough manner).

So when Ananse go up an' pull some of the fruit, at that time Tiger was standing underneath the tree.

Ananse look down on Tiger head an' said, 'Look lice in . . . Brar Tiger head!'

Tiger said, 'Come down an' ketch it, sah!'

Ananse come down an' said to Tiger he kyan't ketch it without he lean on the tree.

Tiger said, 'Lean on the tree, sah!'

The hair on Tiger head is very long. So whil[e] Ananse ketchin' the lice, Tiger fell asleep. Ananse now take the hair an' lash it round the tree . . .

After he done that he wake up Tiger an' say that he kyan't ketch any more.

Tiger in a rough manner say, 'Come an' ketch it, sah!'

Ananse say, 'I won't!'

So Ananse run off, Tiger spring after him, an' fin' out that his hair is tied on the tree.

So Tiger say, 'Come an' loose me, sah!'

Ananse say, 'I won't!' . . .

An' Ananse leave him go home, an' a hunter-man come an' see Tiger tie on the tree, [an'] make kill him.[7]

And this is how the second story goes:

A man plant a big field of [tall] gub-gub peas. He got a watchman put there. This watchman can't read. The peas grow lovely an' bear lovely; everybody pass by, in love with the peas.

Ananse himself pass an' want to have some. He beg the watchman, but the watchman refuse to give him.

[Ananse] went an' pick up an' old envelope, present it to the watchman an' say the master say to give [to] the watchman.

The watchman say, 'The master know that I cannot read an' he sen' this thing come an' give me?'

Ananse say, 'I will read it for you . . . The master say, 'You mus' tie Mr

Ananse at the fattest part of the gub-gub peas an' when [his] belly full, let him go."

The watchman did so; when Ananse belly full, Ananse call to the watchman, an' the watchman let him go.

After Ananse gone, the master of the peas come an' ask the watchman what was the matter with the peas. The watchman tol' him.

Master say he see no man, no man came to him an' he send no letter, an' if a man come to him like that, he mus' tie him in the peas but no let him away till he come.

The nex' day, Ananse come back with the same letter an' say, 'Master say, give you this.' Ananse read the same letter an' [the] watchman tie Ananse in the peas. An' when Ananse belly full, him call to the watchman to let him go, but [the] watchman refuse.

Ananse call out a second time, 'Come, let me go!'

The watchman say, 'No, you don' go!'

Ananse say, 'If you don' let me go, I spit on the groun' an' you rotten!' [i.e. I'll put a curse on you.] Watchman get frighten an' untie him.

Few minutes after that the master came; an' tol' [the watchman] if [Ananse] come back the nex' time, no matter what he say, hol' him.

The nex' day, Ananse came back with the same letter an' read the same story to the man.

The man tie him in the peas, an', after him belly full, [Ananse] call to the man to let him go; but the man refuse . . . all that [Ananse] say he refuse until the master arrive.

The master take Ananse an' carry him to his yard an' tie him up to a tree, take a big iron an' put it in the fire to hot.

Now while the iron was heating, Ananse was crying . . .

Lion was passing then, see Ananse tie up underneath the tree, ask him what cause him to be tied there.

Ananse said to Lion[,] from since him born he never hol' knife an' fork, an' de people wan' him now to hol' knife an' fork.

Lion said to Ananse, 'You too wort'less man! Me can hol' it. I will loose you and then you tie me there.'

So Lion loose Ananse an' Ananse tied Lion to the tree.

So Ananse went away, now, far into the bush an' climb upon a tree to see what [is] taking place.

When the master came out, instead of seeing Ananse he see Lion. He took . . . the hot iron out of the fire an' shove it in Lion ear. An' Lion make a plunge an' pop the rope an' away gallop in the bush[.][8]

In this chapter, we've explored *Anansesem*, including what they are, who their main character is, their nature and purpose in Asante culture, and how these changed when they were transported to Jamaica.

In Asante, Ananse is a semi-divine, but troublesome, being who interacts with both the Sky-god Nyame and humankind, and Asante tell his stories to express resentment of other people without offending those people.

In Jamaica, Ananse is more cynical, more earthly, and has more antagonists, often on whom he seeks to avenge himself. Here, Asante told his stories to inspire each other to perform dissident acts.

Having explored various aspects of the almost uniquely African cultural feature that is oral literature, in the next chapter, we're going to look at a cultural feature that, though not even almost uniquely African, characterises many of its cultures: holistic health.

8

WISDOM OF THE ANCIENTS

In many African cultures, health is not confined to the body. For a person to be considered healthy, as well as their body, their mind, spirit, and even relationships with both their living and living dead community members must be in good condition. In healing themselves, then, Africans employ remedies that treat not just the body, but all these aspects. Specifically, it is this attitude to health, and these remedies, that we'll explore in this chapter.

In the West, that health should not be confined to the body has begun to be appreciated only recently. For instance, it's only in the last few years that the public in countries like the United States has shown that it is acceptable for top athletes to drop out of competitions because of mental, and not just physical, ill health.

In July 2021, when the American gymnast Simone Biles dropped out of competitions in the Tokyo Olympics Women's Gymnastics Team Final, she received an outpouring of support.

In the lead-up to and during those competitions, Biles was suffering from a mental block known as the 'twisties'. In the air, gymnasts usually know exactly where they are in relation to the ground. But if they perform while stressed, anxious, or depressed, they can lose this sense of their position. 'Literally can not [sic] tell up from down,' explained Biles. '[The twisties is] the craziest feeling ever. Not having an inch of control over your body. What's even scarier is since I have no idea where I am in the air, I also have NO idea how I am going to land.'[1]

In the vault competition, Biles meant to execute a very difficult move called the 'Amanar', which involves the gymnast in the air spinning their body round two-and-a-half times before landing. Usually, the Amanar is no problem for Biles. But this time, when Biles launched herself off the vault, she spun round only one-and-a-half times before only just managing to land on her feet. If not for her skill, and familiarity with the Amanar, she might have landed on her head, broken her neck, and her career would have been over.

For all athletes, preparation for the Tokyo Olympics, and the Games themselves, was exceptionally difficult. Because of the coronavirus pandemic, the games had been postponed, and training centres closed. Athletes' training schedules had been severely disrupted. Spectators had been banned from attending the games, and the energy that athletes usually feed off to perform their best was non-existent.

Biles was under even more pressure. Her team had won in both the 2012 and 2016 Olympics, and they were expected to win again. Biles was the most high-profile gymnast and Olympian competing in Tokyo. In 2016, she'd won five medals, four of them gold, and she was expected now to win a record-breaking five gold. She was also the only known sexual abuse survivor of Larry Nassar – a convicted paedophile and former USA Gymnastics doctor who sexually assaulted hundreds of female gymnasts – competing that year. 'It's been really stressful, this Olympic Games,' said Biles. 'I think just as a whole, not having an audience, there are a lot of different variables going into it . . . [I]t's been a long Olympic process, it's been a long year . . . I think we're just a little bit too stressed out.'[2]

After the Amanar incident, Biles consulted a USA Gymnastics trainer. They left the building. When Biles returned, she removed her competing gear, and put on her warm-up clothes. The next day, USA Gymnastics released the following statement: 'After further medical evaluation, Simone Biles has withdrawn from the final individual all-around competition at the Tokyo Olympic Games, in order to focus on her mental health.'[3]

As well as members of the American public, support came from Biles's teammates, other athletes, and mental-health campaigners and charities. 'We wholeheartedly support Simone's decision and applaud her bravery in prioritizing her well-being,'[4] read the end of Team USA's statement. '[Biles is] showing us all that maintaining one's mental health is as important as physical health,'[5] said Mental Health America.

Now, we're going to look at a few examples of Africans' holistic view of health, and how they restored it via remedies that healed not the body, but their relationships with either their living or living-dead community members.

We'll begin with the early twentieth-century Azande of the Democratic Republic of the Congo, and how they restored their health via a practice that repaired their relationships with their living kinsfolk.

*

In Azande, *Mangu* ('witchcraft') caused all kinds of misfortunes, including illnesses.

Any Zande (the singular of 'Azande') was capable of witchcraft. Every Zande had inside them a 'witchcraft substance' – a swollen black object above their stomach. Male Azande inherited this witchcraft substance from their fathers, and females inherited it from their mothers.

Each witchcraft substance had its own *mbisimo mangu* ('witchcraft-substance soul'). To bewitch someone, a Zande *no* ('shot') their witchcraft-substance soul towards their victim. *No* can also be translated as 'to bewitch'. This witchcraft-substance soul was a big, bright glowing orb, like an unrealistically large firefly. It entered the victim and removed their *mbisimo pasio* ('flesh soul' – the kind of soul that Christians believe in). Soon afterwards, the victim became ill.

But bewitchment rarely happened. The witchcraft substance was often dormant. The Azande said it's 'cool'. It became active – or 'hot' – only when its possessor felt negatively towards another. A person's annoyance, anger, or resentment towards a friend, family member, or neighbour is what caused their witchcraft-substance soul to be shot out towards that individual. This happened automatically, without the former meaning for it to happen.

When a Zande fell ill, then, they ascertained who felt negatively towards them, and got them to stop. In short, they restored the relationship between themselves and that person.

First, they got one of their family members to consult an oracle. For the oracle to work, the person handling it had to have avoided certain taboos. For instance, he mustn't have had sex, or eaten certain foods, like fish, in the past week. The same restrictions applied to someone in mourning. Thus, often, the sick person asked a family member in mourning to consult the oracle on their behalf.

Early one morning, this family member would travel to the bush with a friend. The family member would carry an open-weave basket full of fowls, and his friend would carry a gourd full of water, and poison – specifically, a strychnine-like red powder made from a forest creeper.

The friend would find a secluded space and step on the grass to flatten it. Then, he'd scratch a hole in the ground, and find, and place over it, a large leaf. From other leaves, he'd make a cup and a filter, and from grass, he'd make a small brush. He'd also collect branches.

The family member would give his friend the fowl-basket, then sit some distance away.

The friend would pour the poisonous powder onto the large leaf. He'd then pour water from the gourd into the cup. He'd empty the cup on top of the poison and stir the mixture into a paste with his finger.

On the family member's orders, he'd pick up a fowl and bind it with some of the branches. He'd pick up the brush, twirl it in the paste, and wrap the filter round it. He'd then open the fowl's beak, put the filter into it, and squeeze.

The family member would then say something like this: 'Was it so-and-so (i.e. this friend or that neighbour) who bewitched my kinsman, making them sick? If so-and-so did indeed bewitch my kinsman, poison oracle, kill the fowl. However, if so-and-so had nothing to do with it, poison oracle, spare the fowl.'

Whether or not the fowl died, the friend would take another fowl and give it the poison, and the family member would ask a confirmation question. Let's say the first fowl died. The family member would then say: 'The poison oracle killed the fowl. Seemingly, so-and-so bewitched my family member. If this is true, poison oracle, spare the second fowl. If this is false, poison oracle, kill the second fowl.' Let's say this second fowl survived. The family member would now know for certain who made their kinsman ill.

In reality, poison oracle consultations took much longer to complete – sometimes days – and were more complex. The family member would ask the oracle not just who caused the illness, but about its exact nature, severity, whether there were other culprits, and so on. In their questions, they often included as much detail as possible. Sometimes, it took them up to five to ten minutes to ask a *single* question. To do them properly, the family member had to be practised in poison oracle consultations.

The Azande had two other oracles.

To consult the rubbing-board oracle (*iwa*), a Zande first crafted the two pieces of the rubbing-board. One of these pieces resembled a hand-sized, three-legged table, and the other, a similarly sized pot lid. The Zande would then hold a fruit – usually, a kei apple – over the table, and squeeze, so that its juice poured onto the table. They'd then pick up the lid, dip it in a gourd full of water, put it on the table, and slide it back and forth. As they did so, they'd ask something like this: 'Was it so-and-so who bewitched my kinsman, making them sick? If so-and-so did indeed bewitch my kinsman, rubbing-board, stick. However, if so-and-so had nothing to do with it, rubbing-board, run smoothly.'

To consult the termite oracle (*dakpa*), a Zande would stick two branches, named *dakpa* and *kpoyo*, into a termite mound. Then they'd say something like, 'Was it so-and-so who bewitched my kinsman, making them sick? If so-and-so did indeed bewitch my kinsman, termites, eat just *dakpa*. However, if so-and-so had nothing to do with it, termites, eat both *dakpa* and *kpoyo*.' The Zande would then leave the sticks in the mound overnight, and return the next morning to see the result.

Of the three oracles, the poison oracle was the most prestigious and authoritative, and the termite oracle was the second most. The poison oracle needed the most materials – which didn't come cheap – and the most practice to consult properly. For most matters, the Zande ordinarily just consulted the much cheaper rubbing-board oracle. But for serious matters, including identifying witches, they consulted the poison oracle.

When the family member who'd consulted the poison oracle got their confirmed answer, his friend would cut off the dead – that is, the first – fowl's wing, put it on the end of a stick, and spread out its feathers, to resemble a fan. He'd then give it to the family member.

Both would return home, the family member taking the wing with him.

Then, the family member would arrange an audience with an official of the Azande royal family. In his audience, he'd put the wing on the ground before this official, and explain everything, from when his kinsman got sick to the poison oracle's result.

After listening intently to what the family member had to say, the official would summon a messenger, tell him to take the wing to the culprit's house and explain to the culprit the poison oracle's result.

When the messenger did so, putting the wing on the ground before the culprit, the culprit would first apologise for having felt negatively towards, bewitched and made sick the family member's kinsman. He'd then say that he did not mean to activate his witchcraft substance and that he would 'cool' it again so that this kinsman might recover.

To 'cool' his witchcraft substance, the culprit would first go to get a gourd full of water. When he returned, he'd take a sip of this water, swill it around his mouth, and spit it out in a thin spray over the wing. His witchcraft substance was now 'cooled'.

The messenger would take the wing back to the official and family member and report on what the culprit had done. Relieved, the family member would return home and wait for his kinsman to recover. If they didn't, he'd consult the poison oracle again with a different culprit in mind.

Through this process, the sick kinsman indirectly approached, resolved the issue with, and restored the relationship between themselves and a fellow community member whom they thought or knew felt negatively towards them. Only when they restored this relationship could they get better.

Now that we've seen an example of an African people who became healthy through restoring their relationships with living community members, let's look at an example of an African people who did the same, but with *living-dead* community members: the late twentieth-century Lobi of Burkina Faso.

*

Like in many African cultures, in Lobi, misfortunes, including illnesses, occurred when ancestors stopped protecting their living descendants. As we saw in Chapter 2 (How the Dead Still Live), usually, African ancestors punish their descendants in this way when they're angry with them, most likely because the descendants have failed to honour said ancestors. In short, damaged relationships between a person and their ancestors cause the individual to become sick.

In Lobi, community ancestors are invisible beings called *thila* (singular, *thil*). According to Lobi tradition, *thila* were a consolation gift from their Supreme Being, Thangba Yu, whose name means 'Sky Above'.

Once upon a time, the Lobi lived carefree, without disease, war, or – because Thangba Yu gave them as much meat as they desired – famine. In return, Thangba Yu asked the Lobi to obey certain rules: don't steal, commit adultery, or kill.

At first, when the Lobi's population was small, they easily followed these rules. But as time went on, and their population grew, and they competed over scarcer resources, they broke them.

Thangba Yu was heartbroken. He took away the Lobi's meat, and gave them diseases and natural disasters. He retreated into the sky so that He could no longer hear the Lobi's prayers. This is how He got His name.

But Thangba Yu couldn't forsake the Lobi completely. As well as crops and farming hoes, He gave them *thila*, who, if honoured, would protect and guide them.

Thus, when a Lobi fell ill, he knew that the relationships between him and one or more of his *thila* had been damaged.

To help ascertain which *thil* this was, and how he could restore their relationship, the sick Lobi consulted a *buor* ('diviner').

A Lobi became a *buor* because, probably in a dream, a *thil* told them that they must. Becoming a *buor* required no formal training. Most Lobi had been to *buors* countless times, and knew how divination worked. But only chosen Lobi divined successfully. To become a *buor*, all a chosen Lobi had to do was complete a divination for a senior *buor*.

When the sick Lobi met the *buor* at the latter's house, he said he had a problem, but didn't explain exactly what this was. He intended to test the *buor*'s skill by having him divine *this*, as well as why it was happening, and how it could be resolved.

The *buor* would lead the Lobi into his ancestral shrine room and tell him to sit on a mat on the floor. When the Lobi did so, the *buor* would lay out in front of him his divining instruments, including an iron bell and leather bottles filled with cowrie shells.

He'd then sit down next to the Lobi, pick up the bell, and shake it, summoning the *thila*.

When the *thila* arrived from the spirit world, the *buor* would greet them, take the Lobi's hand, and begin asking the *thila* yes-or-no questions about the Lobi's condition – for example, 'Is he sick?', or 'Has he had an accident?'.

If the answer was 'Yes', the *buor* would feel the *thila* lift his and the Lobi's joined hands, slowly lower them and jerk them towards the Lobi. If the answer was 'No', the *buor* would feel the *thila* only lift, and slowly lower, the joined hands.

The *buor* would spend forty-five minutes asking around a thousand yes-or-no questions that helped him ascertain not only what exactly the Lobi's problem was, but its severity, cause, and solution.

The *buor* would then let go of the Lobi's hand, and ask the *thila* a final question: 'Have I obtained all the relevant and correct information about my client's condition?' The *buor* would then pick up one of the leather bottles filled with cowrie shells, pour out a handful, and toss them onto the floor in front of him. If only one shell faced upwards, the *thila* had answered yes. But if *more* than one shell faced upwards, the *thila* had answered no, and the *buor* would have to re-start the questioning process.

When he'd obtained from the *thila* all the relevant and correct information about the Lobi's condition, the *buor* would give the Lobi a detailed summary of his questions and the *thila's* answers, including which *thil* is angry with the Lobi, and what he should do to restore their relationship.

The Lobi would go home and do what he had to. For the angry *thil*, he, for instance, would either build a shrine or carve a small statue of them. Appeased, the *thil* resumed their protection of the Lobi, and the Lobi recovered.

Now, as well as an example of an African people who became healthy through restoring their relationships with living community members, we've seen one of an African people who did the same, but with living-dead community members. In both examples, we discussed mainly individual's health. In the next section, we're going to look briefly at the late twentieth-century Lugbara of Uganda, an example of an African people who healed their entire community through a practice that simultaneously restored relationships between living community members, and between those community members and the living dead.

*

Like in Lobi, in Lugbara, a person became sick when the relationships between them and their personal ancestors, whom the Lugbara call *a'bii*, were damaged. In this case, the sick Lugbara knew that, to restore these relationships, he had to appease his ancestors by building them a shrine. However, he didn't immediately know what *kind* of shrine would appease them – that is, how big it should be, what shape, and which materials (wood, or stone) it should be made from.

So, the sick Lugbara went to a diviner, who asked his ancestors on his behalf what kind of shrine he should build, and told him. Usually, the shrines were fifty centimetres tall, thirty centimetres wide, and fifteen centimetres thick, and built of stone, grass, or clay. Others, often built of clay, were as big as a small hut. Sometimes, new shrines were built next to, or on top of, an old one, making a superstructure.

After the sick Lugbara had built the shrine, he gathered at it with his family members and food. He asked his ancestors' forgiveness. Then, he and his family members feasted, leaving some of the food near the shrine for the ancestors. If this food remained untouched by ants as the sick Lugbara and his family ate, the ancestors were considered to have accepted it, and forgiven their descendant. The relationships between the sick Lugbara and his ancestors were restored, and the sick person recovered.

When the community suffered an epidemic, it was the relationships between the Lugbara and one or more of their *community* ancestors, whom they call *ori*, that were damaged. Across Lugbaraland, the Lugbara had built temples dedicated to these community ancestors. To appease an angry community ancestor, the Lugbara knew that they had to perform a sacrifice at their temple. First, though, they had to ascertain which ancestor was angry, and which animal should be sacrificed.

To do the former, an elder consulted the 'chicken oracle'. He began by digging holes, or placing stones, in a circle, each of which represented an ancestor. Then, he took a chicken and cut its throat, and the angry ancestor was the one whose hole, or stone, the chicken died on.

The elder then informed the other elders of the oracle's result. To determine which animal should be sacrificed – usually, a chicken, goat, or cow – they went to a diviner together. The diviner asked the ancestor on their behalf and informed them of the answer. The angrier the ancestor, and the more severe the epidemic, the bigger the animal that needed to be sacrificed.

When the elders had informed the community of everything that had happened, as many of its members as possible gathered at the community ancestor's temple. In complete silence, the elder who probably brought the sacrificial animal sacrificed it, ensuring some of its blood touched the temple. He then butchered the animal, and other community members cooked and served the meat.

As the Lugbara feasted, they caught up with one another. Often, they approached and resolved issues with each other. Then, when everyone had finished eating, one by one, the elders stood up and gave speeches about why they all were gathered at the temple that day, and Lugbara history. In other words, the elders reminded their kinsfolk of what happens if relationships with the ancestors aren't properly maintained. In short, when the living Lugbara gathered for the sacrifice, they talked and restored the relationships between themselves, and when they'd not only completed the sacrifice itself but purposefully remembered their ancestor, they restored the relationship between themselves and that ancestor.

As we've seen with the Azande, Lobi, and Lugbara examples, African peoples' conceptions of health extend beyond the body, and even the mind, encompassing every aspect that could affect a person's well-being, including relationships with others. African health is holistic in the truest sense of the word.

In the next chapter, we'll explore racism, a cultural feature that many people associate only with Africans, even though it hasn't affected them exclusively. More specifically, we'll examine when, and why, anti-African racism came into being.

9

THE INVENTION OF RACISM

First, though, let's look at an example of how racism affected some African people.

From 1934 until 2015, there stood in the University of Cape Town (UCT), South Africa, a bronze statue of Cecil John Rhodes. Rhodes was a nineteenth-century imperialist, businessman and statesman, who contributed largely to Britain's colonisation of southern Africa. He was also a racist – that is, he discriminated against dark-skinned Africans because he thought them naturally inferior to himself.

Rhodes's statue, therefore, pained many of UCT's dark-skinned African students. After all, it represented an individual who had discriminated against their ancestors and, had he been alive in their time, would have discriminated against them, too. 'Seeing [Rhodes's] statue every day [for years] ... made me very angry,'[1] said Chumani Maxwele. In 2015, Maxwele was a thirty-year-old, dark-skinned African politics student in his fourth year at UCT. Angered by Rhodes's statue, he decided to do something about it.

On 9 March 2015 – a Monday morning – Maxwele dressed in protest gear – shirtless, black trousers, trainers, a pink helmet, a whistle, and a drum – and took a bus to Khayelitsha, a township (i.e. ghetto) on the edge of Cape Town. Lacking basic amenities, most dark-skinned African residents of Khayelitsha poo in plastic buckets that, once a week, are collected from outside their shacks. Having grown up in Delft, a township next to Khayelitsha, Maxwele had often passed through Khayelitsha and probably knew that Monday was collection day.

When Maxwele reached Khayelitsha, he picked up one of the poo containers and took a bus back to UCT. He walked up to Rhodes's statue and, while blowing his whistle and beating his drum, flung the container's contents on the statue. Gradually, a crowd of students gathered around him. "'Where are *our* heroes and ancestors?'"[2] Maxwele shouted to them.

Maxwele's protest started a conversation about the Rhodes statue. A few days after his protest – at midday on 12 March – over a thousand UCT students and staff assembled on the university's main quad, where a microphone and speakers had been set up. The energy was tense but excited. The crowd booed, cheered and jeered. One by one, students took the microphone and shared their thoughts on Maxwele's protest and Rhodes's statue. Some agreed wholeheartedly with Maxwele's protest, deriding Rhodes's statue and the racism it represented. Some shared Maxwele's sentiment but thought his protest method crass. Others disagreed entirely with Maxwele's protest, which, they argued, would only divide students.

By the end of the debate two hours later, most students had decided that the Rhodes statue had to go. "'[What] we want is a date when Cecil John Rhodes will fall,'"[3] said Maxwele. He then started the chant, "'[W]e want a date!'"[4]

At five o'clock that evening, students tied red and white cloths over Rhodes's statue with rope. Others then founded the 'Rhodes Must Fall' (RMF) movement, which they described as, 'an independent collective of students, workers and staff who have come together to end institutionalised racism ... at UCT[, whose] movement was sparked by ... Maxwele's radical protest against the statue of ... Rhodes ... [One of our] immediate demands,' they continued, '[is] that we receive a date for the removal of [Rhodes's] statue[.]'[5]

On 15 March, RMF members replaced the cloth on the Rhodes statue with bin bags and began twenty-four-hour sit-ins at its site.

Meanwhile, UCT's management resisted removing the statue.

On 20 March, students, including RMF, and SRC (Student Representative Council) members, marched from the Rhodes statue into Bremner – the building where all UCT's administration is handled. Once they'd packed out Bremner's reception area, they cheered and clapped, and sang protest songs. When it got too hot, some of them went outside and sang victory and anti-apartheid songs.

For over two weeks, the students occupied Bremner. They renamed the building 'Azania House' – 'Azania' is a traditional name for South Africa – and protested in shifts. While some students went to lectures or to get food, others remained behind in Azania House, eating, studying and sleeping. UCT's administrators were unable to enter the building, let alone work, and the university ground to a halt. Simultaneously, other students further defaced Rhodes's statue, graffitiing it with anti-apartheid slogans, and throwing paint on it.

Management capitulated. On 8 April, UCT's Council – the university's highest governing authority made up of about thirty individuals, including staff, students and alumni – voted unanimously for the removal of the Rhodes statue.

The next day, Rhodes's statue was bound in green twine, and a cordon was set up around it. Thousands of people, including students, staff, local politicians, and Cape Town residents, gathered round the statue. Maxwele himself milled round the crowd, encouraging people to come as close as possible. The atmosphere was festive and filled with anticipation. Crowd members sang struggle and victory songs and stamped their feet.

As a crane moved beside the statue, crowd members took pictures and shot videos with their phones. When the crane lifted the statue, the crowd's cheers echoed throughout the campus. Students broke through the cordon. Some flung white paint and rubbish on the statue and put a bucket on its head. Others climbed on its plinth and punched the air in victory. As the crane lowered the statue onto the back of a flatbed truck, other students climbed onto the back of the truck, threw red paint on the statue, wrapped paper round its head, and while ululating and crying *Amandla* ('power'), slapped it. More students climbed onto the truck, beat the statue with wooden sticks, covered its head with a black plastic bag, and put a sign over it which read, 'This Is Only The Beginning.' 'It was a joy, because something you envisaged happening did happen,'[6] said Maxwele.

Rhodes's statue pained UCT's dark-skinned African students to the extent that they were compelled to campaign for its removal. Considering the impact the Rhodes statue had on UCT's dark-skinned African students in particular, and, more generally, the impact racism like that which Rhodes exhibited has had on African peoples, we'd be forgiven for thinking that, in African peoples' histories, this racism was widespread and longstanding. But, as we'll see in the following sections, this couldn't be further from the truth. Racism is a primarily eighteenth- and nineteenth-century phenomenon that had initially only a handful of proponents.

*

Perhaps racism's most important proponent was Edward Long, an eighteenth-century English lawyer, West Indian planter, and enslaver.

Long was born in Cornwall on 23 August 1734. He had three elder brothers, and two sisters. He was educated at Bury St Edmunds and Gray's Inn. In 1757, not long into his pupillage, his father, Samuel, died. The year before, it had been Charles, his eldest brother.

Shortly after his father's death, on his uncle's insistence, Long, now in his mid-twenties, went to Jamaica. Long's great-grandfather, also called Samuel, had been a lieutenant in the army that in 1655 had taken Jamaica from the Spanish. Samuel senior became Chief Justice of Jamaica, and a member of its governing council. Long's father – Samuel junior – had also been a member of this council. Charles, Long's brother, had been a member of the House of Assembly – the colonial Jamaican parliament. By the time of Samuel junior's death in 1757, the Longs' estate of seven thousand acres and four hundred enslaved Africans was worth about four million pounds in today's money. One of Long's sisters married Jamaica's governor, Sir Henry Moore. Long himself was also elected a House of Assembly member, and its Speaker. Also, Moore appointed him Judge of the Admiralty Court. Long then married Mary Ballard Beckford, sole heiress of the sugar baron Thomas Beckford, who belonged to the Beckford-Ballard-Palmers, one of Jamaica's wealthiest and most important planting families, which owned fifty thousand acres. Mary's first husband had also been a wealthy planter, as well as the Chief Justice's son.

Long had mixed feelings about Jamaica. When he was a young boy, his mother, Mary, often described it to him as an idyllic place: lush forests, tall mountains, white beaches, and clear waters. She told him nothing of African enslavement.

On the island, Long's parents had separated painfully. Long's father had been a tyrant. Once, Jamaica's governor, who sided with its rich merchants, decided to move the government's seat from St Jago de la Vega to, probably, Kingston, where these merchants lived. The move would destroy St Jago, which had nothing else. Samuel supported it, and ordered his son Charles to do the same. But when the matter reached the House of Assembly, Charles, sympathising with St Jago's residents, voted against it. Samuel disowned him. Shortly after that, Charles fell ill. Samuel didn't care, and Charles died before he and his father reconciled.

When Long got to Jamaica, his brother Robert gave him half an estate called Longville, as well as the Lucky Valley plantation. Long lived and worked on the island until 1769, when poor health prompted him to retire in England.

While Long was in England, the abolitionist movement was fast gaining ground.

The same year Long himself returned to England, Charles Stewart, a Scottish planter, enslaver, and customs paymaster, travelled from Boston, where he was based, to London for business. Stewart took with him James Somerset, an African he kept in enslavement.

In February 1771, Stewart had Somerset baptised in London. In October of that year, Somerset ran away from Stewart. For his freedom, Somerset appealed to his godparents, as well as Granville Sharp, one of England's most passionate abolitionists.

In November 1771, Stewart had Somerset recaptured, and put in chains aboard the *Ann and Mary*, a ship that was to head to Jamaica, where Stewart meant to sell Somerset. When they learnt of this two days later, Somerset's godparents appealed to Lord Mansfield, England's Chief Justice. Mansfield summoned the *Anne and Mary's* captain, John Knowles, and told him to explain himself. When he'd done so, Mansfield decided that, in respect of *habeas corpus* i.e. the right not to be illegally detained, the matter would have to be settled in court.

The so-called Somerset Case had five hearings, and lasted five months.

Stewart's lawyers argued that, having been legally bought in Virginia, Somerset was Stewart's rightful property, and Stewart could do with Somerset what he liked. That they were in England didn't change this. If it did, then it would be practically impossible for anybody to transport their property internationally.

Also, said Stewart's lawyers, freeing Somerset would mean that the other enslaved Africans in ships at England's ports would have to be freed, too. There were about 15,000 of these enslaved Africans, each of which was worth £50 (about £4,500 today). Would it be sensible and fair, said Stewart's lawyers, to take away from these Africans' 'owners' their collective £750,000 in value (about £65 million today)?

On the other hand, Somerset's lawyers, whom Granville Sharp found and paid for, argued that in England there was no law permitting one person to keep another in bondage. As soon as Stewart and Somerset arrived in England, the laws of the colonies ceased to apply to them, and those of England did. Therefore, Somerset was legally a free man, and should be treated as such.

The Somerset Case attracted national attention, and was frequently in the news. During its hearings, all kinds of UK citizens – from British Africans to West-Indian plantation owners (some of whom paid Stewart's lawyers) – packed the court. Seemingly, most people were on Somerset's side. In the third hearing, while Somerset's lawyer was patiently listened to, applauded, and got a standing ovation, Stewart's lawyer was booed, jeered and laughed at. He could hardly get his words out, and had to beg to be allowed to speak. 'It is my misfortune to address an audience, much the greater part of which, I apprehend, wish to find me in the wrong,'[7] he said.

On 22 June 1772, Mansfield ruled that it was illegal for Stewart to have had Somerset captured and removed from England. In other words, the ruling applied to Stewart and Somerset *only*, and the status of neither slavery itself – that is, whether it was legal in the UK to own another person as property – nor the other enslaved Africans in ships in the UK was in said ruling considered. Mansfield avoided ruling on either slavery or these other enslaved Africans on purpose, because he was reluctant to affect the huge worth of both to England's slave traders, enslavers and planters.

Still, the press widely reported Mansfield's ruling as having ended slavery in the UK. A few days after Mansfield gave his ruling, about two hundred British Africans celebrated in a pub in Westminster, where they drank to Mansfield's health. Afterwards, they attended a ball.

Conversely, the West-Indian planters were dismayed that more English than they thought abhorred slavery. They were angry and anxious at the boost the ruling gave the abolitionist movement, and did all they could to counter the ruling's effects, and even reverse the ruling itself.

The planters tried to push through Parliament a Bill that would nullify the ruling, and thus revert the law to the 1729 Yorke-Talbot opinion, which stated that, on being either brought to England, or baptised, an enslaved person still had effectively no rights. They failed.

In England, to avoid pressure to release their enslaved Africans, West-Indian planters classed them as apprentices.

They also wrote pamphlet upon pamphlet, arguing that West-Indian plantations, which weren't profitable without enslaved Africans' labour, were essential to Britain; and that it was okay to keep and treat Africans as property because of their natural inferiority.

In 1772, Samuel Estwick, an assistant agent for planters in Barbados, wrote *Considerations on the Negroe Cause*. In this pamphlet, he argued against Mansfield's ruling, maintaining that, in England, enslaved Africans had no rights at all. He supported this statement by arguing also that Africans were, unlike Englishmen, a non-human species.

Estwick heavily inspired Edward Long.

Back in 1769, when Long returned to England from Jamaica, he almost immediately began writing *The History of Jamaica*, which was essentially a guide to the island, detailing its economy, agriculture, housing, laws and people – including planters and enslaved Africans.

In 1772, when Long read Estwick's tract, he interrupted his writing of *The History of Jamaica* to publish his own pamphlet: *Candid Reflections upon the Negroe Cause*. Here, he argued that Africans had no rights because God had created them as an inferior, non-human species specifically so that they'd be slaves. Moreover, Africans' societies were so savage and backward that bringing them to, and forcing them to work in, the West Indies was merciful.

When Long went back to writing *The History of Jamaica*, which was published eventually in 1774, he included, expanded, and expressed even more intensely, these racist arguments. '[Africans'] noses [are] flat like those of a Dutch dog,' he wrote. '[T]heir lips [are] very thick and big; their teeth [are] exceedingly white, but very long, and ill-set, some of them sticking out of their mouths like boars' tusks ... Their hearing is remarkably quick; their faculties of smell and taste are truly bestial, nor less so their commerce with the other sex; in these acts, they are [as] libidinous and shameless as monkeys, or baboons.'[8]

Long also said that, like monkeys, Africans were tricksters, that they had the mental capacity of orangutans, and so had achieved nothing in either the arts or the sciences, which is why they lacked culture or heritage.

He also asserted that because Europeans and Africans were different species, their children were infertile, like mules, and he decried Europeans and Africans mixing. He wrote that 'lower-class' women especially were attracted to Africans and had by them 'numerous brood[s].' He continued, '[I]n the course of a few generations more, the English blood will become so contaminated with this mixture, and from the chances, the ups and downs of life, this alloy may spread so extensively, as even to reach the middle, and then the higher, orders of the people, till the whole nation resembles the Portuguese ... in complexion of skin and baseness of mind.'[9]

As well as immoral, abusive to their children, gluttonous and lazy, Long dubbed all Africans 'a brutish, ignorant, idle, crafty, treacherous, bloody, thievish, mistrustful, and superstitious, people.'[10]

Although Long wasn't the first European either to have ideas about, argue for or write about Africans' natural inferiority, his extensive use of cultural and biological detail to back up his prejudices made his arguments appear much more fact-based, scientific and thus credible than they really were. Moreover, although Long had never even been to Africa, his and his family's prominence in Jamaica and in the slave trade, which had allowed him to observe Africans first-hand, convinced many he was an African expert. Politicians, civil servants and entrepreneurs eagerly sought, and accepted without question, his opinion on African matters. For instance, in the summer of 1788, before the first Parliamentary debate on the slave trade, William Pitt, the Prime Minister, consulted Long. Then, Lord Hawkesbury, Pitt's President of the Privy Council for Trade, wrote to Long, saying, 'I was certainly impatient to [receive] your opinion on [Africans, West Indian plantations, and the slave trade], with which you are so widely acquainted; as I am so disposed to place confidence in that opinion . . . I shall lose no time in reading and considering the observations you have sent me.'[11] Even abolitionists read, referenced and quoted from Long's works. In the slave-trade debates, no other work was cited as *the* great work on the trade than Long's own *The History of Jamaica*.

For a century after *The History of Jamaica*'s publication, all kinds of eminent European and American academics, from physicians to historians, cited from, and even plagiarised its racist arguments. In his 1799 book, *Account of the Regular Gradation in Man*, the prominent English physician Charles White borrowed heavily from Long to argue that the 'races' of Europeans, Asians, and Africans were different species; and that Africans, being closest evolutionarily to apes, were at the bottom. About ten years earlier, *The History of Jamaica*'s anti-African section was reprinted in America's *Columbia* magazine. In his 1850 work, *Races of Men*, the infamous Scottish doctor, Robert Knox, was inspired by Long to argue that different 'races' are so biologically and culturally different that they should be thought of as different species. These 'species' were in competition with one another, but some were inherently better than others. Unsurprisingly, Anglo-Saxons were at the top, and the races below them were incapable of improvement, but Africans in particular threatened

Anglo-Saxons' natural dominance. White's and Knox's works inspired other thinkers in Europe and America. Because of his extensive influence, Edward Long is considered the godfather of modern pseudo-scientific racism.

But if racism is a primarily eighteenth- and nineteenth-century phenomenon, then what were Europeans' attitudes towards Africans in the preceding eras? That is the subject of the next section, where we'll explore Europeans' attitudes towards Africans in both antiquity – that is, between about the eighth century BC and the sixth century AD – and the Renaissance – that is, between about the fourteenth and seventeenth centuries AD.

*

Seemingly, in both antiquity and the Renaissance, Europeans didn't generally think of Africans specifically as naturally inferior to every other people.

In antiquity – more specifically, between the sixth century BC and the fourth century AD – Greeks and Romans encountered Nubians as ambassadors, governors and especially soldiers. They thus respected, and even feared, Nubians as particularly skilled warriors, most proficient in archery and elephant-riding. Nubia probably actually innovated the warfare-use of elephants. Almost certainly, Nubians used elephants in this way before North Africans and Mediterraneans. The Greeks and Romans (as well as the Egyptians and Persians) thus hired Nubians as mercenaries, or encouraged them to join their armies. In Greece, they painted Nubian soldiers on vases.

But Greeks and Romans also characterised Nubians as wise, noble, just, and pious, their cities as impressive, and their society as wealthy, advanced, and influential. The fifth-century BC Greek historian Herodotus noted the Nubians' piety. He said they worshipped Zeus (i.e. Amun) and Dionysus (i.e. Osiris). He also called Meroë a 'great city'[12]. Herodotus spoke fondly, too, of the 'Macrobians' – ancient Somalis – saying that they are the tallest and most beautiful people on earth, and that their king is profoundly just. The first-century BC Greek historian Diodorus Siculus had met Nubian ambassadors in Egypt. He wrote that the Nubians were first-rate, wise and pious, which is why the gods favoured them. He also noted that they invented many Egyptian customs, including certain funerary rituals, the roles of priests, statue designs, and writing forms. The first-century BC Greek geographer Strabo spoke highly of the eighth-century BC Nubian ruler Piankhy, and included him in his list of the world's greatest conquerors. In his fourth-century AD romance novel, *Aethiopica* (*'Ethiopian Story'*), the Syrian-Greek author Heliodorus of Emesa describes the Nubian king, Hydaspes, as generous, just and peaceful. Hydaspes refuses to kill his enemies and orders his soldiers to take them alive. He also banned human sacrifice and refused to invade others' countries, saying he coveted neither their land nor resources. The first-century AD Roman historian Flavius Josephus described Meroë as a powerful, independent state. The first-century AD Roman philosopher Seneca the Younger described the Nubians as just. The first-century AD Roman naturalist Pliny the Elder described them as wise.

In Renaissance Europe, too, generally, dark-skinned Africans weren't discriminated against. Like in early Virginia, African and European servants had similar lives. That Africans had particular talents or skills was appreciated. These skills were welcomed in different parts of society, where the Africans who possessed them could rise high. Great storytellers became eminent poets and preachers. Great warriors became weapons or sports instructors, or soldiers – even captains. Great drummers became court musicians.

Moreover, African rulers and ambassadors were welcomed with just as much pomp and ceremony as European ones. The story of Prester John – a powerful and pious medieval Ethiopian Christian king – and depictions of one of the Three Wise Men, Balthazar, as a dark-skinned African, signify an appreciation for the existence of wealthy, sophisticated, and important African civilisations.

As we'll see below with the example of Alessandro de' Medici, individuals with African heritage could even become rulers in Renaissance Europe.

Alessandro was born out of wedlock in Florence in 1512. His father was Lorenzo de' Medici, and his mother was Simunetta, a free African who'd worked in the Medici household.

In 1516, Lorenzo became the Medici's chief representative in Florence – essentially, Florence's ruler. His predecessor, and uncle, Giuliano de' Medici, had only had a son, who was also born out of wedlock in 1511 to a noblewoman from the Italian city of Urbino. This son's name was Ippolito.

When Lorenzo died in 1519, Alessandro and Ippolito were the only Medicis who could succeed him. The only child Lorenzo had had with his wife was a daughter, Catherine.

Thus, Ippolito, being older than Alessandro, was groomed as heir, and Alessandro as 'spare'. On the day Lorenzo died, both were legitimised. Ippolito was then made a lord in Naples and archbishop of Avignon. Meanwhile, in the Roman home of Alfonsina, his wealthy paternal grandma, Alessandro was given a first-class education. He was destined for either the military or the Papacy. In 1522, Alessandro was made 'Illustrious Duke of the City of Penne'[13]. In 1524, Ippolito was set up in the Medici's palace in Florence, and was then introduced to elite politicians, and made to do important state duties, including attending council meetings, and entertaining ambassadors.

But a reversal in the Medici's fortunes would change everything.

In May 1527, in Rome, the soldiers of Charles V – king of Spain, and Holy Roman Emperor, which meant he also ruled Germany and the Netherlands – mutinied because they allegedly hadn't been paid. They also besieged the Pope, Clement VII i.e. Giulio de' Medici, in his castle, and sacked Rome. When news of these events reached Florence, the Medici's pro-republican enemies kicked them and their supporters out of power. Ippolito was taken in secret to a villa just outside Florence.

In about early 1528, Clement managed to escape to the tiny hilltop town of Orvieto, north of Rome. About half a year later, when Clement's French allies beat back Charles's mutinying soldiers, he returned to Rome. Still, he was dismayed at the Medici's change in circumstance. In early 1529, he became deathly ill. With Florence all but lost, instead of making Ippolito the Medici's chief representative there, Clement made him a cardinal, hoping he'd one day become Pope.

Unexpectedly, though, Clement recovered. Then, in the summer of 1529, he made a deal with Charles V – the Treaty of Bologna. In exchange for Clement giving Charles more power in Italy, Charles would help the Medici win back Florence. To seal this treaty, Alessandro, now the only Medici heir who could marry, and rule Florence once it had been won back, was betrothed to Charles's seven-year-old daughter, Margaret. (They were wedded in 1536).

In late August 1529, Charles landed in the Italian city of Genoa. Alessandro and Ippolito were part of the delegation that greeted him.

In October 1529, Charles's troops besieged Florence. By August 1530, the pro-republicans, having exhausted their resources, surrendered. In exchange for pardons from the Medici, the pro-republicans let the Medici return to Florence, and Charles decide the new Florentine government.

Meanwhile, ceremonies were held to formalise the Treaty of Bologna. In these, Alessandro, as both Charles V's future son-in-law and soon-to-be ruler of Florence, was given important duties. In the Christmas Eve ceremonies, Alessandro was given the honour of carrying the water the Pope used to cleanse himself. This was the most prestigious role a non-clergyman could perform, and, apart from Charles V himself, made Alessandro the highest-ranking layman present.

In Charles's Iron Crown coronation in February 1530,

Alessandro was given the privilege of carrying the orb – a golden globe, with jewels delineating Asia, Africa, and Europe.

The now eighteen-year-old Alessandro was handsome, athletic, and, above all, charming. '[He's] well-built, stocky, dark-coloured and with a large nose,'[14] wrote one Italian observer. '[He] appears clever, and has this quality: he knows how to accommodate the nature and will of [Pope Clement] than does [Ippolito],' wrote the Venetian ambassador in 1531. '[Pope Clement] has openly shown me that he loves [Alessandro], and holds him in higher account.'[15] The ladies, too, loved Alessandro. Observers commented on how they flocked round him, and how he seduced them. Others rumoured that Alessandro adventured round Florence, sleeping with all manner of women, from married aristocrats to less-noble singletons to even virgins in convents, but evidence for much of this is sparse.

Alessandro's appointments made him extraordinarily wealthy. He had over two hundred courtiers, all of whom wore expensive silks, satins and velvets. These courtiers included fourteen personal attendants (each but one of which had his own personal servants), five chaplains, sixteen pages and their master, a furrier, an armourer, a tailor, a shoe-maker, a painter, a gem-cutter, a gilder, a paymaster, a sommelier, a barber, a mace-bearer, four heralds, a fencing master, over fifty people who looked after Alessandro's horses and dogs, soldiers, messengers, kitchen staff, musicians, *and* a jester. A keen hunter, Alessandro also had an extensive weapons collection, including gilded hand-guns and two-handed swords.

In late 1530, Charles V, very much impressed by Alessandro, invited him on his tour of Germany. Alessandro was meant to stay only about a week, but he so further charmed his future father-in-law that the latter induced him to stay longer. In total, Alessandro spent *six months* with Charles V. 'Many write that the Emperor loves [Alessandro] greatly – and not as a son-in-law but as a son,'[16] wrote one Italian observer.

Charles and Alessandro travelled to Charles's other territories, like Belgium. They feasted, jousted and hunted. In one tournament, Alessandro broke fourteen lances. '[I]n these jousts here, no one has borne himself better than Duke Alessandro,' wrote one Italian observer in the Belgian city of Ghent. 'It makes me glad to be Italian, especially when I hear the Spanish praise him.'[17]

Merely a month into Alessandro and Charles's travels, Charles announced that a Medici dynasty, headed by Alessandro and Charles's daughter Margaret, and passed down to their children, would rule Florence. Charles also announced that he'd give this dynasty his full political and military support.

Alessandro returned to Florence in summer 1531.

As leaving presents, Charles gave Alessandro a Moorish sword with a scabbard and pure gold hilt, a pair of fine horses, elaborate harnesses, and a gold pair of Moorish-style spurs. Meanwhile, Margaret gave him a gold chain with a ruby pendant.

In Florence itself, an eagerly awaiting crowd met Alessandro. Overjoyed at his return, and the peace Charles V had brokered between the Medici and the pro-republicans, the Florentines partied, attending masquerades, letting off fireworks, and firing gun salutes.

On the day Alessandro was to be made officially Florence's ruler, he travelled with Charles V's ambassador to Italy and the *papal nuncio* (Pope's envoy in Florence) to the Palazzo Vecchio – the building that is the heart of Florence's government. '*Palle, Palle*, Medici, Medici, *Viva, Viva*[!]'[18] ('Long live the Medici!') shouted the crowd.

In the oldest part of the Vecchio, Florence's ruling council and magistrates were gathered. Both Charles's ambassador and the chancellor of Florence announced Charles's decision for the city's rulership, which was accepted, wrote one observer, with 'universal satisfaction'[19].

Alessandro was then handed the key to Florence's fortresses. He then made a speech, in which he thanked Charles V, and pledged to him his loyalty and everlasting service. To Florence, he promised, said one observer, 'entire justice and every best comportment that he owed to his fatherland . . . a fatherland that had elected him to such honour and to a perpetual dictatorship, and that was so noble, and dignified, and full of such excellent personages and treasures.'[20]

After the ceremony, Alessandro donated to religious institutions. He announced a cut in grain price. Fires were lit all around the city. Prisoners were pardoned. Masses were held.

Pope Clement was absolutely delighted with Alessandro's achievements. After Alessandro's election as Florence's ruler, Clement worked behind the scenes to increase Alessandro's power even more.

In 1532, Clement pushed for a reform of Florence's constitution, removing any remaining checks and balances that might have stalled Alessandro. The Supreme Magistracy – a governmental body made up of Alessandro, his lieutenant and a handful of councillors – obtained unbridled power, including the ability to handpick the members of Florence's councils. Due to these changes, Alessandro was no longer simply the Medici's chief representative in Florence, but, on 1 May 1532, became officially its prince, and the first person *ever* to be given the title Duke of Florence.

As can be seen from the above, even in Europe, at a time when some Europeans were enslaving and trafficking some Africans, Alessandro faced *no* discrimination because of his African heritage. Few even talked about it.

Alessandro's heritage didn't prevent Clement from legitimising him, grooming him into a leader, making him the Medici heir and Duke of Florence, and favouring him over the non-African Ippolito. Alessandro's African heritage also didn't prevent Charles V from accepting him as the Medici heir, spending time with him, loving him, marrying him to his daughter, and installing him as the head of a new Florentine dynasty.

Even those who, for one reason or another, sought to oppose Alessandro hardly mentioned his African heritage, and never put it forward as a reason he was unfit to rule. Rather, the only issue these opposers had with Alessandro's ancestry was that he was born of a servant, i.e. a non-aristocrat. However, that she was African specifically was immaterial. To Renaissance Italy, enslaved people from all over the world, including Arabia, Turkey, the Balkans, and North and West Africa, were trafficked. Alessandro's mother may have been a Greek, Turkish, or Eastern-European servant, and his opposers still would have held it against him. Sometimes, to emphasise that Alessandro's blood was neither fully aristocratic nor Italian, they called him 'the mule' or the 'Moor'. The latter was an ethnic term that Europeans applied to everyone from dark-skinned East Africans to light-skinned North Africans to olive-skinned Andalusian Muslims.

Even Ippolito, who turned out to be Alessandro's bitterest enemy, wasn't racist towards him. As we'll see below by following Ippolito's story, he was mostly jealous.

*

In 1537, aged only twenty-six, Alessandro was brutally murdered.

Ippolito had always coveted the position of Florence's ruler. He'd always felt this position was his birthright. Not only was he older than Alessandro, but despite also being born out of wedlock, Ippolito felt he had a greater claim to this position because his mother was a noblewoman, not a mere servant. Moreover, his father, Giuliano de' Medici, had been older than, and uncle to, Alessandro's father, Lorenzo de' Medici, and had also been the Medici's chief representative in Florence first.

Ippolito also resented the Church, because he'd never wanted to be Pope, let alone a cardinal. In 1530, he skipped the College of Cardinals' regular meeting, going hunting instead. This annoyed Pope Clement, who felt Ippolito's misbehaviour was embarrassing the Medici. To punish Ippolito for skipping the meeting, Clement cut him off, and refused to pay his debts. Just beforehand, Clement had made Alessandro governor of the Italian town of Spoleto, which had increased Alessandro's income.

In April 1531, Ippolito travelled from Rome to Florence with a few trusted men. There were rumours that he planned to seize Florence, and that the French king – an enemy of Charles V – backed him. Alarmed, Clement ordered Florence's commander to ready his troops. He was furious. Ippolito threatened the alliance – that is, the 1529 Treaty of Bologna – Clement had made with Charles. Clement sent a cardinal to intercept his nephew. Ippolito told the cardinal that he only wanted to talk to Alessandro. But this was probably a lie, as, by this time, Alessandro was touring Europe with Charles V, and everybody close to Clement knew this. To get Ippolito to return to Rome, Clement paid his debts, and increased his income.

But, in July 1532, painfully aware that Ippolito would continue to be a source of trouble, especially since Alessandro was now back in Florence, Clement sent him as *legate a latere* – a high-ranking Papal diplomat – to Hungary, where Charles V was.

In October 1532, Charles's Italian troops, angry at not having been paid, started marching from Hungary back to Italy. Ippolito, seeing an opportunity to sneak back into Florence, followed them. At one point during the march, Ippolito rode out ahead of four hundred gunners. Thinking Ippolito was leading the gunners in an attack on Florence, Charles V's officers arrested him.

Clement was mortified.

Nearly crying, he complained to Charles's ambassadors of being disrespected. They replied that the arrest had been a mistake, and Charles, who didn't know about it, hadn't ordered it. But, the ambassadors added, it had probably been sensible to arrest Ippolito, because everyone knew he wanted Florence, and could very well have been leading an attack. On Charles's orders,

Ippolito was freed. He went to Venice, where he consoled him-self with a courtesan, and plotted Alessandro's downfall with Florentine allies.

In January 1534, Ippolito returned to Rome, angry, with an abscess on his leg, and syphilis. In summer 1534, he sent Medici agents to ask Charles V what he thought of replacing Alessandro as Duke of Florence with Ippolito. Charles responded that such a change would only make Florence unstable, and that Ippolito should remain a cardinal. If Ippolito behaved, said Charles, he – Charles – would be more likely to back Ippolito's election as Pope.

But, in September 1534, Pope Clement, who had fallen ill, died, and the new non-Medici Pope, Paul III, wanting to promote his own family members, sidelined Ippolito. Now that his prospect of becoming Pope had all but vanished, an increasingly desperate Ippolito attempted to have Alessandro assassinated. The plot was discovered, and the hitman arrested, and tortured till he con-fessed. The hitman's confession, plus his belonging to an impor-tant Florentine family, meant his life was spared. However, Pope Paul III used the plot as an excuse to expel Ippolito from Rome. It was only when some Roman nobles complained that Ippolito was allowed to return.

In August 1535, on his way back to Rome, Ippolito stopped at a house in Itri, a small town halfway between Rome and Naples.

He ate a light dinner of chicken broth and bread.

He fell ill.

A few days later, he was dead.

He'd been poisoned.

In his death throes, Ippolito had accused his steward, Giovan Andrea. After Ippolito died, his attendants tortured Andrea, tying his hands behind his back, and hanging him by his wrists until his shoulders dislocated. Andrea confessed that Alessandro's courtier had ordered him to poison Ippolito, saying that this would be to Alessandro's 'great pleasure'[21].

Alessandro's government bribed or threatened a senior Roman

judge to rule Andrea's confession as invalid, because it had been obtained by torture. They also bribed or threatened the doctor that had performed Ippolito's autopsy to change his statement that he'd detected poison. When Andrea was released, he was spirited off to Florence, where he remained under Alessandro's protection.

Now that Ippolito was dead, Alessandro mistakenly believed he was no longer a threat and let down his guard. Alessandro forgot that there remained still some of Ippolito's determined agents.

One of these agents was Lorenzino ('Little Lorenzo') de' Medici, Alessandro's and Ippolito's distant cousin.

Born in 1514, Lorenzino belonged to the Medici's junior branch. He was pale, well-mannered and intelligent. By eighteen, he was fluent in Latin and Greek. People called him 'The Philosopher'.

Lorenzino's and the main Medici families didn't get on. The former Pope Clement, who belonged to the main Medici family, gave Lorenzino's family little financial support, and even refused to pay back fully a loan from Lorenzino's uncle. Then, in 1533, Clement revoked Lorenzino's appointment as governor of Fano, a town in east Italy, and gave it instead to a cardinal who'd bribed him for it.

In 1534, Lorenzino acted out, secretly removing the heads of several Roman statues. An angry Clement, not thinking it could be Lorenzino, ordered that, when found, the culprit be executed without trial. Ippolito, who'd discovered that the culprit was indeed Lorenzino, privately told this to Clement. But he also begged Clement to take it easy on Lorenzino, who was young, had only wanted busts like his ancestors', and, with time, would change. Convinced not so much by Ippolito's appeal, but by a desire not to scandalise further the Medici, Clement dropped the matter, sparing Lorenzino.

But word that Lorenzino was the culprit eventually got out. Rome's lawmakers, even angrier than Clement at the vandalism, expelled Lorenzino from Rome, and decreed that any Roman who killed him wouldn't just avoid punishment but would be rewarded. Lorenzino fled to Florence and managed to join Alessandro's entourage.

Alessandro and Lorenzino soon became good friends, and Lorenzino even agreed to spy for the duke. But, because Ippolito had essentially saved his life, Lorenzino's true allegiance would always lie with Ippolito. Therefore, Lorenzino became rather a double agent, pretending to spy for Alessandro, when he was spying *on* Alessandro for Ippolito, looking for an opportunity to get rid of him.

Two years after Ippolito's unexpected death in 1535, Lorenzino made his move. On the night of 5 January 1537, Lorenzino convinced Alessandro that Caterina de' Ginori, a beautiful noble-woman whose husband was in Naples on business, could be per-suaded to sleep with Alessandro, and suggested setting up a meet. Lorenzino told Alessandro to head to his – Lorenzino's – room in Alessandro's palace, and that he'd sneak in Caterina by the back door. When Alessandro reached Lorenzino's room, he took off his sword, lay on the bed and soon fell asleep.

Lorenzino entered the room.

He moved Alessandro's sword away from the bed.

Then, he ushered in his accomplice, Scoronconcolo, an impov-erished thug he'd groomed into his henchman.

They crept up to the sleeping Alessandro.

Lorenzino drew his sword and stabbed Alessandro in the stomach.

Alessandro lurched forward and made for the door. But Scoronconcolo drew his knife and slashed Alessandro's left cheek.

Lorenzino pushed his cousin back onto the bed and leapt on top of him. He forced his hand over Alessandro's mouth to cover his screams.

Alessandro bit Lorenzino's thumb and Lorenzino rolled off him.

They struggled.

With his knife, Scoronconcolo aimed carefully and stabbed Alessandro in the throat.

The floor was flooded with blood.

The assassins fled.

A month later, Alessandro was buried next to his father, Lorenzo de' Medici.

Lorenzino made it to Mirandola, a city in northern Italy. When his role in Alessandro's murder was discovered, he became in Florence *persona non grata*. The Florentines labelled him a traitor and nicknamed him 'Lorenzaccio' ('bad Lorenzo'). In Florence, above the fortress gates, someone painted Lorenzino hanging by one foot. The Florentine government put a bounty on his head. Unable to return to Florence, Lorenzino spent ten years roaming Italy, Turkey and France, trying to put together a coalition that would defeat Florence's government. All the while, Charles V's spies tailed him. In 1548, they assassinated Lorenzino.

In this chapter, we've seen that in African peoples' histories, racism wasn't widespread or longstanding. Ideas about Africans' natural inferiority proliferated mainly in Western Europe in the eighteenth and nineteenth centuries. In preceding eras, Europeans didn't necessarily think that Africans were naturally inferior to every other people. Because of the eighteenth-century English planter and enslaver Edward Long's background, and his extensive use of cultural and biological detail when arguing for Africans' natural inferiority in his book, *The History of Jamaica*, this book, more than most, encouraged the spread of racist ideas. But, as we've seen from the sixteenth-century Alessandro de' Medici's story, in Europe, before Long's day, being African meant little to no discrimination. An African could be legitimised in a powerful family, be married to a European princess, and even become a European ruler.

Just as, in this chapter, we tackled the general historical misunderstanding that racism is an age-old phenomenon, in our final chapter, we're going to tackle another – namely, that in the seventeenth and eighteenth centuries, like European merchants, every African ruler sought to profit from the Transatlantic Slave Trade. More specifically, we're going to look at how, in the eighteenth century, one African king in particular – Agaja, of the Dahomey kingdom (now Benin) – didn't just seek *not* to profit from this trade, but tried to stop it.

10

AN AFRICAN END TO SLAVERY

Born in 1673, Agaja was crowned king of Dahomey in 1708.

He was of average height, broad-shouldered and muscular. He was also handsome and majestic but had smallpox scars on his face.

He was charming and magnanimous. 'Though I do nothing for [His Majesty], he has put me into a house, and given me half a dozen men and women servants,'[1] wrote Bulfinch Lambe, a Royal African Company agent who lived with Agaja for three years. 'His Majesty [also] ordered me a horse, and told me, whenever he went out, I should go with him.'[2] 'He ... gives great encouragement to all [African] strangers, and is extremely kind to some Malay people who are now here.'[3]

As well as charming and magnanimous, Agaja was curious, intelligent and fun-loving. He taught himself to read and write English. '[He also] takes great delight in trifling toys and whims,'[4] wrote Lambe. 'His Majesty ... [once] got from me the greatest part of [my] paper, having a notion in his head of a kite, which, though I told him was only fit for boys to play with, yet he says, I must make one for him and [me] to play with.'[5]

Also, Agaja was extraordinarily wealthy. He had eleven palaces, two of which were, said Lambe, 'in circumference larger than St James's Park[.]'[6] Agaja was carried between these palaces in, 'a fine hammock with gilded awnings and curtains.'[7] He also owned, 'great quantities of plates, wrought gold and other rich things, also all sorts of fine gowns, cloaks, hats, caps ... [and] brandy[.]'[8] Moreover, he had, 'at least two thousand wives ... [who] wear rich silk waist-cloths[.]'[9]

When Agaja held court, he wore, wrote Archibald Dalzel, an eighteenth-century Scottish doctor, slave trader and historian, 'a gown, flowered with gold, that reached to his ankles; [a] European embroidered hat; and sandals on his feet.'[10] He sat in, 'a fine gilt chair,'[11] and had, '[t]hree large umbrellas . . . held over his head, by women, to shade him from the sun . . . [These] women were finely dressed . . . their arms were adorned with many large . . . bracelets of gold . . . ; and round their necks, and in their hair, were [an] abundance of beads, of diverse colours[.]'[12]

Lastly, Agaja was a highly skilled and ruthless leader and military commander, with one of the best West African armies at the time. '[This army] was not numerous . . . but they were select troops, both brave and well disciplined, led by . . . experienced officers,'[13] wrote one French observer. '[A]rmed with muskets, cutting swords, and shields[, Agaja's troops] were divided into companies; each having their proper officers and colours,' wrote Dalzel. 'Their marching was in a much regular order than . . . ever seen before[.]'[14] Agaja also had his own spy network, the *Agbadjigbeto*. '[He has, too,] twenty-five cannon[s], some of which are upwards of a thousand weight,'[15] wrote Lambe.

In the 1720s, Agaja invaded the nearby kingdoms of Allada and Whydah.

Allada was then known as the 'father-kingdom' of both Dahomey and Whydah. This was because, in Alladan, Dahomean, and Whydah tradition, their kings were descended from a prince who had migrated to, and ruled, Allada. Therefore, as the Alladan kings occupied the original ancestor's throne, they were seen as the 'fathers' of Dahomey's and Whydah's kings. This meant that, traditionally, the latter had to show respect and deference to the former. Both Dahomey and Whydah even paid tributes to Allada.

Allada was, wrote Dalzel, 'beautiful . . . abound[ing] with hill and dale . . . [and had an] army consist[ing] of more than fifty thousand men.'[16] Meanwhile, Whydah was a 'great park,'[17] whose 'beauty and fertility [were] almost beyond description.'[18] '[Having] a very rich soil, and well cultivated by [its] inhabitants, [Whydah] looked like an entire garden,'[19] wrote William Snelgrave, an eighteenth-century English slave trader. '[It] appeared full of towns and villages,'[20] Snelgrave continued, and was, wrote Dalzel, 'so populous, that one village contained as many inhabitants as a whole kingdom on the Gold Coast [i.e. Ghana].'[21] '[The Whydah] could have [easily] brought at least one hundred thousand men into the field [of battle],'[22] said Snelgrave.

Agaja invaded Allada in March 1724. In one day, he reached its capital, and defeated and captured its king, Soso. Two days later, he beheaded Soso, and his army set Soso's palace on fire and looted everything they could, including the houses of Alladan chiefs. Thousands of Alladans were slain and captured. '[T]here was scarce any stirring for bodies without heads, and had it rained blood, it could not have lain thicker on the ground,'[23] wrote Lambe.

In 1727, Agaja invaded Whydah. Whydah's king, Huffon, was the opposite of Agaja. Born in 1695, Huffon was forcibly crowned king of Whydah when he was only thirteen. Ordinarily, in Whydah, when the heir was a minor, the Gogan ('Lord') of Savi – Whydah's capital – was supposed to rule as regent until the former came of age. But, in Huffon's case, a Whydah chief called Assu, who intended to rule Whydah through Huffon, rebelled against and defeated the Gogan of Savi, and installed Huffon as puppet king.

To ensure Huffon's dependence on and loyalty to him, Assu taught the young king nothing about kingship, and spoilt him. By the time he was thirty, Huffon was overweight, arrogant and incompetent. Rather than ruling his kingdom, he preferred to be, wrote Dalzel, 'shut up in his [harem], amongst thousands of women.'[24] The result was that Whydah's officials, wrote Snelgrave, 'played the petty tyrants, often falling out, and pursuing their particular interests, without regarding the good of their King or Country.'[25]

Huffon tried to bring these officials in line, applying autocratic laws and customs. This included that, when speaking to him, his subjects had to be prostrate on the ground. But it was too late. The officials' lack of respect for Huffon meant that they only resented his disciplinary actions. '[N]ot one of [these officials] ... minds any law [Huffon] makes,' wrote an English observer. '[S]ome of the greatest men in [Whydah] ... assure me [that] if [Huffon] continues his tyranny much longer, they'll be obliged to take a violent course with him.'[26] By 1726, Huffon had faced at least two rebellions, one of which had forced him to flee Savi for a short while.

The night before his attack on Whydah, Agaja sent orders to his daughter, Na Gueze, who, for about ten years, had been married to Huffon, to pour water on the gunpowder in Whydah's arsenal.

The next day, Agaja marched into north Whydah. When the governor of north Whydah, Lord Appragah, saw the Dahomeans approaching, he sent a messenger to Savi to ask for Huffon's support. But Appragah's enemies at court convinced Huffon to refuse. Appragah decided to fight Agaja alone, and put up a little resistance, but was soon overpowered and surrendered. Admiring Appragah's bravery, Agaja, wrote Snelgrave, 'received him very kindly.'[27]

Agaja continued marching into Whydah, and, by the afternoon, had reached the river that was only half a mile away from Savi. Only at one point was this river shallow enough to be crossed. Savi was therefore very easy to defend, because almost all you had to do was station a few hundred soldiers in front of this point. But Huffon and his officials hadn't even done *that*.

Agaja ordered two hundred of his soldiers to cross the river. When they did so without encountering any opposition, they felt emboldened to continue to Savi without the rest of Agaja's army, or even awaiting further orders!

Shouting and playing their battlefield musical instruments, the two hundred reached Savi by about three o'clock. '[Savi's guards] were almost all asleep,' wrote Snelgrave. '[B]ut being roused by the noise of the enemy's music and shouts, they fled into the town, reporting that . . . the Dahomean army [had] got over the river.'[28]

The Whydahs scattered. Huffon had attendants carry him on a hammock to the coast. There, they boarded canoes and sailed safely to nearby islands. '[B]ut a great many [Whydahs] that could not have the same benefit . . . drowned . . . in attempting to swim to [these islands],'[29] wrote Snelgrave.

The two hundred marched into Huffon's palace, looted it and set it ablaze. Over the next five days, the rest of Agaja's army marched into Savi, and those Whydah who could not escape were either killed or captured. In total, in Savi, the Dahomeans slayed almost five thousand Whydahs. The ground, wrote Snelgrave, '[was] strew[n] with their bones.'[30] The Dahomeans then marched ten thousand imprisoned Whydahs to Allada.

Agaja was ecstatic that it had taken only two hundred of his soldiers to defeat a nation as big and populous as Whydah. He rewarded his officers handsomely, and then had four thousand of the imprisoned Whydahs executed. '[T]wo heaps of [the executed Whydahs'] heads [were] piled up on two large stages, and [soon] covered with swarms of . . . flies,'[31] wrote Dalzel.

To prevent Huffon and any other Whydah from returning to their kingdom, Agaja stationed in Whydah a large regiment. Cut off from their homeland and its resources, Whydah refugees were, wrote Dalzel, 'reduced to the utmost extremity, and obliged to sell their servants, and even their children to purchase subsistence from the neighbouring [peoples].'[32]

But why did Agaja rain so much destruction on Allada and Whydah?

Since the late seventeenth century, both Allada and Whydah had been important trade partners of Europeans, including the Portuguese, Dutch, French and English. By the early eighteenth century, Europeans had established trade headquarters in Whydah. They'd also signed a treaty declaring that, even if their countries were at war, they wouldn't attack each other's ships docked at Whydah's ports. In 1709, to augment their trade with Whydah, the English Royal African Company gifted Huffon a crown. Meanwhile, the French gifted him an entire ship *and* its cargo.

For European goods, the Alladans and Whydahs traded mainly enslaved Africans. By the end of the seventeenth century, both Whydah and Allada were 'exporting' annually 20,000 enslaved Africans. Europeans called the region of these kingdoms the 'Slave Coast' because it was, wrote Snelgrave, 'the principal part of all the [West African coast] for the slave trade. It was a pleasure to deal with them.'[33]

According to Dalzel, the reason why Agaja conquered Allada and Whydah was that he wanted to monopolise this trade with Europeans, which would mean an increase in the number of good-quality European weaponry – guns especially – he imported, allowing him to make Dahomey even more formidable.

Indeed, just before he invaded Allada in 1724, Agaja had sent ambassadors to both Allada's king, Soso, and Huffon, asking for a greater share of the European trade. But he'd been rebuffed. '[I]n an audience I had of [Huffon], soon after the [Dahomean] ambassador's departure, he told me; if [Agaja] should [then] offer to invade him, he would not . . . cut off [Agaja's] head[, as is customary,] but . . . keep him for a slave to do the vilest [duties],'[34] wrote Snelgrave. 'This foolish speech, which, no doubt, reached [Agaja's] ears . . . probably [angered] him,'[35] wrote Dalzel.

However, as we'll see in the next section, this answer fails to explain Agaja's actions following his conquests of Allada and Whydah. What these actions demonstrate is that, far from wanting to trade more with Europeans, Agaja conquered Allada and Whydah because he wanted to put an *end* to European trade in his region.

*

When Agaja invaded Allada and Whydah, he thought nothing of preserving their trading infrastructures, selling to Europeans those Alladans and Whydahs he captured, or even maintaining good relationships with Europeans. He destroyed ports and slaving-forts, had thousands of people executed who otherwise might have been sold, and even took Europeans prisoner.

By 1735, Agaja had destroyed most ports and forts in Allada and Whydah that had survived his invasions and had even expelled Europeans from his region, including the Dutch and the French. He'd also had arrested, and sometimes even executed, Dahomeans, including his chief jailer, that sold or attempted to sell other Africans into slavery. He ordered his soldiers to stop African slave traders who marched enslaved Africans to the coast. When Europeans begged him to hire experienced Whydah slave traders, he refused. To prevent Europeans from going to other kingdoms to trade enslaved Africans, he stationed soldiers on his borders with instructions to stop any foreigners from leaving. Lastly, he ensured that Europeans discussed all trade matters exclusively with him. He often demanded goods on credit, called outrageous prices and levied heavy customs. If defied, he punished Europeans with expulsion.

Agaja's measures to reduce European trade in his region soon bore fruit. 'It was from this impolitic conduct, of destroying the nations he subdued, that the European trade ... gradually fell off,'[36] wrote Dalzel. '[F]rom two thousand slaves a year, transported from Whydah only, in 1726, the greatest number now sent off from this and the two great kingdoms of Allada and Dahomey, together with several other small ones united to them, is only five thousand five hundred; little more than one-fourth part of the former.'[37]

As for why Agaja wanted to put an end to this European trade, the answer is simpler. Since Dogbagri-Genu, Agaja's grandfather, had founded Dahomey in 1625, the Dahomeans had hated Allada,

Europeans, and the trade in enslaved Africans that encouraged the latter to interfere in their region.

Before he founded Dahomey, Dogbagri-Genu was an Alladan prince. He had an older brother, Te-Agbalin, with whom he disagreed about many things. Chief among these was whether to welcome the Dutch, already established further west, to Allada.

Dogbagri-Genu had heard of the upheaval the Dutch's presence caused in the western kingdoms and was against welcoming them. On the other hand, Te-Agbalin, who saw mostly the Dutch's wealth, and feared their strength, was in support of it.

Most Alladans agreed with Dogbagri-Genu. When, by 1620, Kokpon – the Alladan king, and Dogbagri-Genu and Te-Agbalin's father – died, the Alladans elected Dogbagri-Genu king. Behind his brother's back, Te-Agbalin met the Dutch, and, with their support, deposed and exiled Dogbagri-Genu, seizing the throne for himself.

Dogbagri-Genu and his supporters migrated north to the Igede kingdom, where they founded Dahomey.

The Dahomeans sought revenge against the Alladans and Europeans. In the late seventeenth century, the Dahomeans conquered and shut down various slave-trading routes, preventing Alladan slave traders from bringing to the coast enslaved Africans. In 1715 – some ten years before he conquered it – Agaja stopped paying the customary tribute to Allada.

Unfortunately, though, Agaja was unable to succeed in finishing what his ancestors had started.

Between 1725 and 1740, the Oyo – i.e. Yoruba based in the city-state of Oyo in what's now Nigeria – crushed Dahomey no less than *five* times.

In the eighteenth century, Oyo was arguably the most powerful West African kingdom. '[Oyo's] people are numerous and warlike, and ... their arm[y] totally consist[s] of cavalry,'[38] wrote Dalzel. This cavalry was perhaps Oyo's most famous, and terrifying, feature. '[Besides being] well mounted, [Oyo's cavalry was] armed with bows, javelins, and cutting swords ... [, was] courageous, and had spread terror through the adjacent countries.'[39]

Like Dahomey and Whydah, Oyo had its own father-kingdom – the Yoruba city-state of Ife. Unlike Dahomey's king, though, Oyo's *Alafin* ('king') respected deeply his father-kingdom. Thus, he was angry at Dahomey, and particularly at Agaja, for having disregarded Allada, by, for instance, ceasing to pay tribute, and decided to punish them.

In 1726, the *Alafin* invaded Dahomey. Agaja, wrote Dalzel, '[with] daring spirit[,] marched boldly to face the [Oyo]; and, on meeting them, supported such a fire from his musketry as effectually affrighted the horses so that their riders could never make [a] regular charge[.]'[40] But the Oyo were, said Dalzel, 'many thousands,'[41] and, having fought for four days outnumbered, Agaja was in danger of losing the battle.

'[A]t this critical moment[,] a stratagem entered the mind of [Agaja], worthy of the most enlightened general,'[42] continued Dalzel. At night, Agaja collected from his war camp brandy – which he'd obtained from the French – and other treasures, and took them to a nearby town, where he placed them. He then retreated from both this town and his camp.

The next morning, the Oyo, seeing that the Dahomeans weren't at their camp, and thinking that the Dahomeans had fled, and that they – the Oyo – had won the battle, pillaged the town. Many of them drank the brandy, and got so drunk that they passed out. 'At this juncture, the Dahomeans, who had timely intimation of the [Oyo's] disorder, fell upon them with redoubled fury, destroyed a great number, [and] completely routed the rest,' wrote Dalzel. '[T]hose that escaped, owed their safety to their horses.'[43]

Although he'd won, Agaja was aware that the Oyo were much stronger than Dahomey, and he tried to make peace with them, sending the *Alafin* gift-laden ambassadors. However, unsure that the *Alafin* would go for this, Agaja made plans in case the former decided to invade Dahomey again.

Agaja was right to be prepared. In early 1728, in Oyo, wrote Dalzel, '[a] great army was raised with all expedition, and ordered to make a second descent on Dahomey.'[44] Heavily weakened from the previous battle, Agaja merely retreated to the forest hideouts he'd earlier prepared. 'The [Oyo], disappointed [that Agaja had escaped], fought the Dahomeans in [these] retreats, and destroyed many of them,' wrote Dalzel. '[B]ut [the Dahomeans] bore these hardships with patience, knowing that the rainy season, and [diminishing supplies], would soon drive [the Oyo] away[.]'[45] When, in early May, that season came, the Oyo, as expected, retreated. '[T]he Dahomeans [were left] to ... repair ... their towns and villages, from which they had now been driven several months,'[46] wrote Dalzel.

Meanwhile, the Europeans, who despised Agaja because of his anti-trade policies, exploited the Oyo invasions to re-settle the Whydahs, who, wrote Dalzel, 'had been at once the most com-mercial ... people on the whole coast'.[47]

In 1728, at the request of Dupetitval, a high-ranking French official, several thousand Whydahs came to stay in a French fort in Whydah. For whatever reason, Huffon was not among them. When Agaja discovered this re-settlement following the Oyo's retreat in May, he besieged the fort. Two weeks later, their resources running low, the French abandoned the fort without informing the Whydahs. For two more weeks, the Whydahs resisted Agaja's siege, until their ammunition caught fire and exploded, killing three thousand of them. The Dahomeans then captured the fort.

In 1729, the Oyo invaded Dahomey yet again, forcing Agaja back into his forest retreats. This time, it was Testefole, a high-ranking English official, who encouraged the Whydahs' re-settlement.

More than any other European, Testefole, who was, wrote Dalzel, 'a hot and unthinking man,'[48] hated Agaja because of his anti-trade policies. '[He] was so far exasperated at [these policies], together with the [uncommercial] behaviour of the Dahomean traders ... that he took every opportunity of testifying his displeasure,' wrote Dalzel. 'He treated any of [these Dahomean traders] that came to [his] fort very roughly; [and even] caused one of [Dahomey's] principal men to be whipped at the flag-staff, telling him, when [the chief] complained of this great indignity, that he [Testefole] would serve [Agaja] in the same manner, if he had him in his power. This foolish conduct . . . [soon] lost [Testefole] his life.'[49]

At Testefole's request, in April, Huffon marched into Whydah at the head of a fifteen-thousand-strong army, which included a few thousand Popoes. The Popo were a people of what's now Togo. The English greeted Huffon with gun salutes and feasts and secured him in their fort.

When Agaja learnt of this in June, he collected together what remained of his army following the Oyo's devastating attacks, and, to make it seem larger than it actually was, even ordered, wrote Snelgrave, 'a great number of women to be armed like soldiers, and appointed officers[.]'[50] He then attacked the Whydah-Popo army.

'Huffon, and the Popo general, [met the Dahomeans] . . . with so much vigour,'[51] wrote Dalzel. But, seeing that Agaja seemed to have many more soldiers than they were led to believe, Huffon's soldiers fled. 'The Dahomeans . . . [then] rallied; and . . . [attacked] the rear of Huffon's troops, [routing] them and the Popoes,' wrote Dalzel. '[Huffon himself] took refuge in the English fort, whence, by the connivance of Testefole, he escaped in the night to his former asylum.'[52]

Angered not just that Testefole had helped Huffon escape, but also by his earlier insult, Agaja besieged the English fort a few months later. When, after six hours, he'd failed to capture it, he called off the siege, and returned to Abomey – Dahomey's capital. But he left behind some soldiers to watch the fort in case an opportunity of taking Testefole arose.

That opportunity came that same night, when Testefole snuck out of the fort, probably to board a ship that would take him back to England. Agaja's soldiers snatched Testefole, bound his hands and feet and took him to Agaja. Agaja told his soldiers to do what they wanted with him.

First, these soldiers pretended to ransom Testefole, by which they got from the English many goods. Then, they tortured Testefole, tying him face down to stakes in the ground, slashing his arms, back and legs, and rubbing into the wounds a mixture of salt, pepper and lime juice. They then beheaded and dismembered him.

When the other English officials found out, horrified, they begged Agaja to punish the executioners. But Agaja refused, and, wrote Dalzel, 'only observed . . . that what had been done to Testefole, his own imprudence had brought upon himself; and hoped the [Royal] African Company would send a fitter person to govern their fort in future.'[53]

Testefole had been dealt with, but the Oyo could not be stopped. Their 1730 invasion so destroyed Abomey that Agaja had no choice but to abandon it. He made Allada his new capital and sent the Oyo a peace offering. '[The gift-laden Dahomean ambassadors] were graciously received . . . [and] obtained for [Agaja] a very advantageous peace,'[54] wrote Dalzel. In return for Agaja paying tribute to Oyo annually, the *Alafin* agreed not to attack Agaja again.

However, this didn't mean Agaja's problems were over. Like the Europeans, many Dahomeans, who thought that the point of conquering Allada and Whydah was to obtain a greater share of the European trade, also hated Agaja because of his anti-trade policies. In 1733, 1735 and 1736, these Dahomeans, including the *Mehy* – Dahomey's second-highest official – rebelled against Agaja, aiming to depose him. Mercilessly, Agaja squashed these rebellions, which only increased these Dahomeans' resentment.

Meanwhile, Europeans armed Dahomey's rival kingdoms, and encouraged them to invade and destroy Dahomey, and kill Agaja. In 1737, with Dutch support, the Popo and the Ewe – a people of what's now Ghana – invaded the Whydah city of Igelefe, killed many Dahomeans and destroyed the city.

Having had to deal with both these internal and external conflicts, as well as the Oyo's attacks and European interference, Agaja was distracted from continuing to implement measures that would reduce European trade. Then, all these conflicts so impoverished him that in 1739, he failed to pay the Oyo's tribute and the *Alafin* ruthlessly invaded his lands again. His army and arms too reduced for him even to put up a fight, Agaja could only retreat to his forest hideouts and watch as the Oyo laid waste to his kingdom. In May 1740 – aged sixty-six – Agaja, poor, tired and depressed, died of an unspecified illness.

But his impact, either on European trade or on those around him, was far from negligible. Though this trade continued under Agaja's successors, its volume was much reduced. It never again reached the heights it had attained in the early eighteenth century, when the Alladan and Whydah kings ruled the coast. Because of his ambition, bravery and political and military skill, Agaja was for many later Dahomean kings a role model. Even Europeans, who had cause to dislike him, could not deny his ability. 'Agaja, considered as a conqueror, seems little inferior to any other of that class which has swollen the page of history,' wrote Dalzel. 'Like them he waded to glory through an ocean of innocent blood; and like them experienced the vicissitudes of fortune. Yet he never lost his magnanimity nor wept like Alexander when his general refused to follow him; he knew how to enforce obedience and drove when he could not lead them to conquest.'[55]

CONCLUSION: MOTHERLAND

What a journey we've been on.

Covering hundreds of thousands of years, we travelled to almost every part of Africa.

In East Africa, we evolved with our earliest ancestors. We lived in medieval stone towns with international traders and prayed in stone mosques. We bartered shells for ivory, and that ivory for Iranian bottles, Indian beads, and Chinese pottery. We might have even sailed to these countries themselves.

In North Africa, we met ancient female rulers and warrior-queens. With the best-known among them, we campaigned against and defeated the Romans.

In West Africa, we met these queens' more modern equivalents. We also met the wealthiest person who's ever lived, accompanied him on his splendid pilgrimage, and attended one of the world's first universities he helped found. We also learnt about his court, customs and people, including their guild of hereditary story-tellers. We saw these storytellers' training and the diverse roles they play. We watched their performances and heard their songs, stories and instruments.

We mourned, but also celebrated, our family members' passage from the mortal to the spirit world. We welcomed the most respected of them back. We prayed for their protection and blessings. We learnt of a trickster hero and experienced his exploits. We rooted for him, and he inspired us to seek freedom. We also joined the army of a great conqueror, and his mission to destroy a pernicious trade. First-hand, we saw skill, valour and determination almost unrivalled.

In Central Africa, we consulted oracles and discovered who had bewitched us.

In South Africa, we migrated with Bantu. We encountered long-forgotten hunter-gatherers and gave them knowledge of ironworking and farming, or else forced it on them. We started our journey thousands of years ago in a western rainforest, and eventually spread over most of the continent.

Despite all we've seen, this represents just a fraction of the African past. To demonstrate its richness, other aspects of African peoples' histories and cultures I could have covered in this book include the art of the Yoruba, the architecture of the Shona in Zimbabwe, Christianity in Ethiopia, the migration of the Masai, and the exploits of Shaka Zulu.

And this, really, is the point of the book. There's so much more to the African past than the Transatlantic Slave Trade and colonialism, and, crucially, so much more to these subjects than the victimisation of Africans. Instead of seeing Africans as enslaved people and colonial subjects, we should see them as accomplished traders, travellers, warriors, artists, scholars and rulers, to name but a few. This is not only a more inspirational view of Africans, but a much more accurate one.

My hope is that through this book I've given you a glimpse of this view.

LIST OF IMAGES

1. A contemporary map of Africa. (Calvin Dexter/iStock)
2. *Mansa* Musa, depicted on Abraham Cresques's Catalan Atlas. (Alamy)
3. Léon Benett's illustration of Ibn Battuta and his tour guide in Egypt. In Jules Verne's *Great Travels and Great Travellers. Discovering the Earth*. Page 81. Dates to 1878. (Alamy)
4. 'Portrait of a Humanist' by Venetian artist Sebastiano del Piombo. Dates to 1520. Allegedly depicts Leo Africanus. (Samuel H. Kress Collection, National Gallery of Art)
5. Thirteenth-century Timbuktu astronomy manuscript – Knowledge of the Movement of the Stars and What It Portends in Every Year. (The Picture Art Collection/Alamy)
6. The Golden Stool carried in procession. (Black Star/Alamy)
7. *Egungun* masquerade dance costume. (EMU History/Alamy)
8. The 'Meroë Head'. (© The Trustees of the British Museum)
9. Stela of Kandake Amanishakheto. (Khruner/Wikicommons CC 4.0)
10. Portrait of Queen Njinga. (Alamy)
11. Engraving of Queen Njinga sitting on her attendant, negotiating with the Portuguese governor of Angola. (Bridgeman Images)
12. An example of Urewe ware from Lydenburg, South Africa. (Nkansah Rexford/Wikicommons CC 4.0)

13. Documents – 'Anthony Johnson versus John Casar, Northampton County Court Case, 1655', Document Bank of Virginia. (Alamy)
14. Ming dynasty painting of the giraffe gift for Yongle. Unknown artist's copy of Shen Du's original. (Alamy)
15. Photograph of Mwamaka Sharifu and other students at Nanjing University of Chinese Medicine graduation ceremony. (Imaginechina Limited/Alamy)
16. Ruins of Husuni Kubwa. (Ulrich Doering/Alamy)
17. Inside the Great Mosque of Kilwa. (Jon Arnold Images Ltd/Alamy)
18. Image of Kool Moe Dee. (Michael Benabib/Michael Ochs Archives/Getty Images)
19. Nineteenth-century Wolof griots playing a *kora* and *guimbris*. (Alamy)
20. Eighteenth-century Wolof griot playing a *balafon*. (Alamy)
21. Gold staff with Ananse motif. (Museum of Fine Arts, Houston/Gift of Alfred C. Glassell, Jr./Bridgeman Images)
22. A protestor slaps Rhodes's statue with his belt as the statue is about to be transported away. (Rodger Bosch/AFP via Getty Images)
23. Portrait of Alessandro de' Medici. (Alamy)

SELECT BIBLIOGRAPHY

1. Our Lost Millennia

Allen, A.R., *Leo's Travels in the Sudan: Being the Seventh Book of Leo Africanus Simplified, Abridged and Done into Modern English from the Translation of John Pory* (Oxford, 1962).

Battuta, Ibn, *Travels in Asia and Africa 1325–1354*, trans. and ed. Gibb, Hamilton (London: Broadway House, 1929).

Niane, Djibril (ed.), *General History of Africa IV: Africa from the Twelfth to the Sixteenth Century*, (UNESCO, University of California Press, Heinemann Educational Books, 1984).

Stringer, Chris, *The Origin of Our Species*, (London: Penguin, 2012).

2. How the Dead Still Live

Kopytoff, Igor, 'Ancestors as Elders in Africa', *Africa: Journal of the International African Institute*, Vol. 41, Issue 2, (April 1971), pp. 129–142.

Mbiti, John, *African Religions and Philosophy*, (Nairobi: East African Educational Publishers Ltd., 1969).

Morgan, Stephen and Okyere-Manu, Beatrice, 'The Belief in and Veneration of Ancestors in Akan Traditional Thought: Finding Values for Human Well-being', *Alternation – Interdisciplinary Journal for the Study of the Arts and Humanities in Southern Africa* Special Edition, 30, (November 2020) pp. 11–31.

3. Queenmothers and Warrior-Queens

Heywood, Linda, *Njinga of Angola: Africa's Warrior Queen*, (Harvard, 2017).

Lohwasser, Angelika, 'The Role and Status of Royal Women in Kush', *The Routledge Companion to Women and Monarchy in the Ancient Mediterranean World*, ed. Carney, Elizabeth and Müller, Sabine, (Routledge, 2021), pp. 61-73.

Meyerowitz, Eva, *The Sacred State of the Akan*, (Faber & Faber, 1951).

Török, László, *The Kingdom of Kush: Handbook of the Napatan-Meroitic Civilization*, (Brill: New York, 1997).

4. We Are More Than Skin Colour

Berlin, Ira, *Many Thousands Gone: The First Two Centuries of Slavery in North America*, (Harvard University Press, 1998).

Choudhury, Ananyo *et al.*, 'African Genetic Diversity Provides Novel Insights into Evolutionary History and Local Adaptations', *Human Molecular Genetics*, Vol. 27, Issue R2, (August 2018), pp. R209–R218.

Heine, Bernd and Nurse, Derek, *African Languages: An Introduction*, (Cambridge University Press, 2000).

Phillipson, David, 'The Spread of the Bantu Language', *Scientific American*, Vol. 236, No. 4, (April 1977), pp. 106–115.

5. Merchants, Traders and Navigators

Battuta, Ibn, *Travels in Asia and Africa 1325–1354*, trans. and ed. Gibb, Hamilton (London: Broadway House, 1929).

Middleton, John, *The World of the Swahili: An African Mercantile Civilization*, (New Haven: Yale University Press, 1992).

Middleton, John and Horton, Mark, *The Swahili: The Social Landscape of a Mercantile Society* (John Wiley & Sons Ltd., 2001).

6. Rappers, Singers and Storytellers

Finnegan, Ruth, *Oral Literature in Africa*, (Oxford University Press, 1970).

Hale, Thomas, *Griots and Griottes: Masters of Words and Music*, (Bloomington: Indiana University Press, 1998).

Wald, Elijah, *Talking 'Bout Your Mama: The Dozens, Snaps, and the Deep Roots of Rap*, (Oxford, 2014).

7. Story of the Spider-God

Beckwith, Martha and Roberts, Helen, *Jamaica Anansi Stories*, (New York: The American Folk-lore Society, 1924).

Rattray, Robert, *Akan-Ashanti Folk-Tales*, (Oxford: Clarendon Press, 1930).

Vecsey, Christopher, 'The Exception Who Proves the Rules: Ananse the Akan Trickster', *Journal of Religion in Africa*, Vol. 12, Fasc. 3, (Brill, 1981), pp. 161–177.

Zobel Marshall, Emily, *Anansi's Journey: A Story of Jamaican Cultural Resistance*, (Kingston, Jamaica: University of the West Indies Press, 2012).

8. Wisdom of the Ancients

Evans-Pritchard, Edward, *Witchcraft, Oracles, and Magic among the Azande*, abridged with an introduction by Gillies, Eva, (Oxford University Press, 1976).

Peek, Philip (ed.), *African Divination Systems: Ways of Knowing*, (Indiana University Press, 1991).

Westerlund, David, *African Indigenous Religions and Disease Causation: From Spiritual Beings to Living Humans*, (Brill, 2006).

9. The Invention of Racism

Fletcher, Catherine, *The Black Prince of Florence: The Spectacular Life and Treacherous World of Alessandro de' Medici*, (The Bodley Head, 2016).

Shyllon, Folarin, *Edward Long's Libel of Africa: The Foundation of British Racism*, (Cambridge Scholars Publishing, 2021).

Snowden, Frank, *Before Color Prejudice: The Ancient View of Blacks*, (Harvard University Press, 1983).

10. An African End to Slavery

Akinjogbin, Isaac, *Dahomey and its Neighbours, 1708–1818*, (Cambridge University Press, 1967).

Dalzel, Archibald, *The History of Dahomy: An Inland Kingdom of Africa* (London, 1793; reprinted, with a new introduction by Fage, John, 1967).

Polanyi, Karl, *Dahomey and the Slave Trade: An Analysis of an Archaic Economy*, (Seattle: University of Washington Press, 1966).

ACKNOWLEDGEMENTS

Once I'd written this book, I fully understood why the acknowl-edgements in books I've read are *so* gushing. Writing a book is an immensely rewarding, but challenging, endeavour, whose com-pletion is impossible without the support of many who've touched the author's life.

If not for the love, patience and guidance of the many people who've touched *my* life, *Motherland* would never have come into being. So, I feel privileged to be given here the opportunity to thank them for all that they've done for me.

First, I'd like to thank my family: my brother, William, for helping to expand my worldview with his bright mind and our stimulating conversations; my sister, Clara, for tirelessly and, without complaint, shouldering burdens that otherwise might've fallen on only me; my mother, Kwan, for bringing me into the world; and, most especially, my father, Mark, for raising me with a confidence and a perspective without which I couldn't have even conceived of *Motherland*, for guiding me so that I remained focused on the ambitions I've had since childhood, and for edu-cating and supporting me, which gave me the skills, time and headspace necessary to complete this book.

Next, I'd like to thank Bob Roberts and Tony Chan, my won-derful, talented and passionate English teachers who taught me about – and instilled in me a love of – language, literature and storytelling. I miss our lessons dearly!

Thank you, too, to my amazing university professors – par-ticularly, Amy Bogaard, Elizabeth Ewart, Tim Clack, and Peter Mitchell – who taught me almost everything I know about not just academic rigour, including how to research, verify information, and present an evidence-based argument, but also archaeology, anthropology, the deep African past and a host of African cultures.

I'd also like to thank world-class professors Benjamin Kankpeyeng and Irene Odotei of the University of Ghana for generously sharing their expertise with me when I was sixteen, which first made me aware intellectually of the depth and breadth of African cultures and encouraged me to study them at university.

Thank you to my sterling agents at United Agents, and, most especially, to my literary agent, Robert Kirby, who, from the very beginning, has championed my ideas, perspective and career. For your guidance, I'm forever grateful.

Thank you, too, to the brilliant team at Weidenfeld & Nicolson, and, particularly, to my editor, Maddy Price, who've shown me such kindness, patience and understanding, and *Motherland* such heart-warming enthusiasm. To have you as my publishers, I'm so lucky.

Lastly, thank you to the many awesome historians, all of whom I've looked up to since I was a young teenager, who've graciously given me knowledge, advice and guidance. Truly, it's an honour to know you all.

Among these superb historians, I'd like to give special thanks to two: first, to Dan Jones, who read the first draft of *Motherland's* first chapter, and gave feedback that not only made the book better, but hugely accelerated my writing of it. And second, and most especially, to Kate Williams, without whom I probably wouldn't have a *career*, let alone a completed book.

In the summer of 2020, I was maintaining a blog about African history and cultures but was lost. In various ways, I'd tried to interest people, including those in the same field as me, in the research I was doing, but was largely ignored and rebuffed.

Then, I messaged Kate, asking simply for advice on how to share my research more widely.

That one message changed my life.

Kate not only gave me advice, but introduced me to those, including my excellent agent, who have enabled me to take my writings about African history and cultures from an obscure WordPress blog to an international audience.

Modest as she is, Kate has always maintained that she did nothing special, and that I would have got to where I am without her. Of course, this is very kind of her to say, but whether it's true is difficult to determine.

Whatever the case, it *is* largely because of her that I am where I am, and, to her, I couldn't be more grateful.

NOTES

1: Our Lost Millennia

1   Djibril Niane, *Mali and the Second Mandingo Expansion*, in *General History of Africa IV: Africa from the Twelfth to the Sixteenth Century*, ed. Djibril Niane (UNESCO, University of California Press, Heinemann Educational Books, 1984), 149.

2   Mohammed Hamidullah, 'Muslim Discovery of America Before Columbus', *Journal of the Muslim Students' Association of the United States and Canada*, 4:2 (1968), 7–9.

3   Tahar Abbou, *Mansa Musa's Journey to Mecca and Its Impact on Western Sudan 1324-5*, The International Conference on 'The Routes of Pilgrimage in Africa', organised by the International University of Africa, Khartoum, Sudan, (November 2016), 5.

4   Abbou (2016), 7.

5   Niane (1984), 149.

6   Nehemia Levtzion and J. F. P. Hopkins, *Corpus of early Arabic sources for West African History*, (Cambridge, 1981), 269–273.

7   Levtzion and Hopkins, (1981), 269–273.

8   Ibid.

9   Ibid.

10 Niane (1984), 149.

11 Levtzion and Hopkins (1981), 269–273.

12 Ibid.

13 Abbou, (2016), 7–8.

14 Niane (1984), 149.

15 Levtzion and Hopkins, (1981), 269–273.

16 Nathaniel Harris, *Mapping the World: Maps and their History* (San Diego: Thunder Bay Press, 2002), 7.

17 Tor Benjaminsen, Gunnvor Berge, and Erling Dugan, 'Myths of Timbuktu: From African El Dorado to Desertification', *International Journal of Political Economy*, 34:1; Political Ecology: Global, Historical, and Economic Perspectives (2004) 31–59, 35.

18 Richard Smith, 'The Image of Timbuktu in Europe before Caillié', *Proceedings of the French Colonial Historical Society*, 8 (1985) 18.

19 Ibn Battuta, *Travels in Asia and Africa 1325–1354*, trans. and ed. Hamilton Gibb, (London: Broadway House, 1929), 324.

20   Battuta, (1929), 325.
21   Ibid.
22   Niane (1984), 152.
23   Battuta, (1929), 326.
24   Ibid., 328.
25   Ibid., 327.
26   Ibid., 329–30.
27   Ibid., 330.
28   Ibid., 330.
29   Ibid., 330–331.
30   Robert Brown, *The History and Description of Africa and of the Notable Things Therein Contained Volume I, written by Al-Hassan Ibn-Mohammed Al-Wezaz Al-Fasi, a Moor, baptised as Giovanni Leone, but better known as Leo Africanus. Done into English in the Year 1600, by John Pory* (The Hakluyt Society, London, 2010), 128.
31   A.R. Allen, *Leo's Travels in the Sudan: Being the Seventh Book of Leo Africanus Simplified, Abridged and Done Into Modern English from the Translation of John Pory* (Oxford, 1962), 7–9.
32   Allen, (1962), 9.
33   Maniraj Sukdaven, Asgher Mukhtar, and Hamid Fernana, 'A Timbuktu Manuscript Expressing the Mystical Thoughts of Yusuf-ibn-Said', *Journal for the Study of Religion*, 28:2, (2015), 181–201; 187.
34   Allen, (1962), 9.
35   Brent Singleton, 'African Bibliophiles: Books and Libraries in Medieval Timbuktu', *Libraries & Culture*, 39:1 (2004) 1–12; 6.
36   Singleton, (2004), 1–12; 1.

2: How the Dead Still Live

1   George Hagan, 'The Golden Stool and the Oaths to the King of Ashanti', *Research Review*, 4:3, MSU Libraries Digital Collections, (University of Ghana, Institute of African Studies, 1968), 1–33; 14.
2   Augustine Abasi, "'Lua-Lia", The "Fresh Funeral": Founding a House for the Deceased among the Kasena of North-East Ghana', *Africa: Journal of the International African Institute*, 65:3 (Cambridge on behalf of the International African Institute, 1995), 448–475; 455.
3   Abasi, (1995), 448–475; 460.
4   Igor Kopytoff, 'Ancestors as Elders in Africa', *Africa: Journal of the International African Institute*, 41:2 (Cambridge on behalf of the International African Institute, Apr. 1971), 129–142; 130.
5   Stephen Morgan and Beatrice Okyere-Manu, 'The Belief in and Veneration of Ancestors in Akan Traditional Thought: Finding Values for Human Wellbeing', *Alternation Special Edition*, 30 (2020), 11–31; 12.

6   Josh Eells, 'The "Black Panther" Revolution', *Rolling Stone*, (18 February 2018), https://www.rollingstone.com/tv-movies/tv-movie-features/the-black-panther-revolution-199536/

7   The Newsroom, 'Obituary: Chadwick Boseman, Star of Marvel's Black Panther', *Scotsman*, (3 September 2020), https://www.scotsman.com/news/people/obituary-chadwick-boseman-star-of-marvels-black-panther-2959233

8   Eells, (2018).

9   Julie Miller, '42 Star Chadwick Boseman on Playing Jackie Robinson, Copying His Baseball Moves, and Being Stood Up by the President', *Vanity Fair*, (12 April 2013), https://www.vanityfair.com/hollywood/2013/04/chadwick-boseman-42-interview

10   Derrik J. Lang, 'Chadwick Boseman is Making his Mark', *American Way*, (1 February 2018), https://derrikjlang.com/wp-content/uploads/2018/06/awchadwickboseman.pdf

11   Ron Halper, 'Chadwick Boseman: A Tribute for a King', *ABC*, (30 August 2020).

12   Eells, (2018).

13   American Film Institute, 'Chadwick Boseman: "There is no BLACK PANTHER without Denzel Washington"', YouTube, (28 June 2019), https://www.youtube.com/watch?v=fWIgdO9LhKQ

14   Lang, (2018), 46.

15   Eells, (2018).

16   Howard University, 'Chadwick Boseman's Howard University 2018 Commencement Speech', YouTube, (14 May 2018), https://www.youtube.com/watch?v=RIHZypMyQ2s

17   Howard University, (2018).

18   Ibid.

19   Ibid.

20   Ibid.

21   Ibid.

22   Ibid.

23   Ibid.

24   Ibid.

25   Ibid.

26   Ibid.

27   Ibid.

28   Ibid.

29   Daniel Riley, 'The Surprisingly Sudden Arrival of Chadwick Boseman', *GQ*, (22 September 2014), https://www.gq.com/story/chadwick-boseman

30   Quinn Peterson, 'Actor Chadwick Boseman Talks Playing Jackie Robinson in '42'', *Life + Times*, (4 March 2013), https://lifeandtimes.com/actor-chadwick-boseman-talks-playing-jackie-robinson-in-42

31   Riley, (2014).

32   Peterson, (2013).
33   Gary Thompson, 'Meet Chadwick Boseman, Star of "42"', *The Philadelphia Inquirer*, (12 April 2013), https://www.inquirer.com/philly/entertainment/20130412_Meet_Chadwick_Boseman__star_of__42_.html
34   Thompson, (2013).
35   Peterson, (2013).
36   Steve Rose, 'I got the feelin' – Chadwick Boseman on Playing James Brown', *Guardian*, (20 November 2014), https://www.theguardian.com/film/2014/nov/20/james-brown-chadwick-boseman-get-on-up
37   Rose, (2014).
38   Sarah Halley Finn, as told to Chris Lee, 'Why Chadwick Boseman Was Always the "Unanimous" Choice for Black Panther', *Vulture*, (30 August 2020), https://www.vulture.com/2020/08/how-chadwick-boseman-was-cast-as-marvels-black-panther.html
39   Jimmy Kimmel, 'Chadwick Boseman on Playing Black Panther', *Jimmy Kimmel Live*, (29 April 2016), https://www.youtube.com/watch?v=Xl1y-ZzITaU 9
40   Megha Mohan, 'Black Panther: The "Weird Signs" That Led Chadwick Boseman to Wakanda', *BBC News*, (5 September 2020), https://www.bbc.co.uk/news/stories-54014997
41   Mohan, (2020).
42   Mohan, (2020).
43   LiveKellyandMark, 'Chadwick Boseman on Black Panther Role in "Captain America: Civil War"', YouTube, (2 May 2016), https://www.youtube.com/watch?v=bLQavRhiCzo
44   LiveKellyandMark, (2016).
45   Ibid.
46   Ibid.
47   Ibid.
48   Ibid.
49   Ibid.
50   Kimmel, (2016).
51   LiveKellyandMark, (2016).
52   Ibid.
53   Ibid.
54   Ibid.
55   Mohan, (2020).
56   Mohan, (2020).
57   Josh Eells, 'The "Black Panther" Revolution', *Rolling Stone*, (18 February 2018), https://www.rollingstone.com/tv-movies/tv-movie-features/the-black-panther-revolution-199536/
58   Ramin Setoodeh, 'Chadwick Boseman and Ryan Coogler on How "Black Panther" Makes History', *Variety*, (5 February 2018), https://variety.com/2018/

film/features/black-panther-chadwick-boseman-ryan-coogler-interview-1202686402/

59   The Newsroom, 'Obituary: Chadwick Boseman, Star of Marvel's Black Panther', *The Scotsman*, (3 September 2020), https://www.scotsman.com/news/people/obituary-chadwick-boseman-star-of-marvels-black-panther-2959233

60   The Late Show with Stephen Colbert, 'Chadwick Boseman on Bringing Humanity To "Black Panther"', YouTube, (17 May 2018), https://www.youtube.com/watch?v=YCf_dMfAeuE

61   Eells, (2018).

62   Ryan Coogler, 'Chadwick Boseman: Black Panther director Ryan Coogler pays emotional tribute', *BBC News*, (30 August 2020), https://www.bbc.co.uk/news/entertainment-arts-53968816

63   Eells, (2018).

64   Coogler, (2020).

65   Ibid.

66   Finn, (2020).

67   Rose, (2014).

68   Riley, (2014).

69   Ryan Gilbey, 'Black Panther's Chadwick Boseman: "Everybody's minds are opening up"', *Guardian*, (15 February 2018), https://www.theguardian.com/film/2018/feb/15/black-panther-chadwick-boseman-interview-everybodys-minds-are-opening-up

70   Reggie Ugwu and Michael Levenson, '"Black Panther" Star Chadwick Boseman Dies of Cancer at 43', *The New York Times*, (17 December 2020), https://www.nytimes.com/2020/08/28/movies/chadwick-boseman-dead.html

71   Kirsten Chuba, 'Chadwick Boseman's Agent: He Chose Roles "Always Bringing About Light"', *Hollywood Reporter*, (2 September 2020), https://www.hollywoodreporter.com/movies/movie-features/chadwick-bosemans-agent-he-chose-roles-always-bringing-about-light-4053475/

72   Coogler, (2020).

3: Queenmothers and Warrior-Queens

1   Eva Meyerowitz, *The Sacred State of the Akan*, (London: Faber and Faber, 1951), 53.

2   A. A. Hakem, 'The civilization of Napata and Meroe', *General History of Africa II: Ancient Civilizations of Africa*, Ed. Mokhtar, G., (UNESCO, University of California Press, Heinemann Educational Books, 1981), 298–299.

3   Duane Roller, *The Geography of Strabo*, (Cambridge, 2014), 759.

4   Roller (2014), 759–760.

5   Ibid., 760.

6   Ibid., 760.

7   Roller (2014), 760.

8   Linda Heywood, *Njinga of Angola: Africa's Warrior Queen*, (Harvard, 2017), 57.

9 Heywood, (2017), 26.

10 Ibid., 125.

11 Ibid., 129.

12 Ibid., 151.

13 Ibid., 188–189.

14 Heywood, (2017), 201.

15 Ibid.

16 Ibid.

17 Ibid.

4: We Are More Than Skin Colour

1 Nisha Chittal, 'The Kamala Harris Identity Debate Shows How America Still Struggles to Talk About Multiracial People', *Vox*, (20 January 2021), https://www.vox.com/identities/2020/8/14/21366307/kamala-harris-black-south-asian-indian-identity

2 Kevin Sullivan, '"I am who I am": Kamala Harris, Daughter of Indian and Jamaican Immigrants, Defines Herself Simply as "American"', *The Washington Post*, (2 February 2019), https://www.washingtonpost.com/politics/i-am-who-i-am-kamala-harris-daughter-of-indian-and-jamaican-immigrants-defines-herself-simply-as-american/2019/02/02/0b278536-24b7-11e9-ad53-824486280311_story.html

3 Sullivan, (2019).

4 Ibid.

5 Ibid.

6 Ibid.

7 Beatrice Peterson, 'Sen. Kamala Harris Questions Whether America Would Elect a Woman of Color as President', *ABC News*, (16 November 2019), https://abcnews.go.com/Politics/sen-kamala-harris-questions-america-elect-woman-color/story?id=66610615

8 Dana Goodyear, 'Kamala Harris Makes Her Case', *New Yorker*, (15 July 2019), https://www.newyorker.com/magazine/2019/07/22/kamala-harris-makes-her-case

9 Gerry Shih, 'San Francisco District Attorney Is Tireless in State Campaign', *The New York Times*, (30 September 2010), https://www.nytimes.com/2010/10/01/us/01bckamala.html

10 Joseph Deal, *Race and Class in Colonial Virginia: Indians, Englishmen, and Africans on the Eastern Shore During the Seventeenth Century* (New York: Garland, 1993), 226.

11 Aloysius Higginbotham, *In the Matter of Color: Race and the American Legal Process: The Colonial Period* (New York: Oxford University Press, 1978), 39.

12 Higginbotham, (1978), 52.

5: Merchants, Traders and Navigators

1   James Kirkup and Robert Winnett, 'Theresa May Interview: "We're Going to Give Illegal Migrants a Really Hostile Reception"', *The Telegraph*, (25 May 2012), https://www.telegraph.co.uk/news/0/theresa-may-interview-going-give-illegal-migrants-really-hostile/

2   Alan Travis, 'Immigration Bill: Theresa May Defends Plans to Create "Hostile Environment"', *Guardian*, (10 October 2013), https://www.theguardian.com/politics/2013/oct/10/immigration-bill-theresa-may-hostile-environment

3   Amelia Gentleman, 'Mother of Windrush Citizen Blames Passport Problems for His Death', *Guardian*, (18 April 2018), https://www.theguardian.com/uk-news/2018/apr/18/mother-of-windrush-citizen-blames-passport-problems-for-his-death?trk=public_post_comment-text

4   Gentleman, (2018).

5   Ibid.

6   Ibid.

7   Ibid.

8   Ibid.

9   May Bulman, 'Windrush Man Who Suddenly Died Did Not Access Healthcare For Two Years Due To Immigration Concerns, Inquest Hears', *Independent*, (20 July 2018), https://www.independent.co.uk/news/uk/home-news/windrush-scandal-latest-name-death-racist-gp-home-office-a8457006.html

10   'Windrush: Migrant Dexter Bristol's family walk out of inquest', *BBC News*, (28 August 2018) https://www.bbc.co.uk/news/uk-england-london-45332410

11   Bulman, (2018).

12   Tom Foot, 'Dexter Bristol Inquest: Mother of Windrush Scandal Victim Says "Justice Has Not Been Done"', *Camden New Journal*, (10 October 2019), https://www.camdennewjournal.co.uk/article/dexter-bristol-inquest-mother-of-windrush-scandal-victim-says-justice-has-not-been-done

13   Foot, (2019).

14   Gentleman, (2018).

15   Ibid.

16   Greville Freeman-Grenville (ed.), *The East African Coast: Select Documents from the First to the Earlier Nineteenth Century*, (Oxford: Clarendon Press, 1962), 2

17   Freeman-Grenville, (1962), 16.

18   Ibid 54.

19   Freeman-Grenville, (1962), 16.

20   Ibid. (1962), 1.

21   Ibid. (1962), 14.

22   Ibid. (1962), 55.

23   Edward Dreyer, *Zheng He: China and the Oceans in the Early Ming Dynasty, 1405–1433*, (New York: Pearson Longman, 2006), 18–19.

24 Sally Church, "Zheng He: An Investigation into the Plausibility of 450-ft Treasure Ships", *Monumenta Serica*, 53, (2005), 1–43, 13.

25 Church, (2005).

26 'Girl's Journey to Ancestral Land in China', *Nation*, (21 July 2012) https://nation.africa/kenya/life-and-style/lifestyle/girl-s-journey-to-ancestral-land-in-china-820958

27 *Nation*, (2012).

28 Huaxia, 'Kenyan Doctor to Promote Chinese Medicine in Kenya', *Xinhua*, (22 March 2017) http://www.xinhuanet.com/english/2017-03/22/c_136146526.htm

29 Ibn Battuta, *Travels in Asia and Africa 1325–1354*, trans. and ed. Hamilton Gibb, (London: Broadway House, 1929), 110.

30 Freeman-Grenville, (1962), 2.

31 Ibid.

32 Ibid., 14.

33 Ibid., 15–16.

34 Ibid., 15.

35 Ibid., 8.

36 Battuta, (1929), 110–111.

37 Ibid., 110.

38 Ibid.

39 Ibid., 111.

40 Ibid., 111–112.

41 Ibid., 112.

42 Ibid.

43 Ibid.

44 Ibid.

45 Freeman-Grenville, (1962), 66.

46 Ibid., 60.

47 Edward Dreyer, *Zheng He: China and the Oceans in the Early Ming Dynasty, 1405–1433*, (New York: Pearson Longman, 2006), 88.

48 John Middleton, *The World of the Swahili: An African Mercantile Civilization*, (New Haven: Yale University Press, 1992), 40.

49 Freeman-Grenville, (1962), 60.

50 Ibid., 66.

51 Neville Chittick, *Kilwa: An Islamic Trading City on the East African Coast, Volume I: History and Archaeology* (Nairobi: The British Institute in Eastern Africa, 1974), 249.

52 Chittick, (1974), 248.

53 Ibid.

54 Ross Dunn, *The Adventures of Ibn Battuta: A Muslim Traveler of the 14 Century*, (University of California Press, 1989), 128.

55 Battuta, (1929), 112–113.

56 Chittick, (1974), 185.

57   Chittick, (1974), 250.
58   Freeman-Grenville, (1962), 14.
59   John Middleton, *The World of the Swahili: An African Mercantile Civilization*, (New Haven: Yale University Press, 1992), 40.
60   Chittick, (1974), 250.

6: Rappers, Singers and Storytellers
1   Chris Wilder, 'Mutual Respect: Kool Moe Dee', *The Source*, (November 1993).
2   WBLS, 'Grandmaster Caz opens up about the Kool Moe Dee & Busy Bee rap battle', YouTube, (23 March 2015), https://www.youtube.com/watch?v=zBp5aniNa2I
3   Geoff Edgers, 'They took Grandmaster Caz's rhymes without giving him credit. Now, he's getting revenge', *Washington Post*, (29 September 2016), https://www.washingtonpost.com/entertainment/music/they-took-grandmaster-cazs-rhymes-without-giving-him-credit-now-hes-getting-revenge/2016/09/29/f519c35a-7f3e-11e6-8d0c-fb6c00c90481_story.html
4   Troy Smith, 'Interview with the Bronx African American History Project', BAAHP Digital Archive at Fordham University, (3 February 2006), 16.
5   Smith, (2006), 16.
6   Smith, (2006), 17.
7   Troy Smith, 'Charlie Rock of "The Harlem World Crew" and Harlem World', *The Foundation*, (Autumn, 2003).
8   Smith, (2003).
9   djvlad, 'Grandmaster Caz: Kool Moe Dee Upped Standard for Battle Rap', *VladTV*, (14 June 2015), https://www.vladtv.com/article/212731/grandmaster-caz-kool-moe-dee-upped-standard-for-battle-rap
10   WBLS, (2015).
11   djvlad, (2015).
12   WBLS, (2015).
13   djvlad, (2015).
14   Smith, (2003).
15   Peter Spirer, *Beef*, (Aslan Productions, Open Road Films, QD3 Entertainment, Image Entertainment, 2003).
16   Spirer, (2003).
17   Ibid.
18   Ibid.
19   WBLS, (2015).
20   Wilder, (1993).
21   Spirer, (2003).
22   Unique Access Ent., 'Busy Bee on Kool Moe Dee Sabotaging Him & How Kid Rock Changed His Life With "Bawitdaba"', YouTube, (12 November 2019), https://www.youtube.com/watch?v=4GXJ4JhZXXU
23   Chris Wilder, 'Mutual Respect: Kool Moe Dee', *The Source*, (November 1993).

24 Spirer, (2003).
25 Ibid.
26 Ibid.
27 Ibid.
28 realhiphop3000, 'Kool Moe Dee Live At Harlem World 1981 (Busy Bee VS Kool Moe Dee Battle) Old School Hip Hop/Hiphop', YouTube, (2 April 2009), https://www.youtube.com/watch?v=86XG7gw4RIA
29 realhiphop3000, (2009).
30 Kool Moe Dee, 'Battle w/Busy Bee (Harlem World, 1981)', Track 2, *Pioneers of Hip-Hop: Volume One*, Urban Gold Music Inc., Genius, (1 December 1981).
31 Spirer, (2003).
32 Ibid.
33 Ibid.
34 Ibid.
35 Kool Moe Dee, (1981).
36 WBLS, (2015).
37 Spirer, (2003)
38 Smith, (2003).
39 Wilder, (1993).
40 Spirer, (2003).
41 djvlad, (2015).
42 WBLS, (2015).
43 djvlad, (2015).
44 Smith, (2003).
45 Spirer, (2003)
46 Wilder, (1993).
47 WBLS, (2015).
48 djvlad, (2015).
49 ItzYourzMedia, 'Busy Bee Talks Wild Style, Kool Moe Dee, Hip Hop Culture', YouTube, (23 November 2018), https://www.youtube.com/watch?v=dT2jBsdWuZw
50 Wilder, (1993).
51 John Dollard, 'The Dozens: Dialect of Insult', *The American Imago*, 1, (November 1939), 3–25, 11.
52 Roger Abrahams, 'Playing the Dozens', *The Journal of American Folklore*, 75:297, Symposium on Obscenity in Folklore (American Folklore Society, Jul. – Sep. 1962), 209–220; 211.
53 Abrahams, (1962), 209–220; 210.
54 Elijah Wald, *Talking 'Bout Your Mama: The Dozens, Snaps, and the Deep Roots of Rap*, (Oxford, 2014), 21.
55 Wald, (Oxford, 2014), 22.
56 Amuzie Chimezie, 'The Dozens: An African-Heritage Theory', *Journal of Black Studies*, 6:4 (Sage Publications, Inc., Jun. 1976) 401–420; 403–404.

57 James Agbájé, 'Proverbs: A Strategy for Resolving Conflict in Yorùbá Society', *Journal of African Cultural Studies*, 15:2 (Taylor & Francis, Ltd., Dec. 2002); 237–243; 238.

58 Felicia Ohwovoriole, 'Peacemaking and Proverbs in Urhobo and Yoruba Marital Conflicts: Part 1', *African Conflict and Peacebuilding Review*, 1:2, Special Issue on West African Research Association Peace Initiative Conference in Dakar (2009) (Indiana University Press, Fall 2011), 122–135; 126.

59 Ohwovoriole, (2011), 122–35; 127.

60 Ibid., 122–135; 127.

61 Ibid.

62 Ibid.

63 Ibid.

64 Ibid., 122–135; 127–128.

65 Thomas Hale, *Griots and Griottes: Masters of Words and Music*, (Bloomington: Indiana University Press, 1998), 84.

66 Hale, (1998), 99.

67 Ibid., 100.

68 Ibid., 100–101.

69 Ibid., 92.

70 Ibid., 90.

71 Ibid., 92.

72 Ibid.

73 Ibid., 100.

74 Ibid., 77.

75 Ibn Battuta, *Travels in Asia and Africa 1325–1354*, trans. and ed. Hamilton Gibb, (London: Broadway House, 1929), 328.

76 Hale, (1998), 112.

77 Ibid., 101.

78 Ibid., 112.

79 Ibn Battuta, *Travels in Asia and Africa 1325–1354*, trans. and ed. Hamilton Gibb, (London: Broadway House, 1929), 329.

80 Hale, (1998), 49.

81 Ibid., 111.

82 Ibid., 89–90.

83 Ibid., 92.

84 Ibid., 94.

85 Ibid., 46.

86 Ibid., 77.

87 Ibid., 77.

88 Ibid., 77.

89 Ibid., 173.

7: Story of the Spider-God

1   Robert Rattray, *Akan-Ashanti Folk-Tales*, (Oxford: Clarendon Press, 1930), 55.
2   Rattray, (1930), 77.
3   Christopher Vecsey, 'The Exception Who Proves the Rules: Ananse the Akan Trickster', *Journal of Religion in Africa*, 12:3 (Brill, 1981), 161–177, 166.
4   Vecsey, (1981), 161–177, 170.
5   Rattray, (1930), 55–59.
6   Rattray, (1930), 5–7.
7   Martha Beckwith and Helen Roberts, *Jamaica Anansi Stories*, (New York: The American Folk-lore Society, 1924), 1–2.
8   Beckwith and Roberts, (1924), 4–5.

8: Wisdom of the Ancients

1   Rosa Sanchez, 'Simone Biles Explains Competition Withdrawal at Olympics: "My Mind and Body are Simply Not in Sync"', *ABC News*, (30 July 2021), https://abcnews.go.com/Sports/simone-biles-explains-withdrawal-olympics-mind-body-simply/story?id=79157744
2   Bill Chappell, 'Read What Simone Biles Said After Her Withdrawal from The Olympic Final', *NPR*, (28 July 2021), https://www.npr.org/sections/tokyo-olympics-live-updates/2021/07/28/1021683296/in-her-words-what-simone-biles-said-after-her-withdrawal
3   Ben Church, and Jill Martin, 'Simone Biles Withdraws From All-Around Final at Tokyo 2020 to Focus on Mental Health', *CNN*, (28 July 2021), https://edition.cnn.com/2021/07/28/sport/simone-biles-gymnastics-tokyo-2020-mental-health-spt-intl/index.html
4   Church and Martin, (2021).
5   Clea Skopeliti, 'Simone Biles Receives Praise for Prioritising her Mental Health', *Guardian*, (28 July 2021), https://www.theguardian.com/sport/2021/jul/28/simone-biles-receives-praise-for-prioritising-her-mental-health

9: The Invention of Racism

1   Newsmaker, 'Chumani Maxwele: No Regrets for Throwing Faeces at Rhodes Statue', *News24*, (29 March 2015), https://www.news24.com/News24/Newsmaker-Chumani-Maxwele-No-regrets-for-throwing-faeces-at-Rhodes-statue-20150429
2   Eve Fairbanks, 'The Birth of Rhodes Must Fall', *Guardian*, (18 November 2015), https://www.theguardian.com/news/2015/nov/18/why-south-african-students-have-turned-on-their-parents-generation
3   Raeesa Pather, 'That Shitty Rhodes Statue: What Students Think Of The UCT Poo Protest', *The Daily Vox*, (13 March 2015).
4   Newsroom, 'Students Campaign For Rhodes Statue Removal', *UCT News*, (16 March 2015), https://www.news.uct.ac.za/article/-2015-03-16-students-campaign-for-rhodes-statue-removal
5   The Poor Print, 'Rhodes Must Fall UCT: Mission Statement', *The Poor*

Print, (28 April 2017), https://thepoorprint.com/2017/04/28/rhodes-must-fall-uct-mission-statement/

6   Fairbanks, (2015).
7   Folarin Shyllon, *Black Slaves in Britain*, (Oxford University Press, 1974), 107.
8   Folarin Shyllon, *Edward Long's Libel of Africa: The Foundation of British Racism*, (Cambridge Scholars Publishing, 2021), 47.
9   Shyllon, (2021), 54.
10   Ibid., 44.
11   Ibid., 92.
12   Frank Snowden , *Before Color Prejudice: The Ancient View of Blacks*, (Harvard University Press, 1983), 46.
13   Catherine Fletcher, *The Black Prince of Florence: The Spectacular Life and Treacherous World of Alessandro de' Medici*, (The Bodley Head, 2016), 30.
14   Fletcher, (2016), 253.
15   Ibid., 76–77.
16   Ibid., 72.
17   Ibid., 70.
18   Ibid., 78.
19   Ibid., 78.
20   Ibid., 78–79.
21   Ibid., 202.

10: An African End to Slavery

1   William Smith, *A New Voyage to Guinea*, (London: Psychology Press, 1744; reprinted 1967), 177.
2   Smith, (1967), 179.
3   Ibid., 184.
4   Ibid., 182.
5   Ibid., 181.
6   Ibid., 173.
7   Ibid., 179.
8   Isaac Akinjogbin, *Dahomey and its Neighbours, 1708–1818*, (Cambridge: Cambridge University Press, 1967), 75.
9   Smith, (1967), 183.
10   Archibald Dalzel, *The History of Dahomy: An Inland Kingdom of Africa* (London, 1793; reprinted, with a new introduction by John Fage, 1967), 33.
11   Dalzel, (1967), 33.
12   Ibid.
13   Robin Law, 'Dahomey and the Slave Trade: Reflections on the Historiography of the Rise of Dahomey', *The Journal of African History*, 27:2, Special Issue in Honour of J.D. Fage (Cambridge University Press, 1986), 237–267; 248.
14   Dalzel, (1967), 47.
15   Smith, (1967), 182.
16   Dalzel, (1967), 5.

17 Ibid.

18 Ibid.

19 William Snelgrave, *A New Account of Some Parts of Guinea, and the Slave Trade*, (London, 1734; reprinted 1971), 3.

20 Snelgrave, (1734; reprinted 1971), 3.

21 Dalzel, (1967), 5.

22 Snelgrave, (1734; reprinted 1971), 4.

23 Isaac Akinjogbin, *Dahomey and its Neighbours, 1708–1818*, (Cambridge: Cambridge University Press, 1967), 65.

24 Dalzel, (1967), 17.

25 Snelgrave, (1734; reprinted 1971), 5.

26 Akinjogbin, (1967), 52.

27 Snelgrave, (1734; reprinted 1971), 10.

28 Ibid., 14.

29 Ibid., 14–15.

30 Ibid., 19.

31 Dalzel, (1967), 32.

32 Ibid., 50–51.

33 Snelgrave, (1734; reprinted 1971), 2–3.

34 Ibid., 6.

35 Dalzel, (1967), 17.

36 Ibid., 57.

37 Ibid., 27.

38 Ibid., 12.

39 Ibid., 14.

40 Ibid.

41 Ibid.

42 Ibid.

43 Dalzel, (1967), 15.

44 Ibid., 52.

45 Ibid.,53.

46 Ibid.

47 Ibid., 54.

48 Ibid.

49 Ibid., 57–58.

50 Stanley Alpern, 'On the Origins of the Amazons of Dahomey', *History in Africa*, 25 (Cambridge University Press, 1998), 9–25, 18.

51 Dalzel, (1967), 55.

52 Ibid., 56.

53 Ibid., 58.

54 Ibid., 59.

55 Akinjogbin, (1967), 107–108.

INDEX

Funji, sister of Njinga Mbande 68, 69, 70, 72, 74

Gabon 86
Gaby, Father Jean-Baptiste 151
Gallus, Aelius 62
Gallus, Cornelius 62, 64
Gambia 152
Gao 17
genetic diversity of African peoples 80–2, 85, 102
Gersheene, Mary 91
Get On Up (film) 50–1
Ghana ix, 23–33, 53, 82, 133, 155, 217
Ghana Empire 139, 140, 142
ghosts 28
God's Wife of Amun 59–60, 62
gold 6, 7, 9–10, 11, 18, 24, 116
Goldberry, Silvestre 140
Golden Stool 24–6
Granada 16
Grandmaster Caz 125–6, 128, 129
Great Zimbabwe 116
Greeks 191, 192
Greene, Michael 42, 44, 47, 51
Grenada 104
griots 139–53
   advisory and diplomatic roles 150
   battlefield musicians 151
   becoming a griot 151–3
   epic story-telling 144–5
   female 139, 140
   griot academies 152–3
   griot by birth 141, 152
   linguistic roles 149, 151
   mastery of genealogies 148–9
   musicianship 142–4, 148, 150, 152
   origin stories 140, 142
   patrons 142, 145, 146–7, 148–9, 150
   praise-singing 145–7, 148–9, 150, 151
   rewards 147
   social standing 141
   specialisation 153
   witness role 149–50
   wrestling, role in 150–1
Guinea 5, 144, 147
Guinea-Bissau 48
Gye Nyame symbol 24

Haidara, Abdel Kader 20–1
Halley Finn, Sarah 46, 47
Hamet-Dou, Chief of Brakna 142, 145, 146
Hari a Kiluanje 71
Harlem World Club, New York ('The World') 124–5
harp-lute 143
Harris, Donald 78
Harris, Kamala 78–9, 102
Harris, Shyamala 78, 79
Hausa people 134
Hawkesbury, Lord 190
health 168, 169–80
   holistic 169, 171–80
   mental 169–71
   restoring relationships with the ancestors 175–9
   restoring relationships with the community 172–5, 179–80
Hehe people 133
Helgeland, Brian 44, 45
Heliodorus of Emesa 192
Herodotus 191–2
Herto 1
hierarchy
   social (Akan) 162
   universal 34, 38
Hip-Hop 124–5
Hispaniola 97
historical epics 144–5
Holocene epoch 86
Homo erectus 2
Homo heidelbergensis 2
Homo helmei 2, 3
Homo sapiens 1, 2, 3, 84–5
Hongwu Emperor 108